I0126886

# THE U.S. PRESIDENTS AND PRESIDENTIAL ELECTIONS

Facts, Figures, and Analyses
about the Presidency,
Presidents and Presidential Families,
Vice Presidents,
and about Presidential Elections

B. C. JACKSON

London Tudor Publishers
New York
2017

The author encourages readers to submit questions,
comments, and suggestions about this book to:
u.s.presidency.book@gmail.com

Third Edition:  May 2017

Copyright © 2017
by B. C. Jackson and London Tudor Publishers
All Rights Reserved

Published by London Tudor Publishers
ISBN 978-0-615-62862-2

Without limiting the rights under copyright reserved above, no part of this publication may be reproduced, stored in, or introduced into a retrieval system, or transmitted, in any form or by any means (electronic, mechanical, photocopying, recording, or otherwise), without the prior written permission of the copyright owner and publisher of this book.

The scanning, uploading, and distribution of this book via the Internet or via any other means without the permission of the publisher is illegal and punishable by law. Please purchase only authorized electronic editions and do not participate in or encourage electronic piracy of copyrightable materials. Your support of the author's rights is appreciated.

*Dedicated to*

*the memory of my beloved parents,*

who instilled in me the curiosity
that led to writing this book
as well as the discipline
to carry this project
through to the end.

# CONTENTS

# LIST OF TABLES AND FIGURES

# PREFACE

This book is meant to satisfy the curiosity of anyone who has ever thought about the Presidents or a Presidential election and said, "I wonder what / when / if ?" It will captivate those who want to understand the history of Presidential elections and how elections work. It is for those who want to know interesting facts about the Presidency, the Presidents, their families, the Vice Presidents, and Presidential elections. This book is for all curious people.

This book can be read cover to cover, back to front, one chapter at a time, one page at a time, or one list, graph, or table at a time. Use it the way that is most useful, and the most fun.

In Chapter I we learn how the Presidents got to the White House, how long they stayed, and why they left. We learn about their education, military service, careers prior to becoming President, some key developments during their terms in office, and about their personal lives and families. Chapter II discusses Presidential succession as a transition to Chapter III about the Vice Presidents. Chapter IV analyzes party control of the Presidency. Chapter V presents detail about Presidential elections from the beginning of the republic through the present day.

The appendices include a number of tables presenting data on the Presidents, their families, the Vice Presidents, the candidates, and each election result from 1789 to present, as well as the text of those portions of the U.S. Constitution and its amendments that deal with the Presidency and Presidential elections.

I owe a debt of deep gratitude to two young Americans. As a young boy just becoming politically aware during the run-up to the 2008 Presidential election, my son Andrew Jackson peppered me with endless questions about politics and presidential elections. I knew many of the answers but had to don my researcher's hat to adequately answer some of his questions. I kept detailed records of my research and that information formed the basis for the First Edition of this book. The many conversations with him also underscored the need for an accessible resource on the Presidents and elections. My daughter, Alexa Jackson, read the manuscript of the First Edition with an extraordinarily keen eye and offered many invaluable comments on editorial content, the text, the data, and the presentation of data. All surviving errors in this book are my responsibility solely. Finally, I owe thanks to my entire family, who endured my process of writing.

## A Note about the Data on Popular Votes

The Constitution says that Electoral College electors shall be chosen by the states. Early on, state legislators chose the electors. By the 1824 election all but one of the states had made the change to selecting electors by popular vote. South Carolina was the one hold-out and it made the switch in 1860. (When Colorado joined the Union just before the election of 1876, the legislators chose the electors since there was insufficient time to hold a popular vote.) Thus, prior to 1824, popular-vote data were scant, and for much of the rest of the 19th century the data on popular votes may not be comparable from election to election because the popular vote of a varying number of states is included in the results. In this book, analyses of the popular vote are based on elections from 1860 to present.

Pinpointing even the 20th century popular-vote data is not always an exact science. When we vote in a Presidential election our votes are tallied locally. Local election authorities then report data to state authorities. In addition, the various sources of election data apply differing methodologies for compiling and presenting the data. This book uses data reported in the *Congressional Record* and the *Federal Register* for elections in and after 1920. For elections prior to 1920 this book uses data compiled by researchers who collected data from local and state-level election records.

Determining the voter turn-out rate can present challenges. That rate is the ratio of total votes cast to the number of potential voters, and it is the latter that is often the issue. Sometimes the turn-out rate is presented on the basis of the voting-age population but this measure understates the turn-out rate because the denominator is inflated by people who are ineligible to vote. To be accurate, that denominator must exclude U.S. residents who are not citizens and those otherwise ineligible to vote (felons, for example). This is called the "voting-eligible population" or VEP, and it is the measure employed in this book.

## A Note about the Data on Electoral Votes and Electoral College Procedures

Before 1804, each elector cast two votes. The candidate with the most votes became President and the one with the second-most votes became Vice President. After ratification of the 12th Amendment in 1804 (prior to that year's election), electors voted separately for President and Vice President. Thus, electoral-vote results for elections before ratification – *i.e.,* the elections of 1789, 1792, 1796, and 1800 – and after it are not strictly comparable. For this reason, those four elections are excluded from some of the analyses in this book. In addition, the elections of 1824 and 1876 are excluded in some cases because those elections were decided by the House of Representatives rather than the Electoral College.

## A Note about the Several Eras in U.S. Electoral History

In segmenting the timeline of U.S. history for purposes of electoral analysis, this book recognizes three inflection points:

❖ 1860 was the election best representing the watershed between the multi-party system that marked elections before that date, and the two-party system that characterized most elections after that date; 1860 was also the first election in which all states chose their electors via a popular vote.

❖ 1948 was the first election in the post war period and hence the beginning of the "modern era."

❖ 1964 was the first election in which all 50 states and the District of Columbia voted in Presidential elections and hence the beginning of the "538 era" during which there have been 538 electoral votes.

## A Note about the Relevant Constitutional Amendments

Nine amendments refine, alter, or add to the Constitutional provisions relating to the Presidency and Presidential elections.

**The 12th Amendment** changed the electoral voting system from the "first place, second place" process that prevailed in Presidential elections from 1789 to 1800. Under the revised system electoral votes are cast for President and Vice President separately.

**The 15th Amendment** prohibits denying voting rights based on race, color, or previous condition of servitude.

**The 19th Amendment** gave women the right to vote.

**The 20th Amendment** moved Presidential inauguration day from 4th March to 20th January.

**The 22nd Amendment** established a Presidential term limit: No person can be elected President more than twice. However, if a Vice President were to ascend to the Presidency and serve as President – or if someone else were to act as President – for more than two years remaining in a term, he/she would then be eligible to be elected only once.

**The 23rd Amendment** gave the District of Columbia the right to vote in Presidential elections.

**The 24th Amendment** prohibits denying voting rights based on non-payment of poll taxes.

**The 25th Amendment** codified the Tyler Precedent and defines procedures for filling vacancies in the Presidency and Vice Presidency.

**The 26th Amendment** established the voting age at 18 years of age.

*See the appendices for the full text of these amendments and Article II, Section 1 of the Constitution.*

## A Note about Abbreviations and Other Conventions Used in this Book

Throughout this book the following abbreviations are used to refer to political parties:

| | | | |
|---|---|---|---|
| A | American | L | Libertarian |
| AF | Anti-Federalist | N | National Republican |
| AI | American Independent | NU | National Union |
| AM | Anti-Masonic | P | Progressive |
| C | Constitutional Union | PE | People's |
| D | Democrat | PR | Prohibition |
| DP | Democrat-Populist | R | Republican |
| DR | Democratic-Republican | SR | States Rights |
| F | Federalist | W | Whig |
| I | Independent | | |

Presidents and Vice Presidents are referred to by their first (or middle) and last names. However, to distinguish father from son, throughout this book the Bush Presidents bear their middle initials and John Quincy Adams bears his full name. Nicknames are not used. The Appendices entitled "Personal Data" list each President's and Vice President's full name.

Unless otherwise noted, in discussing candidates and data on election results, we refer only to the winner and the second-place loser in the general election. In other words, we exclude losers who placed third or below, and we exclude candidates who ran in a primary but did not participate in the general election.

# I. The Presidents

## Curious Facts About the Presidents

➢ The United States of America has been led by 44 Presidents, from George Washington to Donald Trump. But there have been…

- ❖ 45 Presidencies
- ❖ 58 Presidential elections and Presidential terms
- ❖ 39 Presidential election winners

➢ Twice, the United States has had three Presidents in a single calendar year:

1. 1841: Martin Van Buren's term expired; he was succeeded by William Harrison, who died 31 days later, whereupon Vice President John Tyler ascended to the Presidency.
2. 1881: Rutherford Hayes's term expired; he was succeeded by James Garfield, who was assassinated later that year, whereupon Vice President Chester Arthur ascended to the Presidency.

➢ Twice, the President and Vice President were from different parties:

1. President John Adams (F) and Vice President Thomas Jefferson (D-R), who were elected in 1796 when the "first place, second place" voting system was in effect.
2. Abraham Lincoln (R) and Andrew Johnson (D). In an effort to reunite the country after the Civil War, Lincoln ran in 1864 as a member of the National Union Party and chose "War Democrat" Johnson as his Vice President.

➢ No future President signed *both* the Declaration of Independence and the Constitution.

➢ Two future Presidents signed the Declaration of Independence:

1. John Adams
2. Thomas Jefferson

➢ Two future Presidents signed the Constitution:

1. George Washington
2. James Madison

- Two father/son pairs, and one grandfather/grandson pair, have been President:
  - John, and son John Quincy, Adams
  - George H.W., and son George W., Bush
  - William Henry, and grandson Benjamin, Harrison

- Each member of the Adams family was defeated when he ran as an incumbent:
  - John in 1800
  - John Quincy in 1828

- John Adams and Thomas Jefferson both died on the Fourth of July, 1826, the fiftieth anniversary of the Declaration of Independence, which they had each signed.

- John Adams died while his son John Quincy Adams was President.

- William Harrison was the last President born a British subject.

- Martin Van Buren was the first natural-born U.S. citizen to become President, having been born after the signing of the Declaration of Independence.

- Martin Van Buren is the only President who spoke English as a second language. (Dutch was his mother tongue.)

- Andrew Johnson was the only southerner who did not resign his seat in the U.S. Senate during the Civil War.

- Three Presidents have been career military men:
  1. Zachary Taylor
  2. Ulysses Grant
  3. Dwight Eisenhower

- Charles Evan Hughes is the only Supreme Court Justice ever to be nominated for President. He was the Republican nominee in 1916.

- William Taft is the only President who later served as a Supreme Court Justice.

- James Polk is the only President who had also been Speaker of the House of Representatives. He held that position from 1835 to 1839.

➢ Two Presidents served in Congress *after* their Presidency:

1. John Quincy Adams served as a Representative from Massachusetts. (Prior to his Presidency, he served as a Senator from Massachusetts.)
2. Andrew Johnson was a Senator from Tennessee. (Prior to his Presidency, he served as both a Senator and a Representative from Tennessee.)

➢ Only once in the history of the United States have two future Presidents faced each other in a Congressional election. In 1789 James Madison defeated James Monroe for Virginia's Fifth Congressional District's seat in the first Congress.

➢ Five Presidents were never elected to that office:

| | | | |
|---|---|---|---|
| 1. | John Tyler | 4. | Chester Arthur |
| 2. | Millard Fillmore | 5. | Gerald Ford |
| 3. | Andrew Johnson | | |

➢ When he prevailed in 1904, Theodore Roosevelt became the first un-elected President to win a term of his own. The previous four men who ascended to the Presidency had not even won nomination at the end of their partial term.

➢ The second Nixon-Agnew Presidency is the only administration from which both the President and Vice President resigned, each under a cloud of potential (Nixon) or actual (Agnew) criminal charges. Agnew resigned a few months after his second inauguration; his replacement, Gerald Ford, ascended to the Presidency when Nixon resigned less than a year later.

➢ Gerald Ford is the only man in history who . . .

❖ was President and Vice President but was never elected to either office.
❖ was President and Vice President but did not serve a full term in either job.
❖ as Vice President, neither began nor ended his service at the beginning or end of a term. His partial term began in the middle of a term (by appointment) and he left office (by ascending to the Presidency) before the end of the same term.
❖ ascended to the Presidency, then ran for President as an incumbent, and lost.

➢ Six U.S. Presidents were also college presidents:

| | | |
|---|---|---|
| 1. | Thomas Jefferson | University of Virginia |
| 2. | James Madison | University of Virginia |
| 3. | Millard Fillmore * | University of Buffalo (now SUNY Buffalo) |
| 4. | James Garfield * | Hiram College |
| 5. | Woodrow Wilson * | Princeton University |
| 6. | Dwight Eisenhower * | Columbia University |

    * served prior to being President of the United States

- Four Presidents have won the Nobel Peace Prize:
    1. Theodore Roosevelt    in 1906    (won while in office)
    2. Woodrow Wilson    in 1919    (won while in office)
    3. James Carter    in 2002    (won 21 years after leaving office)
    4. Barack Obama    in 2009    (won while in office)
    - ❖ Carter was the first President to accept the prize in person and the only one to win the prize after leaving office.
    - ❖ Obama was the first to win as a sitting President *and* accept the prize in person.

- No President has won any other Nobel Prize.

- No President has served without at least one living predecessor in the background (except, of course, George Washington).

- Four Presidents served while five former Presidents were alive:
    1. Abraham Lincoln
    2. William Clinton
    3. George W. Bush
    4. Donald Trump

- An additional five Presidents had four former Presidents milling about:
    1. John Quincy Adams
    2. James Polk
    3. James Buchanan
    4. George H.W. Bush
    5. Barack Obama

- Ten Presidents labored in the shadow of only one living predecessor:
    1. John Adams
    2. Thomas Jefferson
    3. Rutherford Hayes
    4. Grover Cleveland (2nd Presidency)
    5. Theodore Roosevelt
    6. William Taft
    7. Calvin Coolidge
    8. Franklin Roosevelt
    9. Harry Truman
    10. Gerald Ford

- Nine Presidents were targeted by assassins. Four of the attempts were successful:
    1. Abraham Lincoln
    2. James Garfield
    3. William McKinley
    4. John Kennedy

➤ One President – Gerald Ford – was targeted twice; both assailants were female and both were unsuccessful. The other eight Presidents were attacked by male assailants.

### Attempts on the Life of U.S. Presidents

| President | Assailant(s) | Attack Date | Location | Result |
|---|---|---|---|---|
| 1. Andrew Jackson | Richard Lawrence | 30-Mar-1835 | Washington, DC | Weapons misfired |
| 2. Abraham Lincoln | John Wilkes Booth | 14-Apr-1865 | Washington, DC | Fatally wounded; died the next morning |
| 3. James Garfield | Charles Guiteau | 2-Jul-1881 | Washington, DC | Fatally wounded; died 79 days later |
| 4. William McKinley | Leon Czologosz | 6-Sep-1901 | Buffalo, NY | Fatally wounded; died 8 days later |
| 5. Franklin Roosevelt * | Guiseppe Zangara | 15-Feb-1933 | Miami, FL | Shot missed |
| 6. Harry Truman | Oscar Collazo and Griselio Torresola | 31-Oct-1950 | Washington, DC | Attempt prevented |
| 7. John Kennedy | Lee Harvey Oswald | 22-Nov-1963 | Dallas, TX | Killed instantly |
| 8. Gerald Ford | Lynette Fromme | 5-Sep-1975 | Sacramento, CA | Attempt prevented |
| 9. Gerald Ford | Sara Jane Moore | 22-Sep-1975 | San Francisco, CA | Shot missed |
| 10. Ronald Reagan | John Hinckley, Jr. | 30-Mar-1981 | Washington, DC | Wounded |

* The attempt on Roosevelt's life occurred after he was elected but before he was inaugurated and took office.

➤ Four Presidents died in office of natural causes:
1. William Harrison
2. Zachary Taylor
3. Warren Harding
4. Franklin Roosevelt

➤ Only two Presidents are buried in Arlington Cemetery.
1. William Taft
2. John Kennedy

> Many Presidents served without a Vice President.

### Presidents Who Served Alone

| President | Days without Vice President | Reason |
|---|---|---|
| James Madison (1st term) | 318 | Vice President George Clinton died. |
| James Madison (2nd term) | 832 | Vice President Elbridge Gerry died. |
| Andrew Jackson | 66 | Vice President John Calhoun resigned |
| John Tyler | 1,430 | President William Harrison died. |
| Millard Fillmore | 969 | President Zachary Taylor died. |
| Franklin Pierce | 1,416 | Vice President William King died. |
| Andrew Johnson | 1,419 | President Abraham Lincoln was assassinated. |
| Ulysses Grant | 468 | Vice President Henry Wilson died. |
| Chester Arthur | 1,262 | President James Garfield was assassinated. |
| Grover Cleveland | 1,195 | Vice President Thomas Hendricks died. |
| William McKinley | 468 | Vice President Garret Hobart died. |
| Theodore Roosevelt | 1,267 | President William McKinley was assassinated. |
| William Taft | 125 | Vice President James Sherman died. |
| Calvin Coolidge | 580 | President Warren Harding died. |
| Harry Truman | 1,379 | President Franklin Roosevelt died. |
| Lyndon Johnson | 425 | President John Kennedy was assassinated. |
| Richard Nixon | 57 | Vice President Spiro Agnew resigned. |
| Gerald Ford | 132 | President Richard Nixon resigned. |
| Note: The full four-year Presidential term is 1,461 days. | | |

> James Madison is the only President who had two Vice Presidents, both of whom died in office:
>  1. George Clinton
>  2. Elbridge Gerry

# Presidential Inaugurations

➢ Inaugurations originally took place on 4th March. The 20th Amendment changed that date to 20th January, motivated by a desire to reduce the "lame duck" period between election day and inauguration day.

➢ The only Presidents who were not inaugurated on either 4th March or 20th January were George Washington and the nine men who ascended to the office upon the death or resignation of the President:

1. John Tyler
2. Millard Fillmore
3. Andrew Johnson
4. Chester Arthur
5. Theodore Roosevelt
6. Calvin Coolidge
7. Harry Truman
8. Lyndon Johnson
9. Gerald Ford

➢ Franklin Roosevelt's first inauguration (in 1933) was the last one held on 4th March and his second inauguration (in 1937) was the first one held on 20th January.

➢ All but seven Presidential inaugurations have taken place in Washington, DC.

❖ Three inaugurations took place prior to Washington becoming the U.S. capital:

| | | | |
|---|---|---|---|
| 1. | George Washington's first inauguration | in New York City | in 1789 |
| 2. | Washington's second inauguration | in Philadelphia | in 1792 |
| 3. | John Adams' inauguration | in Philadelphia | in 1796 |

❖ Four inaugurations took place outside of Washington when a Vice President had to be inaugurated upon the death of the President:

| | | | |
|---|---|---|---|
| 1. | Chester Arthur | in New York City | in 1881 |
| 2. | Theodore Roosevelt | in Buffalo, NY | in 1901 |
| 3. | Calvin Coolidge | in Plymouth, VT | in 1923 |
| 4. | Lyndon Johnson | in Dallas, TX | in 1963 |

➢ A Supreme Court Justice has administered all oaths of office except the first one, which was handled by Robert Livingston, New York Chancellor, in 1789.

➢ Supreme Court Chief Justice John Marshall administered nine Presidential oaths of office, which is more than any other person. He swore in each of the five Presidents from Thomas Jefferson to Andrew Jackson.

➢ William Taft is the only former President to administer the Presidential oath of office. As Chief Justice of the Supreme Court he swore in Calvin Coolidge and Herbert Hoover.

## Presidential Tenure

➤ Of the 43 men who served as President from 1789 to 2017 (from Washington to Obama), almost one-quarter did not even serve one full term.

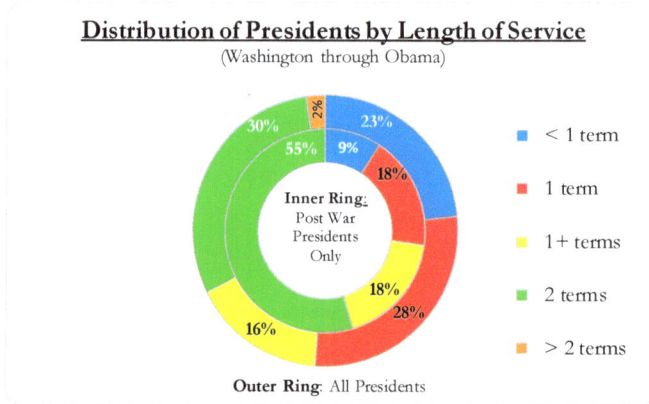

**Distribution of Presidents by Length of Service**
(Washington through Obama)

Inner Ring:
Post War
Presidents
Only

23%
9%
18%
18%
28%
16%
55%
30%
2%

- ■ < 1 term
- ■ 1 term
- ■ 1+ terms
- ■ 2 terms
- ■ > 2 terms

**Outer Ring**: All Presidents

➤ Five of the 10 Presidents who served less than one term had been *elected* President and then died in office:
1. William Harrison
2. Zachary Taylor
3. James Garfield
4. Warren Harding
5. John Kennedy

➤ Five of the 10 Presidents who served less than one term had *ascended* to that office, completed a term, and were then not nominated or elected in their own right:
1. John Tyler      (not nominated)
2. Millard Fillmore (not nominated)
3. Andrew Johnson (not nominated)
4. Chester Arthur (not nominated)
5. Gerald Ford      (ran and lost)

➤ Twelve Presidents served one term:
1. John Adams
2. John Quincy Adams
3. Martin Van Buren
4. James Polk
5. Franklin Pierce
6. James Buchanan
7. Rutherford Hayes
8. Benjamin Harrison
9. William Taft
10. Herbert Hoover
11. James Carter
12. George H.W. Bush

- ➤ Seven Presidents served more than one term but less than two.
  - ❖ Three of the seven served a full term and then part of a second term:
    1. Abraham Lincoln  (assassinated)
    2. William McKinley  (assassinated)
    3. Richard Nixon  (resigned)
  - ❖ Four of the seven started mid-term and thereafter served a full term:
    1. Theodore Roosevelt
    2. Calvin Coolidge
    3. Harry Truman
    4. Lyndon Johnson

## Presidents Served Only One Term, Even Less, or More

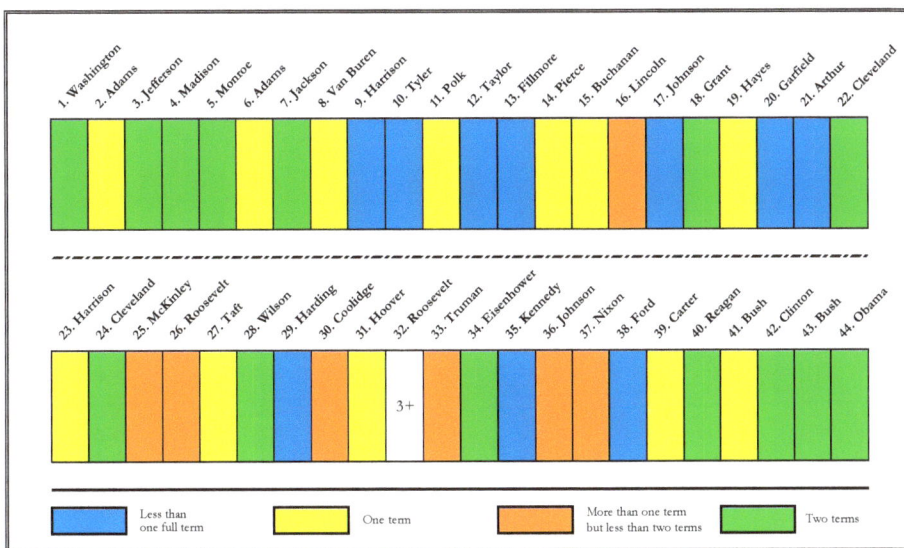

- ➤ Thirteen Presidents served two full terms:
  1. George Washington
  2. Thomas Jefferson
  3. James Madison
  4. James Monroe
  5. Andrew Jackson
  6. Ulysses Grant
  7. Grover Cleveland (non-consecutive)
  8. Woodrow Wilson
  9. Dwight Eisenhower
  10. Ronald Reagan
  11. William Clinton
  12. George W. Bush
  13. Barack Obama

- ➤ Franklin Roosevelt was the only President who served more than two terms. He was elected four times but died 82 days into his fourth term.

- Only twice in its history has the United States had three two-term Presidents in a row: once in the early days of the republic and then not again until the most recent three Presidents:
  1. Thomas Jefferson (3rd President), James Madison (4th), James Monroe (5th)
  2. William Clinton (42nd), George W. Bush (43rd), Barack Obama (44th)
    - ❖ There has been no other time when even two Presidents in a row served two full consecutive terms.

- In the middle of the 19th century, eight consecutive Presidents – from Martin Van Buren to James Buchanan – served only one term or less.

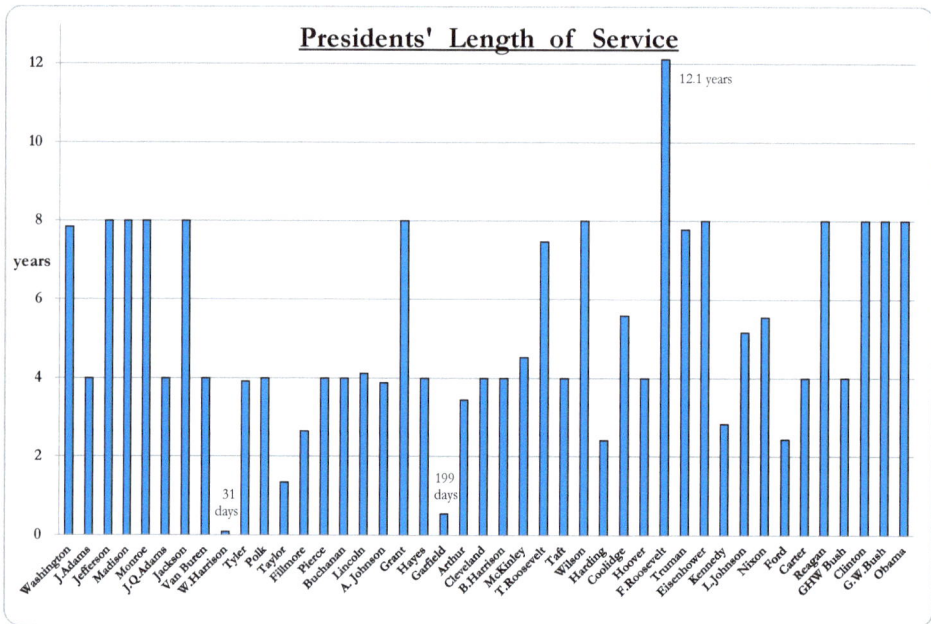

Presidents' Length of Service

- Franklin Roosevelt had the longest tenure, having spent a robust 4,422 days (that is, 12 years, 1 month, and 8 days) in office.
    - ❖ Roosevelt will hold this record for eternity unless the 22nd Amendment is repealed or amended.

- William Harrison had the briefest tenure, having spent a scant 31 days in office.

- Franklin Roosevelt's tenure was 143 times as long as the shortest Presidential tenure.

- The five shortest Presidencies:
    1. William Harrison        31 days     (died)
    2. James Garfield          199 days    (assassinated)
    3. Zachary Taylor         492 days    (died)
    4. Warren Harding        881 days    (died)
    5. Gerald Ford             895 days

- The Presidential term is four years; *i.e.,* 1,461 days. Four terms have been shorter:
    - ❖ The 1$^{st}$:     In his first term George Washington was not inaugurated until 30$^{th}$ April, so that term was only 1,404 days in length.
    - ❖ The 3$^{rd}$:     1800 was not a leap year so this term was only 1,460 days in length. John Adams was President.
    - ❖ The 28$^{th}$:     1900 was not a leap year so this term was only 1,460 days in length. William McKinley was President.
    - ❖ The 37$^{th}$:     The 38$^{th}$ term was the first for which inauguration day was moved from 4$^{th}$ March to 20$^{th}$ January, so the 37$^{th}$ term was only 1,418 days. Franklin Roosevelt was President.

*See the Appendices for more on the flow of Presidents and Vice Presidents in and out of office.*

# Presidential Timelines

➢ Presidents have tended to be in their fifties when they took office, although post war Presidents have been older.

**Distribution of Presidents' Ages at First Inauguration**
(Washington through Trump)

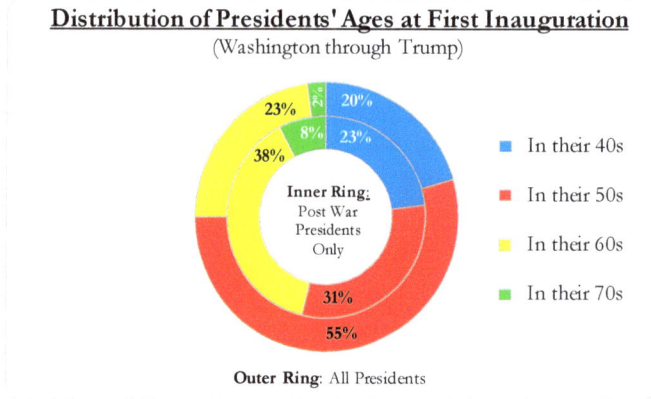

Inner Ring: Post War Presidents Only

Outer Ring: All Presidents

Legend:
- ■ In their 40s
- ■ In their 50s
- ■ In their 60s
- ■ In their 70s

➢ The five youngest Presidents:
  1. Theodore Roosevelt   first sworn in at 42.9 years of age
  2. John Kennedy       first sworn in at 43.6 years of age
  3. William Clinton     first sworn in at 46.4 years of age
  4. Ulysses Grant      first sworn in at 46.9 years of age
  5. Barack Obama      first sworn in at 47.5 years of age
  ❖ John Kennedy was the youngest man to be *elected* President.

➢ The five oldest Presidents:
  1. Donald Trump      first sworn in at 70.6 years of age
  2. Ronald Reagan     first sworn in at 69.95 years of age
  3. James Buchanan    first sworn in at 65.9 years of age
  4. George H.W. Bush   first sworn in at 64.6 years of age
  5. Zachary Taylor     first sworn in at 64.3 years of age

➢ The oldest President was 65% older than the youngest.

## Presidents' Ages at First Inauguration

- ➤ The average age of the Presidents on the date of their first inauguration:

| All Presidents | | Post War Presidents | |
|---|---|---|---|
| ❖ Average: | 55.5 years of age | ❖ Average: | 57.3 years of age |
| ❖ Median: | 54.9 years of age | ❖ Median: | 56.0 years of age |

- ➤ Some Presidents died shortly after leaving office; others enjoyed decades of retirement:

  - ❖ The Five Shortest Retirements
    1. James Polk                    103 days
    2. Chester Arthur          1 year, 259 days
    3. George Washington    2 years, 285 days
    4. Woodrow Wilson       2 years, 335 days
    5. Calvin Coolidge         3 years, 337 days

  - ❖ The Five Longest Retirements
    1. James Carter          36 years,   0 days  (as of 20th January 2017)
    2. Herbert Hoover       31 years, 230 days
    3. Gerald Ford            29 years, 340 days
    4. John Adams            25 years, 122 days
    5. George H.W. Bush    24 years,   0 days  (as of 20th January 2017)

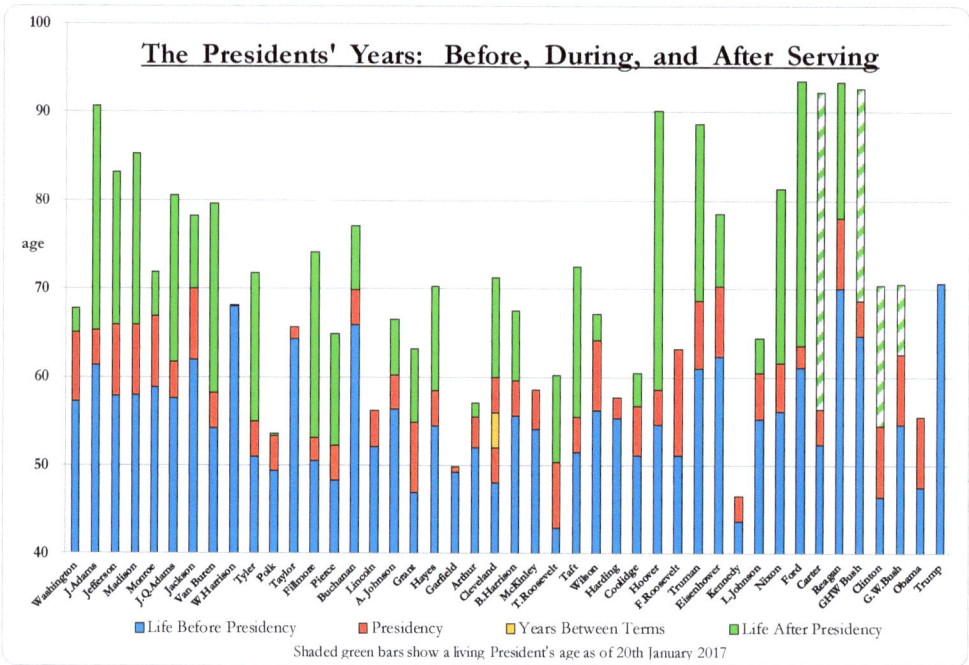

**The Presidents' Years: Before, During, and After Serving**

Life Before Presidency ■   Presidency ■   Years Between Terms ■   Life After Presidency ■

Shaded green bars show a living President's age as of 20th January 2017

➤ The five youngest President - Vice President teams:

| President / Vice President | First Sworn In | Total Age |
|---|---|---|
| 1. William Clinton and Albert Gore | 20 January 1993 | 91.2 years |
| 2. Ulysses Grant and Schuyler Colfax | 4 March 1869 | 92.8 years |
| 3. Theodore Roosevelt and Charles Fairbanks | 4 March 1905 | 95.7 years |
| 4. John Kennedy and Lyndon Johnson | 20 January 1961 | 96.0 years |
| 5. John Quincy Adams and John Calhoun | 4 March 1825 | 100.6 years |

➤ The five oldest President - Vice President teams:

| President / Vice President | First Sworn In | Total Age |
|---|---|---|
| 1. Harry Truman and Alben Barkley | 20 January 1949 | 132.1 years |
| 2. Donald Trump and Michael Pence | 20 January 2017 | 128.2 years |
| 3. Ronald Reagan and George H.W. Bush | 20 January 1981 | 126.6 years |
| 4. Herbert Hoover and Charles Curtis | 4 March 1929 | 123.7 years |
| 5. James Madison and George Clinton | 4 March 1809 | 123.6 years |

➤ The oldest President – Vice President team was about 45% older than the youngest.

➤ The age of the President - Vice President teams as a group:

| All Teams | | Post War Teams | |
|---|---|---|---|
| ❖ Average: | 109.6 years of age | ❖ Average: | 110.6 years of age |
| ❖ Median: | 109.0 years of age | ❖ Median: | 107.7 years of age |

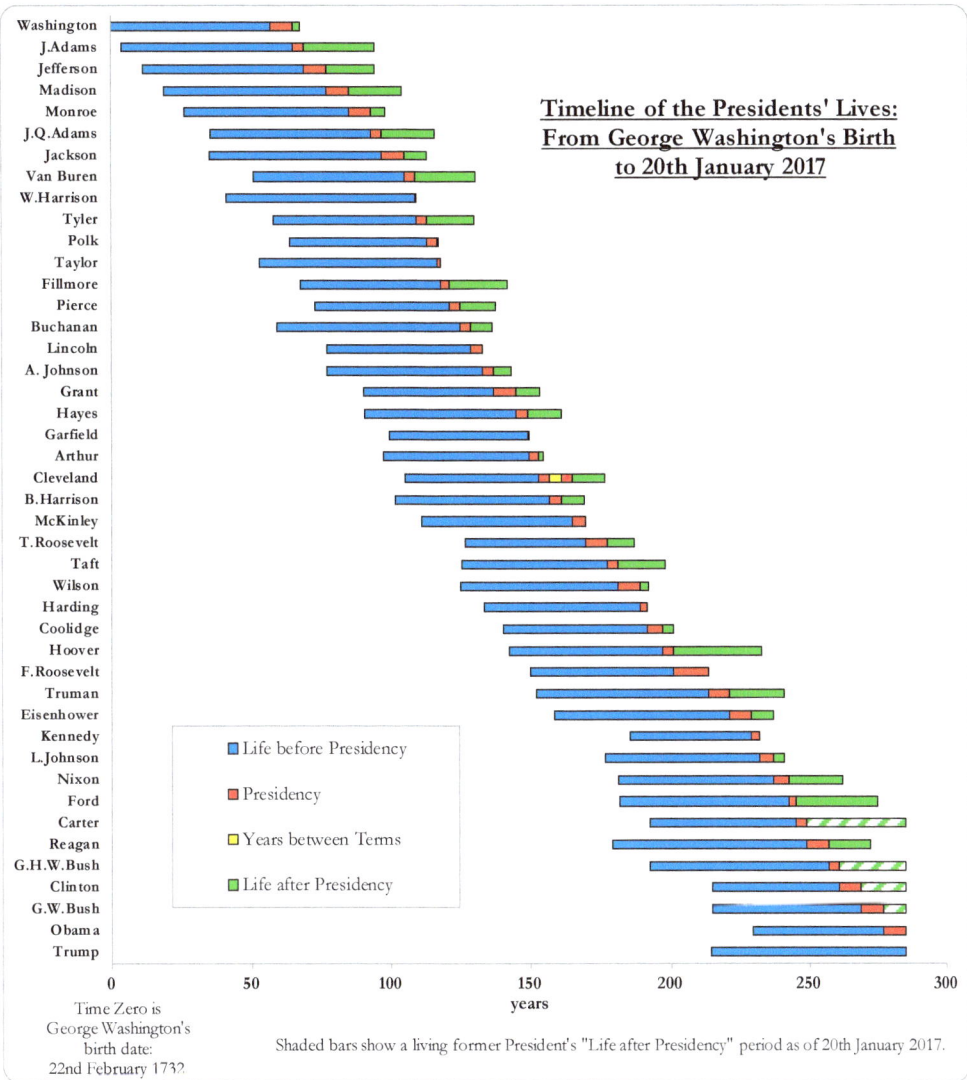

**Timeline of the Presidents' Lives:
From George Washington's Birth
to 20th January 2017**

Time Zero is George Washington's birth date: 22nd February 1732

Shaded bars show a living former President's "Life after Presidency" period as of 20th January 2017.

# The Presidents' Education

➢ Thirty-four Presidents graduated from college; almost one-quarter did not.

➢ With one exception, all Presidents serving in the 20$^{th}$ and 21$^{st}$ centuries went to college. Harry Truman was the exception.

➢ Some of the men who did not have a college degree were self-educated. In the 18$^{th}$ and 19$^{th}$ centuries, several Presidents read the law and became practicing lawyers.

➢ Abraham Lincoln was probably the least formally educated of all Presidents; he is said to have had only one year of formal schooling.

➢ Twenty-four colleges boast a Presidential alumnus; five colleges sent multiple men to the White House:
   1. Harvard sent five.
   2. William and Mary sent three.
   3. Yale sent three.
   4. Princeton sent two.
   5. West Point sent two.

## The Presidents' Undergraduate Education

| President | College | President | College |
|---|---|---|---|
| George Washington | *none* | Grover Cleveland | *none* |
| John Adams | Harvard | William McKinley | Allegheny |
| Thomas Jefferson | William and Mary | Theodore Roosevelt | Harvard |
| James Madison | Princeton | William Taft | Yale |
| James Monroe | William and Mary | Woodrow Wilson | Princeton |
| John Quincy Adams | Harvard | Warren Harding | Ohio Central |
| Andrew Jackson | *none* | Calvin Coolidge | Amherst |
| Martin Van Buren | *none* | Herbert Hoover | Stanford |
| William Harrison | *none* | Franklin Roosevelt | Harvard |
| John Tyler | William and Mary | Harry Truman | *none* |
| James Polk | UNC Chapel Hill | Dwight Eisenhower | West Point |
| Zachary Taylor | *none* | John Kennedy | Harvard |
| Millard Fillmore | *none* | Lyndon Johnson | Southwest Texas State Teachers |
| Franklin Pierce | Bowdoin | | |
| James Buchanan | Dickinson | Richard Nixon | Whittier |
| Abraham Lincoln | *none* | Gerald Ford | Michigan |
| Andrew Johnson | *none* | James Carter | Naval Academy |
| Ulysses Grant | West Point | Ronald Reagan | Eureka |
| Rutherford Hayes | Kenyon | George H.W. Bush | Yale |
| James Garfield | Williams | William Clinton | Georgetown |
| Chester Arthur | Union | George W. Bush | Yale |
| Grover Cleveland | *none* | Barack Obama | Columbia |
| Benjamin Harrison | Miami of Ohio | Donald Trump | Pennsylvania |

➢ Very few Presidents earned graduate or professional degrees.

❖ Woodrow Wilson is the only President who held a Ph.D. (earned in Political Science at Johns Hopkins University).

❖ Only George W. Bush held an M.B.A. (earned at Harvard Business School).

❖ Seven Presidents earned law degrees:

| | | |
|---|---|---|
| 1. Rutherford Hayes (Harvard) | 5. Gerald Ford (Yale) |
| 2. William McKinley (Albany) | 6. William Clinton (Yale) |
| 3. William Taft (Cincinnati) | 7. Barack Obama (Harvard) |
| 4. Richard Nixon (Duke) | |

➢ Only one President has been a Rhodes Scholar: William Clinton, who studied Philosophy, Politics, and Economics at the University of Oxford.

➢ Of the 78 men who have served as President and/or Vice President (through Trump-Pence), 62 of them graduated from college, having attended 42 different colleges. Nine undergraduate institutions produced more than one President and/or Vice President:

1. Harvard produced seven.
2. Princeton produced five.
3. Yale produced four.
4. William and Mary produced three.
5. Columbia produced two.
6. University of Minnesota produced two.
7. University of North Carolina at Chapel Hill produced two.
8. West Point produced two.
9. Hanover College produced two.

## The Presidents' Careers Prior to Entering the White House

➢ Most Presidents entered the White House with experience as an elected politician at the state and/or national level.

➢ Fourteen Presidents had been Vice President.

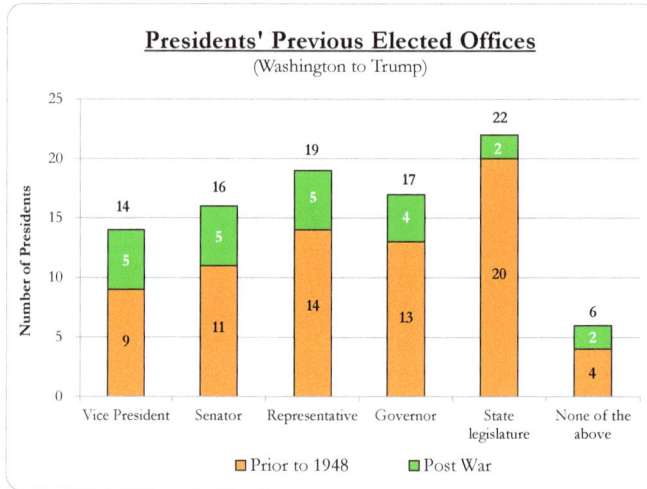

➢ Most Presidents – 57% – had served in Congress.

➢ Taking into account state legislatures, almost three-quarters of Presidents had legislative experience. Twelve had none:

1. Zachary Taylor
2. Ulysses Grant
3. Chester Arthur
4. Grover Cleveland
5. William Taft
6. Woodrow Wilson
7. Herbert Hoover
8. Dwight Eisenhower
9. Ronald Reagan
10. William Clinton
11. George W. Bush
12. Donald Trump

➢ Four of every ten Presidents had been a state Governor.

➢ Two Presidents had been Vice President, a Governor, a Senator, a Member of the House of Representatives, and a state legislator.

1. John Tyler
2. Andrew Johnson

❖ Both men ascended to the Presidency and were not subsequently nominated to run in their own right.

## Presidents with Experience in Three Key Offices

| Of these Three Offices, → <br><br> Presents who had held ↓ | Vice President | | Governor | | Congress | |
|---|---|---|---|---|---|---|
| | All Presidents | Post War Presidents | All Presidents | Post War Presidents | All Presidents | Post War Presidents |
| . . . only this office | 1 | 0 | 7 | 4 | 12 | 2 |
| . . . this office and had served in Congress | 6 | 5 | 4 | 0 | | |
| . . . this office and had served as a Governor | 3 | 0 | | | | |
| . . . this office and had served as a Governor and in Congress | 3 | 0 | | | | |

➢ Six Presidents had no experience as an elected politician:

1. Zachary Taylor
2. Ulysses Grant
3. William Taft
4. Herbert Hoover
5. Dwight Eisenhower
6. Donald Trump

❖ Taylor, Grant, and Eisenhower were career military officers.

❖ Taft and Hoover each had experience in the Federal government, including having served as a Cabinet Secretary.

❖ Donald Trump is the only President who had no government or military experience at all.

❖ While Chester Arthur does not make this list, his only experience in elected office was as Vice President for 199 days prior to ascending to the Presidency when James Garfield was assassinated.

# Each President's Prior Elected Political Offices

| President | Vice President | Senate | House | State Legislature | Governor |
|---|---|---|---|---|---|
| George Washington | | | | ✓ | |
| John Adams | ✓ | | | ✓ | |
| Thomas Jefferson | ✓ | | | ✓ | ✓ |
| James Madison | | | ✓ | ✓ | |
| James Monroe | | ✓ | ✓ | ✓ | ✓ |
| John Quincy Adams | | ✓ | | ✓ | |
| Andrew Jackson | | ✓ | ✓ | | |
| Martin van Buren | ✓ | ✓ | | ✓ | ✓ |
| William Harrison | | ✓ | ✓ | ✓ | |
| John Tyler | ✓ | ✓ | ✓ | ✓ | ✓ |
| James Polk | | | ✓ | ✓ | ✓ |
| Zachary Taylor | | | | | |
| Millard Fillmore | ✓ | | ✓ | ✓ | |
| Franklin Pierce | | ✓ | ✓ | ✓ | |
| James Buchanan | | ✓ | ✓ | ✓ | |
| Abraham Lincoln | | | ✓ | ✓ | |
| Andrew Johnson | ✓ | ✓ | ✓ | ✓ | ✓ |
| Ulysses Grant | | | | | |
| Rutherford Hayes | | | ✓ | | ✓ |
| James Garfield | | | ✓ | ✓ | |
| Chester Arthur | ✓ | | | | |
| Grover Cleveland | | | | | ✓ |
| Benjamin Harrison | | ✓ | | | |
| William McKinley | | | ✓ | | ✓ |
| Theodore Roosevelt | ✓ | | | ✓ | ✓ |
| William Taft | | | | | |
| Woodrow Wilson | | | | | ✓ |
| Warren Harding | | ✓ | | ✓ | |
| Calvin Coolidge | ✓ | | | ✓ | ✓ |
| Herbert Hoover | | | | | |
| Franklin Roosevelt | | | | ✓ | ✓ |
| Harry Truman | ✓ | ✓ | | | |
| Dwight Eisenhower | | | | | |
| John Kennedy | | ✓ | ✓ | | |
| Lyndon Johnson | ✓ | ✓ | ✓ | | |
| Richard Nixon | ✓ | ✓ | ✓ | | |
| Gerald Ford | ✓ | | ✓ | | |
| James Carter | | | | ✓ | ✓ |
| Ronald Reagan | | | | | ✓ |
| George H.W. Bush | ✓ | | ✓ | | |
| William Clinton | | | | | ✓ |
| George W. Bush | | | | | ✓ |
| Barack Obama | | ✓ | | ✓ | |
| Donald Trump | | | | | |

# Presidents' Prior Elected Political Offices . . . by the Numbers

| The Five Offices<br>(Vice President, Governor, Senator, Representative, State Legislator) | All Presidents | | Post War Presidents | |
|---|---|---|---|---|
| | # | % | # | % |
| Number of Presidents | 44 | | 13 | |
| Presidents who had been **Vice President** . . . | 14 | 32% | 5 | 38% |
| . . . and only Vice President | 1 | 2% | 0 | 0% |
| . . . and a Governor only | 0 | 0% | 0 | 0% |
| . . . and a Governor and in Congress only | 0 | 0% | 0 | 0% |
| . . . and a Governor and a state legislator only | 3 | 7% | 0 | 0% |
| . . . and a Governor and in any legislature | 6 | 14% | 5 | 38% |
| . . . and in Congress only | 5 | 11% | 5 | 38% |
| . . . in the Senate only | 1 | 2% | 1 | 8% |
| . . . in the House only | 2 | 5% | 2 | 15% |
| . . . in both the Senate and the House | 2 | 5% | 2 | 15% |
| . . . and in Congress and in a state legislature only | 1 | 2% | 0 | 0% |
| . . . and a state legislator only | 1 | 2% | 0 | 0% |
| . . . and in any legislature only | 2 | 5% | 1 | 8% |
| Presidents who had been a **Governor** . . . | 17 | 39% | 4 | 31% |
| . . . and only a Governor | 5 | 11% | 3 | 23% |
| . . . and in Congress only | 2 | 5% | 0 | 0% |
| . . . in the Senate only | 0 | 0% | 0 | 0% |
| . . . in the House only | 2 | 5% | 0 | 0% |
| . . . in both the Senate and the House | 0 | 0% | 0 | 0% |
| . . . and in a state legislature only | 1 | 2% | 1 | 8% |
| . . . and in a legislature | 12 | 27% | 1 | 8% |
| . . . at the state level only | 5 | 11% | 1 | 8% |
| . . . in Congress | 2 | 5% | 0 | 0% |
| . . . at both the state and Congressional levels | 5 | 11% | 0 | 0% |
| . . . and had no legislative experience | 5 | 11% | 3 | 23% |
| Presidents who had been neither Vice President nor Governor | 19 | 43% | 4 | 31% |
| Presidents who had legislative experience . . . | 32 | 73% | 8 | 62% |
| . . . in the U.S. Congress | 25 | 57% | 7 | 54% |
| . . . in the House | 19 | 43% | 5 | 38% |
| . . . in the Senate | 16 | 36% | 5 | 38% |
| . . . in the Senate and the House | 10 | 23% | 3 | 23% |
| . . . in the House but not the Senate | 9 | 20% | 2 | 15% |
| . . . in the Senate but not the House | 6 | 14% | 2 | 15% |
| . . . in Congress but not in a state legislature | 10 | 23% | 6 | 46% |
| . . . in a state legislature | 22 | 50% | 2 | 15% |
| . . . but not also in Congress | 7 | 16% | 1 | 8% |
| . . . nowhere | 12 | 27% | 5 | 38% |
| . . . but had not been a Governor | 20 | 45% | 7 | 54% |
| Presidents who had been neither Vice President,<br>a Governor, nor a legislator in Congress or at the state level | 6 | 14% | 2 | 15% |
| Presidents who had been a Cabinet member | 8 | 18% | 0 | 0% |

- ➢ Eight Presidents served in a predecessor's Cabinet but none of them was President in the modern era:

  | | | |
  |---|---|---|
  | 1. | Thomas Jefferson | Secretary of State under George Washington |
  | 2. | James Madison | Secretary of State under Thomas Jefferson |
  | 3. | James Monroe | Secretary of State under James Madison |
  | | | Secretary of War under James Madison |
  | 4. | John Quincy Adams | Secretary of State under James Monroe |
  | 5. | Martin Van Buren | Secretary of State under Andrew Jackson |
  | 6. | James Buchanan | Secretary of State under James Polk |
  | 7. | William Taft | Secretary of War under Theodore Roosevelt |
  | 8. | Herbert Hoover | Secretary of Commerce under Calvin Coolidge |

- ➢ Six of the eight Presidents who held Cabinet positions under a predecessor served during the country's first century, and all six were Secretary of State.

- ➢ Five of the eight served in the Cabinet positions immediately prior to being elected President. Three had served earlier:

  1. Thomas Jefferson    2. John Quincy Adams    3. James Buchanan

- ➢ In addition to having served as a legislator and as a Governor, U.S. presidents have come from a wide variety of backgrounds:
  - ❖ Most have been lawyers (27 of the 44 Presidents have been lawyers, but only four in the modern era).
  - ❖ A number have been diplomats, especially in the country's early decades.
  - ❖ Some have served in Federal government departments and agencies.
  - ❖ A number have held state and local government jobs including
    - state attorney general
    - state comptroller
    - mayor
    - postmaster
    - prosecutor
    - sheriff
  - ❖ Many had experience outside of government:
    - actor
    - architect
    - businessman
    - community organizer
    - journalist
    - engineer
    - farmer
    - haberdasher
    - inventor
    - judge
    - professor
    - rancher
    - schoolteacher
    - surveyor
    - tailor
    - university president

➢ Almost two-thirds of Presidents – 28 of the 44 – served in the armed forces.

➢ Sixteen Presidents did not serve in the military:

| | | |
|---|---|---|
| 1. John Adams | 7. Grover Cleveland | 12. Herbert Hoover |
| 2. Thomas Jefferson | 8. William Taft | 13. Franklin Roosevelt |
| 3. John Quincy Adams | 9. Woodrow Wilson | 14. William Clinton |
| 4. Martin Van Buren | 10. Warren Harding | 15. Barack Obama |
| 5. Millard Fillmore | 11. Calvin Coolidge | 16. Donald Trump |
| 6. Andrew Johnson | | |

➢ Almost three-quarters of those who served in the military – 20 of the 28 – saw combat action. Thus, nearly one-half of all Presidents saw combat action.

## The Presidents and Military Service

| President * | Highest Rank Attained | Armed Service ** |
|---|---|---|
| **George Washington** | General of the Armies of the United States | U.S. Army |
| James Madison | Colonel | Virginia militia |
| **James Monroe** | Major | Continental Army |
| **Andrew Jackson** | Major General (2 stars) | U.S. Army |
| **William Harrison** | Major General (2 stars) | U.S. Army |
| John Tyler | Captain | Virginia militia |
| James Polk | Colonel | Tennessee militia |
| **Zachary Taylor** | Major General (2 stars) | U.S. Army |
| **Franklin Pierce** | Brigadier General (appointed, not earned) | U.S. Army |
| **James Buchanan** | Private | U.S. Army |
| Abraham Lincoln | Captain | Illinois militia |
| **Ulysses Grant** | General (4 stars) | U.S. Army |
| **Rutherford Hayes** | Colonel / Brevet Brigadier General | U.S. Army |
| **James Garfield** | Major General (2 stars) | U.S. Army |
| Chester Arthur | Quartermaster General | New York militia |
| **Benjamin Harrison** | Colonel / Brevet Brigadier General | U.S. Army |
| **William McKinley** | Captain / Brevet Major | U.S. Army |
| **Theodore Roosevelt** | Colonel | U.S. Army |
| **Harry Truman** | Colonel | U.S. Army |
| **Dwight Eisenhower** | General of the Army (5 stars) | U.S. Army |
| **John Kennedy** | Lieutenant | U.S. Navy |
| **Lyndon Johnson** | Commander | U.S. Navy |
| **Richard Nixon** | Commander | U.S. Navy |
| **Gerald Ford** | Lieutenant Commander | U.S. Navy |
| James Carter | Lieutenant | U.S. Navy |
| Ronald Reagan | Captain | U.S. Army |
| **George H.W. Bush** | Lieutenant Junior Grade | U.S. Navy |
| George W. Bush | First Lieutenant | Texas Air National Guard |

| * Boldface type indicates that the President saw combat action. | ** Some Presidents also served in a state militia. |
|---|---|

- George Washington was a Colonel in the Virginia militia, General and Commander-in-Chief of the Continental Army, and died a Lieutenant General in the U.S. Army. The "General of the Armies" title was created by Gerald Ford and bestowed on Washington posthumously. No past, current, or future officer can rise to this rank and no superior rank can be created.

- Ten Presidents held the rank of General, although three of them were either appointed to that rank or were Brevet Generals.

- Andrew Jackson is the only President who was a prisoner of war.

- At not quite 19 years of age, George H.W. Bush was the youngest pilot in the U.S. Navy at that time.

- James Buchanan is the only President who served in the armed forces and did not rise above the rank of Private.

## Some Salient Events During Each Presidency

➢ Almost all Presidents have had the opportunity to appoint at least one Supreme Court Justice.

➢ George Washington appointed the most (10) and Franklin Roosevelt eight.

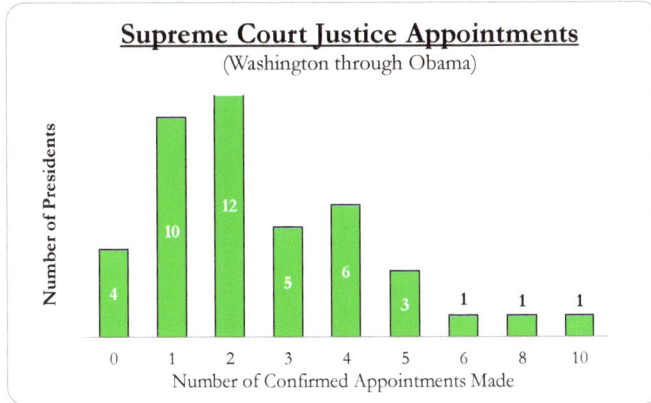

### Supreme Court Justice Appointments
(Washington through Obama)

Number of Presidents

| Number of Confirmed Appointments Made | | | | | | | | |
|---|---|---|---|---|---|---|---|---|
| 0 | 1 | 2 | 3 | 4 | 5 | 6 | 8 | 10 |
| 4 | 10 | 12 | 5 | 6 | 3 | 1 | 1 | 1 |

➢ Four Presidents did not have the chance to appoint a Justice:
   1. William Harrison
   2. Zachary Taylor
   3. Andrew Johnson
   4. James Carter
   ❖ Of the four, only James Carter served a full term as President.

➢ John Tyler had the toughest time with his Supreme Court nominees. He submitted five names to the Senate and . . .
   ❖ Only one was confirmed.
   ❖ One was rejected.
   ❖ One was rejected, then re-nominated, and then withdrawn.
   ❖ One was nominated three times and withdrawn.
   ❖ On one, the Senate took action.

➢ Ten Presidents have had a Supreme Court Justice nominee rejected; some had two.
   1. George Washington
   2. James Madison
   3. John Tyler
   4. James Polk
   5. James Buchanan
   6. Ulysses Grant
   7. Grover Cleveland  (2)
   8. Herbert Hoover
   9. Richard Nixon  (2)
   10. Ronald Reagan

# Supreme Court Justice Appointments, by President

| President | # of Justices | President | # of Justices |
|---|---|---|---|
| George Washington | 10 | Benjamin Harrison | 4 |
| John Adams | 3 | William McKinley | 1 |
| Thomas Jefferson | 3 | Theodore Roosevelt | 3 |
| James Madison | 2 | William Taft | 5 |
| James Monroe | 1 | Woodrow Wilson | 3 |
| John Quincy Adams | 1 | Warren Harding | 4 |
| Andrew Jackson | 6 | Calvin Coolidge | 1 |
| Martin van Buren | 2 | Herbert Hoover | 2 |
| William Harrison | 0 | Franklin Roosevelt | 8 |
| John Tyler | 1 | Harry Truman | 4 |
| James Polk | 2 | Dwight Eisenhower | 5 |
| Zachary Taylor | 0 | John Kennedy | 2 |
| Millard Fillmore | 1 | Lyndon Johnson | 2 |
| Franklin Pierce | 1 | Richard Nixon | 4 |
| James Buchanan | 1 | Gerald Ford | 1 |
| Abraham Lincoln | 5 | James Carter | 0 |
| Andrew Johnson | 0 | Ronald Reagan | 3 |
| Ulysses Grant | 4 | George H.W. Bush | 2 |
| Rutherford Hayes | 2 | William Clinton | 2 |
| James Garfield | 1 | George W. Bush | 2 |
| Chester Arthur | 2 | Barack Obama | 2 |
| Grover Cleveland (both terms) | 4 | Donald Trump * | 1 |

These data exclude nominees who were withdrawn or rejected, confirmed but declined to serve, whose nomination the Senate did not act upon, and Chief-Justice nominations of sitting Associate Justices. There have been nine Justices (eight Associates and the Chief Justice) since the passage of the Judiciary Act of 1869. Prior to that, the number ranged from the initial six to as many as ten.
* As of 30th April 2017. This appointment raised the total number of confirmed appointments to 113.

➤ Of the 37 states admitted to the Union, three joined in the 18th century, 29 in the 19th century, and five in the 20th century. Only 17 Presidents presided over the admission to the Union of a new state.

➤ The greatest number of states was admitted during the Presidency of Benjamin Harrison. Four other Presidents presided over the admission of more than two new states:

1. Benjamin Harrison       6 new states
2. James Monroe            5 new states
3. George Washington       3 new states
4. James Polk              3 new states
5. James Buchanan          3 new states

# States Admitted to the Union During Each President's Tenure

| President | # | State | Date Admitted |
|---|---|---|---|
| George Washington | 3 | Vermont | 4-Mar-1791 |
| | | Kentucky | 1-Jun-1792 |
| | | Tennessee | 1-Jun-1796 |
| John Adams | | | |
| Thomas Jefferson | 1 | Ohio | 1-Mar-1803 |
| James Madison | 2 | Louisiana | 30-Apr-1812 |
| | | Indiana | 11-Dec-1816 |
| James Monroe | 5 | Mississippi | 10-Dec-1817 |
| | | Illinois | 3-Dec-1818 |
| | | Alabama | 14-Dec-1819 |
| | | Maine | 15-Mar-1820 |
| | | Missouri | 1-Aug-1821 |
| John Quincy Adams | | | |
| Andrew Jackson | 2 | Arkansas | 15-Jun-1836 |
| | | Michigan | 26-Jan-1837 |
| Martin Van Buren, William Harrison | | | |
| John Tyler | 1 | Florida | 3-Mar-1845 |
| James Polk | 3 | Texas | 29-Dec-1845 |
| | | Iowa | 28-Dec-1846 |
| | | Wisconsin | 29-May-1848 |
| Zachary Taylor | | | |
| Millard Fillmore | 1 | California | 9-Sep-1850 |
| Franklin Pierce | | | |
| James Buchanan | 3 | Minnesota | 11-May-1858 |
| | | Oregon | 14-Feb-1859 |
| | | Kansas | 29-Jan-1861 |
| Abraham Lincoln | 2 | West Virginia | 20-Jun-1863 |
| | | Nevada | 31-Oct-1864 |
| Andrew Johnson | 1 | Nebraska | 1-Mar-1867 |
| Ulysses Grant | 1 | Colorado | 1-Aug-1876 |
| Rutherford Hayes, James Garfield, Chester Arthur, Grover Cleveland (1st term) | | | |
| Benjamin Harrison | 6 | North Dakota | 2-Nov-1889 |
| | | South Dakota | 2-Nov-1889 |
| | | Montana | 8-Nov-1889 |
| | | Washington | 11-Nov-1889 |
| | | Idaho | 3-Jul-1890 |
| | | Wyoming | 10-Jul-1890 |
| Grover Cleveland | 1 | Utah | 4-Jan-1896 |
| William McKinley | | | |
| Theodore Roosevelt | 1 | Oklahoma | 16-Nov-1907 |
| William Taft | 2 | New Mexico | 6-Jan-1912 |
| | | Arizona | 14-Feb-1912 |
| Woodrow Wilson, Warren Harding, Calvin Coolidge, Herbert Hoover, Franklin Roosevelt, Harry Truman | | | |
| Dwight Eisenhower | 2 | Alaska | 3-Jan-1959 |
| | | Hawaii | 21-Aug-1959 |

**N.B.:** No new states were admitted to the Union during the terms of the Presidents whose names appear in gray or those who served after Eisenhower.

> Fifteen sitting Presidents witnessed the proposal of a Constitutional amendment during their term, and amendments were ratified during 15 Presidencies (although not exactly the same 15).

### Constitutional Amendments Proposed and Ratified During Each President's Tenure

| President | Amendment Proposed | | Amendment Ratified | | Years to Ratify |
|---|---|---|---|---|---|
| | Amend-ment # | Date | Amend-ment # | Date | |
| George Washington | $1^{st} – 10^{th}$ | 25-Sep-1789 | $1^{st} – 10^{th}$ | 15-Dec-1791 | 2.2 |
| | $27^{th}$ | 27-Sep-1789 | | | |
| | $11^{th}$ | 4-Mar-1794 | $11^{th}$ | 7-Feb-1795 | 0.9 |
| John Adams | | | | | |
| Thomas Jefferson | $12^{th}$ | 9-Dec-1803 | $12^{th}$ | 15-Jun-1804 | 0.5 |
| James Madison, James Monroe, John Quincy Adams, Andrew Jackson, Martin Van Buren, William Harrison, John Tyler, James Polk, Zachary Taylor, Millard Fillmore, Franklin Pierce, James Buchanan | | | | | |
| Abraham Lincoln | $13^{th}$ | 31-Jan-1865 | | | |
| Andrew Johnson | | | $13^{th}$ | 6-Dec-1865 | 0.8 |
| | $14^{th}$ | 13-Jun-1866 | $14^{th}$ | 9-Jul-1868 | 2.1 |
| | $15^{th}$ | 26-Feb-1869 | | | |
| Ulysses Grant | | | $15^{th}$ | 3-Feb-1870 | 0.9 |
| Rutherford Hayes, James Garfield, Chester Arthur, Grover Cleveland (both terms), Benjamin Harrison, William McKinley, Theodore Roosevelt | | | | | |
| William Taft | $16^{th}$ | 12-Jul-1909 | $16^{th}$ | 3-Feb-1913 | 3.6 |
| | $17^{th}$ | 13-May-1912 | | | |
| Woodrow Wilson | | | $17^{th}$ | 8-Apr-1913 | 0.9 |
| | $18^{th}$ | 18-Dec-1917 | $18^{th}$ | 16-Jan-1919 | 1.1 |
| | $19^{th}$ | 4-Jun-1919 | $19^{th}$ | 18-Aug-1920 | 1.2 |
| Warren Harding, Calvin Coolidge | | | | | |
| Herbert Hoover | $20^{th}$ | 2-Mar-1932 | $20^{th}$ | 23-Jan-1933 | 0.9 |
| | $21^{st}$ | 20-Feb-1933 | | | |
| Franklin Roosevelt | | | $21^{st}$ | 5-Dec-1933 | 0.8 |
| Harry Truman | $22^{nd}$ | 21-Mar-1947 | $22^{nd}$ | 27-Feb-1951 | 3.9 |
| Dwight Eisenhower | $23^{rd}$ | 17-Jun-1960 | | | |
| John Kennedy | | | $23^{rd}$ | 29-Mar-1961 | 0.8 |
| | $24^{th}$ | 27-Aug-1962 | | | |
| Lyndon Johnson | | | $24^{th}$ | 23-Jan-1964 | 1.4 |
| | $25^{th}$ | 6-Jul-1965 | $25^{th}$ | 10-Feb-1967 | 1.6 |
| Richard Nixon | $26^{th}$ | 23-Mar-1971 | $26^{th}$ | 1-Jul-1971 | 0.3 |
| Gerald Ford, James Carter, Ronald Reagan | | | | | |
| George H.W. Bush | | | $27^{th}$ | 7-May-1992 | 202.7 |
| William Clinton, George W. Bush, Barack Obama | | | | | |

Includes only amendments that were ultimately ratified.
No amendments were proposed or ratified during the terms of the Presidents whose names appear in gray.

- ➢ Amendments to the Constitution occurred in waves:
  - ❖ 13 amendments – including the Bill of Rights – were proposed in the early years of the Republic, covering the administrations of George Washington, John Adams, and Thomas Jefferson.
  - ❖ The next three were proposed in the 1860s when Abraham Lincoln and Andrew Johnson were in office.
  - ❖ Four amendments were proposed in the second decade of the 20th century when William Taft and Woodrow Wilson were President.
  - ❖ The remaining seven amendments were proposed over the 1930s, 1940s, 1960s, and the early 1970s.

- ➢ Most successful amendments were ratified by the required three-quarters of states within a few months to a year or two of being proposed.
  - ❖ The 27th amendment, which governs pay raises for members of Congress, was proposed at the beginning of George Washington's first term and ratified at the end of George H.W. Bush's term. Thus, it took more than 202 years to win ratification.

# The Presidents... Personally

➢ The Presidents were quite tall . . . and very short.

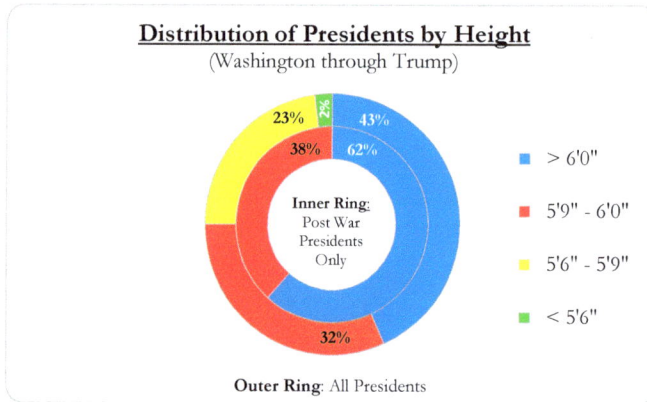

### Distribution of Presidents by Height
(Washington through Trump)

23%  2%  43%

38%  62%

**Inner Ring:**
Post War
Presidents
Only

32%

■ > 6'0"

■ 5'9" - 6'0"

■ 5'6" - 5'9"

■ < 5'6"

**Outer Ring**: All Presidents

➢ A full 12 inches separates the tallest and shortest Presidents.
  ❖ Standing 6'4" tall, Abraham Lincoln and Lyndon Johnson tied for tallest.
  ❖ At 5'4", James Madison was the shortest President.

➢ The five longest-lived Presidents:
  1. Gerald Ford          died when 93.5 years of age
  2. Ronald Reagan        died when 93.3 years of age
  3. John Adams           died when 90.4 years of age
  4. Herbert Hoover       died when 90.2 years of age
  5. Harry Truman         died when 88.6 years of age

➢ The five shortest-lived Presidents:
  1. John Kennedy         died when 46.5 years of age    (assassinated)
  2. William Harrison     died when 48.1 years of age
  3. James Garfield       died when 49.8 years of age    (assassinated)
  4. James Polk           died when 53.6 years of age
  5. Abraham Lincoln      died when 56.2 years of age    (assassinated)

➢ The life span of the Presidents as a group (excluding those still living):

<table>
<tr><td colspan="2">All Presidents</td><td colspan="2">Post War Presidents</td></tr>
<tr><td>❖ Average:</td><td>70.8 years of age</td><td>❖ Average:</td><td>78.0 years of age</td></tr>
<tr><td>❖ Median:</td><td>69.2 years of age</td><td>❖ Median:</td><td>81.3 years of age</td></tr>
</table>

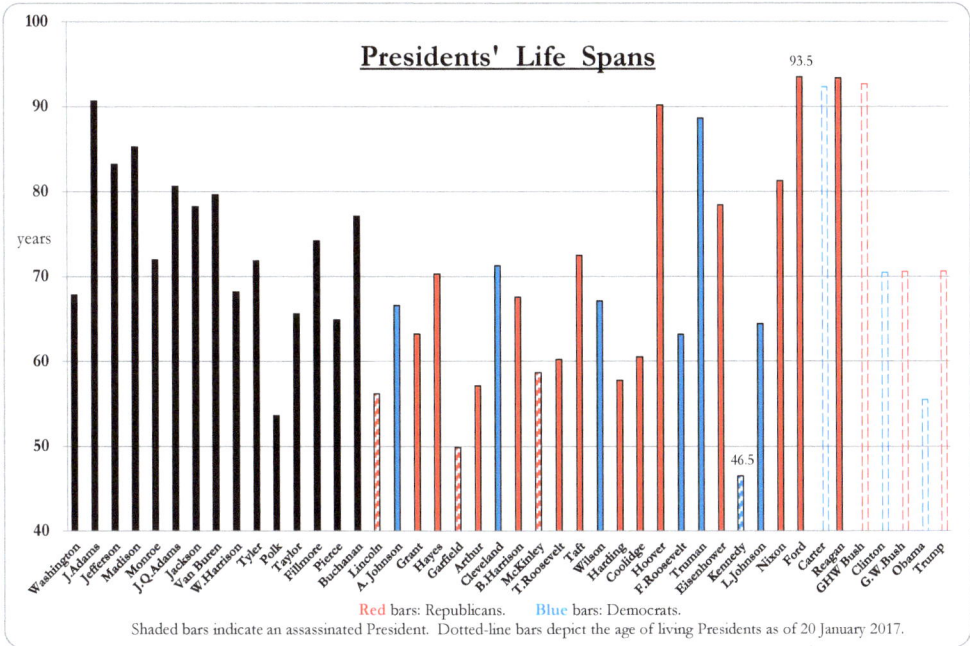

Presidents' Life Spans

Red bars: Republicans.    Blue bars: Democrats.
Shaded bars indicate an assassinated President. Dotted-line bars depict the age of living Presidents as of 20 January 2017.

➢ John Kennedy was the first and, to date, the only Catholic President.

➢ Barack Obama was the first and, to date, the only Black President.

➢ The Presidents are called by 29 different first names, 23 of which are unique.
   ❖ James is the most popular Presidential name; six Presidents bear that name.
   ❖ Four Presidents are named John and four William.
   ❖ Three are named George.
   ❖ Two are named Andrew and two Franklin.

- ➤ The 44 Presidents hailed from 16 different states.
  - ❖ Four states account for more than half of the Presidents:
    1. New York
    2. Ohio
    3. Virginia
    4. Massachusetts

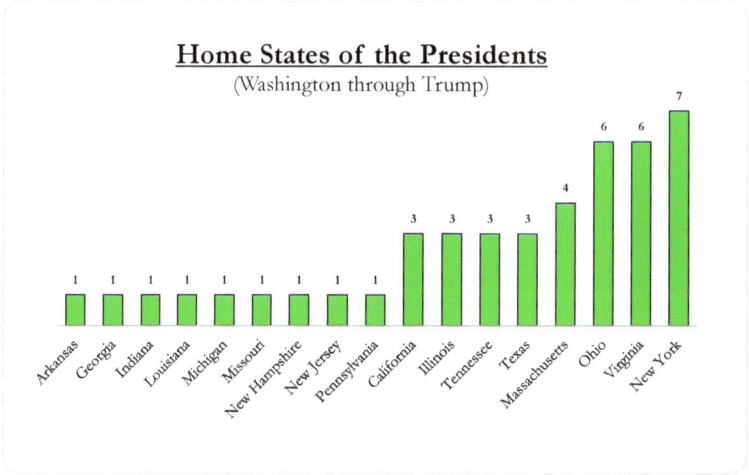

### Home States of the Presidents
(Washington through Trump)

| State | Count |
|-------|-------|
| Arkansas | 1 |
| Georgia | 1 |
| Indiana | 1 |
| Louisiana | 1 |
| Michigan | 1 |
| Missouri | 1 |
| New Hampshire | 1 |
| New Jersey | 1 |
| Pennsylvania | 1 |
| California | 3 |
| Illinois | 3 |
| Tennessee | 3 |
| Texas | 3 |
| Massachusetts | 4 |
| Ohio | 6 |
| Virginia | 6 |
| New York | 7 |

*See the Appendices for a listing of each President's home state.*

- ➤ Four of the first five Presidents hailed from Virginia. Massachusetts native John Adams was the exception.

- ➤ The 13 post war Presidents hailed from nine different states. Texas, California, and New York have sent more than one man to the White House in the post war period.

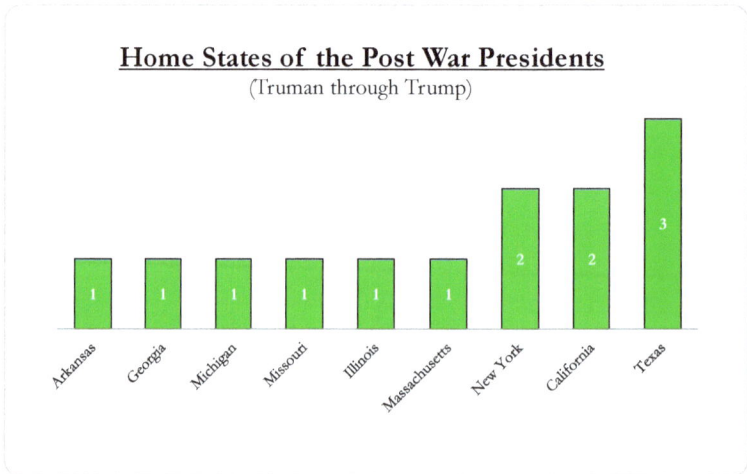

### Home States of the Post War Presidents
(Truman through Trump)

| State | Count |
|-------|-------|
| Arkansas | 1 |
| Georgia | 1 |
| Michigan | 1 |
| Missouri | 1 |
| Illinois | 1 |
| Massachusetts | 1 |
| New York | 2 |
| California | 2 |
| Texas | 3 |

➢ Being born in October seems to be a good omen for Presidential aspirants. But being born in May, June, or September is not as auspicious.

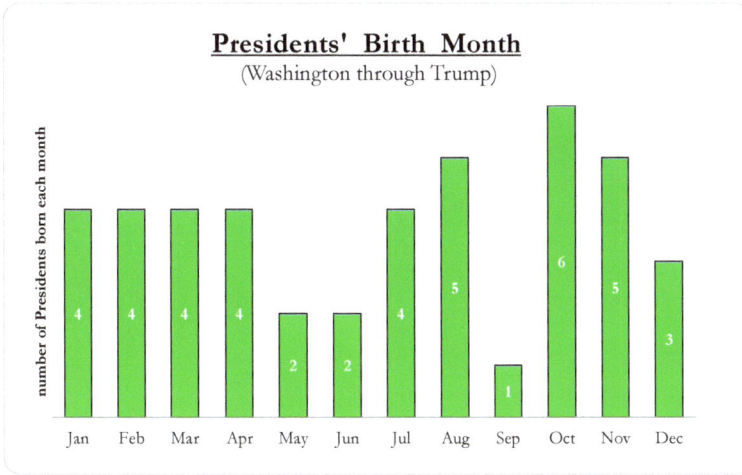

## Presidents' Birth Month
### (Washington through Trump)

number of Presidents born each month

| Jan | Feb | Mar | Apr | May | Jun | Jul | Aug | Sep | Oct | Nov | Dec |
|-----|-----|-----|-----|-----|-----|-----|-----|-----|-----|-----|-----|
| 4 | 4 | 4 | 4 | 2 | 2 | 4 | 5 | 1 | 6 | 5 | 3 |

*See the Appendices for additional "dates and places" information about the Presidents.*

# The Presidents' Families

➢ The Presidential immediate families include 256 people:
  ❖ 44 Presidents
  ❖ 50 wives
  ❖ 93 sons
  ❖ 69 daughters

➢ Six Presidents entered the White House unmarried:
  1. Thomas Jefferson      (widower)
  2. Andrew Jackson      (widower)
  3. Martin Van Buren      (widower)
  4. Chester Arthur      (widower)
  5. Grover Cleveland      (married in office)
  6. James Buchanan      (never married)

➢ Five Presidents were married twice:
  1. John Tyler      (married second wife while President)
  2. Millard Fillmore      (married second wife after his Presidency)
  3. Benjamin Harrison      (married second wife after his Presidency)
  4. Woodrow Wilson      (married second wife while President)
  5. Ronald Reagan      (married second wife prior to Presidency)
  ❖ Of these five, Ronald Reagan was the only divorced President; the other twice-married Presidents buried their first wives.

➢ One President – Donald Trump – was married three times. He married his third wife prior to his Presidency.

➢ Many Presidents have remained married for a long time.
  ❖ Seven deceased Presidents were married for more than half a century.
  ❖ Two living Presidents have been married more than seven decades and are the longest-married Presidents in history:
    1. George H.W. Bush had been married 72 years as of 20th January 2017.
    2. James Carter had been married 70.5 years as of 20th January 2017.

- ➢ Nine Presidential wives had been previously married:
  - ❖ Six buried the first husband:
    1. Martha Washington
    2. Martha Jefferson
    3. Dolley Madison
    4. Caroline Fillmore
    5. Mary (Mrs. Benjamin) Harrison
    6. Edith Wilson
  - ❖ Three were divorcees:
    1. Rachel Jackson
    2. Florence Harding
    3. Betty Ford

- ➢ Three Presidents wed while in office:
  1. John Tyler — second marriage; ceremony not in the White House
  2. Grover Cleveland — first marriage; ceremony in the White House
  3. Woodrow Wilson — second marriage; ceremony not in the White House

- ➢ John Tyler's wedding to Julia Gardiner was the first Presidential wedding.

*See the Appendices for additional information about the wives.*

- ➢ In most cases, the President's wife was the First Lady or White House hostess. Presidents who were unmarried, widowed, or who had a shy or ill wife called on the services of daughters, daughters-in-law, sisters, sisters-in-law, and nieces to act as White House hostess.

- ➢ Two First Ladies were not born in the United States:
  - ❖ Louisa (Mrs. John Quincy) Adams was born in England.
  - ❖ Melania Trump was born in Slovenia.

- ➢ Anna (Mrs. William) Harrison is the only First Lady who never set foot in the White House (excluding the women who were First Lady before the White House was completed in 1800).

- ➢ Anna (Mrs. William) Harrison is the first First Lady to have formal education.

- ➢ Lucy Hayes is often considered the first First Lady to have had a higher education, although there is some question about whether Cincinnati Wesleyan Female College was on a par with four-year colleges.

- ➢ Frances Cleveland is the youngest First Lady, having become First Lady when not quite 22 years of age.

- ➢ Frances Cleveland is the only First Lady whose wedding was held in the White House.

> Edith (Mrs. Theodore) Roosevelt created the Office of the First Lady.

> Standing 5' 11", Eleanor (Mrs. Franklin) Roosevelt, Michelle Obama, and Melania Trump are the tallest First Ladies (from amongst those whose height is known).

> Bess Truman is the longest-lived First Lady.

> Laura Bush is the only First Lady to mother twins.

> Three First Ladies died in the White House:
> 1. Letitia Tyler
> 2. Caroline (Mrs. Benjamin) Harrison
> 3. Ellen Wilson

*See the Appendices for additional information about the First Ladies.*

> Prior to the 20th century, half of all Presidential wives had no formal education and none had a college education.

> Only nine Presidential wives earned a college degree.

> In the post war period more than half of Presidential wives hold a college degree and almost one-third also hold a graduate or professional degree.

### Education Level of the Presidential Wives

| | Highest Formal Education Level Achieved | | | | |
|---|---|---|---|---|---|
| | None | Secondary Education | Post Secondary | College | Graduate / Professional |
| Pre - 1901 | 14 | 8 | 4 | 0 | 0 |
| 1901 - 1948 | 1 | 5 | 1 | 2 | 0 |
| Post War | 0 | 2 | 3 | 3 | 4 |
| All Wives | 15 | 15 | 8 | 5 | 4 |
| Pre - 1901 | 54% | 31% | 15% | 0% | 0% |
| 1901 - 1948 | 11% | 56% | 11% | 22% | 0% |
| Post War | 0% | 17% | 25% | 25% | 33% |
| All Wives | 32% | 32% | 17% | 11% | 9% |

Excludes divorced wives and two second wives whose marriages post dated the husband's Presidency.

*See the Appendices for additional information about the wives' education.*

➢ Four Presidential wives earned a graduate or professional degree:
1. Pat Nixon, the first First Lady to earn a graduate degree, earned a Certificate in Teaching at the University of Southern California, which USC considered a Master's-level program.
2. Hillary Clinton earned a law degree at Yale.
3. Laura Bush earned a Master's in Library Science at the University of Texas at Austin.
4. Michelle Obama earned a law degree at Harvard.

➢ William Harrison had the most children (10) with one wife.
John Tyler had the most children overall (15 with two wives).

➢ Four Presidents had no children:
1. George Washington
2. James Madison
3. James Polk
4. James Buchanan

➢ Three First Children were adopted:
❖ Andrew Jackson's only children, sons Andrew Jr. and Lyncoya
❖ Ronald Reagan's son Michael

➢ Esther Cleveland is the only First Child who was born in the White House.

*See the Appendices for a full listing of all First Children.*

- A total of 22 First Children have married while their father was President; one did so twice. Thus, there have been 23 weddings of a First Child.

- Nine of the 23 wedding ceremonies of First Children were held in the White House. John Adams II was the only male First Child amongst the nine.

- Maria Monroe was the first First Child to wed, and her ceremony was held in the White House.

- With five wives, Franklin Roosevelt, Jr. married more times than any other child of a President.

## Weddings of First Children During Father's Incumbency

|  | First Child | Spouse | Wedding Date |
|---|---|---|---|
| 1 | **Maria Hester Monroe** | Samuel L. Gouverneur | 9-Mar-1820 |
| 2 | **John Adams** | Mary Catherine Hellen | 25-Feb-1828 |
| 3 | Andrew Jackson Jr. | Sarah Yorke | 24-Nov-1831 |
| 4 | Abraham Van Buren | Angelica Singleton | 27-Nov-1838 |
| 5 | **Elizabeth Tyler** | William Nevison Waller | 31-Jan-1842 |
| 6 | **Nellie Grant** | Algernon Charles Satoris | 21-May-1874 |
| 7 | Frederick Grant | Ida Marie Honore | 20-Oct-1874 |
| 8 | **Alice Roosevelt** | Rep. Nicholas Longworth | 17-Feb-1906 |
| 9 | **Jessie Wilson** | Frances Bowes Sayre | 25-Nov-1913 |
| 10 | **Eleanor Wilson** | William Gibbs McAdoo | 7-May-1914 |
| 11 | Anna Roosevelt | John Boettiger | 18-Jan-1935 |
| 12 | Elliot Roosevelt (1st) | Ruth Googins | 22-Jul-1933 |
| 13 | Franklin Roosevelt, Jr. | Ethel duPont | 30-Jun-1937 |
| 14 | John Roosevelt | Anne Lindsay Clark | 18-Jun-1938 |
| 15 | James Roosevelt | Romelle Schneider | 14-Apr-1941 |
| 16 | Elliot Roosevelt (2nd) | Faye Emerson | 3-Dec-1944 |
| 17 | Luci Baines Johnson | Patrick John Nugent | 6-Aug-1966 |
| 18 | **Lynda Bird Johnson** | Charles Spittal Robb | 9-Dec-1967 |
| 19 | **Patricia "Tricia" Nixon** | Edward Ridley Finch Cox | 12-Jun-1971 |
| 20 | Maureen Reagan | Dennis Revell | 25-Apr-1981 |
| 21 | Patricia Ann Reagan, a/k/a Patti Davis | Paul Grilley | 14-Aug-1984 |
| 22 | Dorothy Walker Bush | Robert Koch | 26-Jun-1992 |
| 23 | Jenna Bush | Henry Hager | 10-May-2008 |

The weddings for the children whose names appear in boldface type took place in the White House.

# II.  The Succession

The main body of the U.S. Constitution does not specify who ascends to the Presidency or wields Presidential powers in the case of the death or removal from office of the President. As a result, when the issue first arose upon the death of William Harrison 31 days after his inauguration in 1841, there was significant controversy over the status of Vice President John Tyler. Tyler took the position that he was, in fact, the President and not simply *acting* as President. He prevailed in the face of opposition, and his actions became known as the Tyler Precedent. All subsequent Vice Presidents whose President died or resigned embraced the Tyler Precedent until the issue was formally addressed a century and a quarter later with the ratification of the 25th Amendment.

Only the Vice President can ascend to the Presidency. If both the President and Vice President are unavailable or incapacitated, the next in line becomes merely the *Acting* President.

➤ The line of succession as set forth in the Presidential Succession Act of 1948:

1. Speaker of the House
2. Senate President *pro tempore*
3. Secretary of State
4. Secretary of the Treasury
5. Secretary of Defense
6. Attorney General
7. Secretary of the Interior
8. Secretary of Agriculture
10. Secretary of Commerce
10. Secretary of Labor
11. Secretary of Health and Human Services
12. Secretary of Housing and Urban Development
13. Secretary of Transportation
14. Secretary of Energy
15. Secretary of Education
16. Secretary of Veteran Affairs

*In order to become Acting President, one must first resign*
*from the office that places one in the line of succession.*

➤ The 25th Amendment also empowers the President to nominate a candidate to fill a vacant Vice Presidency. The nominee must then be confirmed by a majority vote of both Houses of Congress.

➤ This provision of the 25th Amendment has been invoked only twice, both within a single Presidential term:

1. Richard Nixon nominated Gerald Ford after Spiro Agnew resigned.
2. Gerald Ford nominated Nelson Rockefeller after Nixon resigned and Ford ascended to the Presidency.

# III.  The Vice Presidents

## Curious Facts About the Vice Presidents

➢ Seventy-seven different men have served as President and/or Vice President, 47 of whom served as Vice President. Of the 47, 33 never served as President.

➢ Only two Vice Presidents – Schuyler Colfax and John Garner – also served as Speaker of the House of Representatives.
 1. Schuyler Colfax served as Speaker from 1863 to 1869.
 2. John Garner served as Speaker from 1931 to 1933.

➢ Only two Vice Presidents – George Clinton and John Calhoun – served under more than one President.
 1. George Clinton was Vice President during Thomas Jefferson's second term and was re-elected in 1808 to serve under James Madison.
 2. John Calhoun served under John Quincy Adams and was re-elected in 1828 to serve under Andrew Jackson.

➢ Only two Vice Presidents – John Calhoun and Spiro Agnew – resigned from that office.
 1. Calhoun resigned near the end of his second term. He had fallen out with President Andrew Jackson and wanted to run for Senator from South Carolina.
 2. Faced with criminal charges, Agnew resigned in the first year of his second term.

➢ Only two Vice Presidents – Gerald Ford and Nelson Rockefeller – were not elected to that office.

➢ Only two Vice Presidents have won the Nobel Peace Prize.
 1. Charles Dawes     in 1925     (won while in office)
 2. Albert Gore      in 2007     (won after leaving office)

➢ Only once did three different Vice Presidents serve during a single Presidential term:  Spiro Agnew, Gerald Ford, and Nelson Rockefeller each served as Vice President during the 47th Presidential term (1973 – 1977).

- Vice President Levi Morton is the only U.S. President or Vice President who died on his birthday – he succumbed on the 96$^{th}$ anniversary of his birth.

- Eight *sitting* Vice Presidents ran for President:
  - ❖ Four won:
    1. John Adams (F)           in 1800
    2. Thomas Jefferson (D-R)   in 1804
    3. Martin Van Buren (D)     in 1836
    4. George H.W. Bush (R)     in 1988
  - ❖ Four lost:
    1. John Breckinridge (D)    in 1860
    2. Richard Nixon (R)        in 1960
    3. Hubert Humphrey (D)      in 1968
    4. Albert Gore (D)          in 2000

- Richard Nixon is the only Vice President who was elected President when he was not the incumbent Vice President.

- Fourteen Vice Presidents subsequently served as President:
  - ❖ Five Vice Presidents first became President via election:
    1. John Adams
    2. Thomas Jefferson
    3. Martin Van Buren
    4. Richard Nixon
    5. George H.W. Bush
  - ❖ Nine Vice Presidents first became President via ascension:
    - Four of the nine ascended when their President died of natural causes.
    - Four of the nine ascended when their President was assassinated.
    - One ascended when his President resigned.

      | Vice President | Reason They Ascended to Presidency |
      |---|---|
      | 1. John Tyler | William Harrison died of natural causes |
      | 2. Millard Fillmore | Zachary Taylor died of natural causes |
      | 3. Andrew Johnson | Abraham Lincoln was assassinated |
      | 4. Chester Arthur | James Garfield was assassinated |
      | 5. Theodore Roosevelt | William McKinley was assassinated |
      | 6. Calvin Coolidge | Warren Harding died of natural causes |
      | 7. Harry Truman | Franklin Roosevelt died of natural causes |
      | 8. Lyndon Johnson | John Kennedy was assassinated |
      | 9. Gerald Ford | Richard Nixon resigned |

- The 14 erstwhile Vice Presidents who became President had varying fates:
  - The men who first became President via election all ran for re-election; two won and three lost:
    1. John Adams — Lost in 1800
    2. Thomas Jefferson — Won in 1804
    3. Martin Van Buren — Lost in 1840
    4. Richard Nixon — Won in 1972
    5. George H.W. Bush — Lost in 1992
  - Of the men who first became President via ascension, some then failed to win nomination and some ran in their own right. Of the latter, only one lost.
    1. John Tyler — Not nominated
    2. Millard Fillmore — Not nominated
    3. Andrew Johnson — Not nominated
    4. Chester Arthur — Not nominated
    5. Theodore Roosevelt — Ran and won
    6. Calvin Coolidge — Ran and won
    7. Harry Truman — Ran and won
    8. Lyndon Johnson — Ran and won
    9. Gerald Ford — Ran and lost
  - Thus, most Vice Presidents who became President failed to remain President after their initial (in some cases, partial) term.

- Nine of the 16 twice-elected Presidents had the same Vice President for both terms:

| President | Vice President |
| --- | --- |
| 1. George Washington | John Adams |
| 2. James Monroe | Daniel Tompkins |
| 3. Woodrow Wilson | Thomas Marshall |
| 4. Dwight Eisenhower | Richard Nixon |
| 5. Richard Nixon | Spiro Agnew |
| 6. Ronald Reagan | George H. W. Bush |
| 7. William Clinton | Albert Gore |
| 8. George W. Bush | Richard Cheney |
| 9. Barack Obama | Joseph Biden |

➤ Seven of the 16 twice-elected Presidents had two different Vice Presidents:

| President | Vice Presidents |
|---|---|
| 1. Thomas Jefferson | Aaron Burr and George Clinton |
| 2. James Madison | George Clinton and Elbridge Gerry |
| 3. Andrew Jackson | John Calhoun and Martin Van Buren |
| 4. Abraham Lincoln | Hannibal Hamlin and Andrew Johnson |
| 5. Ulysses Grant | Schuyler Colfax and Henry Wilson |
| 6. Grover Cleveland | Thomas Hendricks and Adlai Stevenson |
| 7. William McKinley | Garret Hobart and Theodore Roosevelt |

❖ All of these Presidents served in the 19th century.

➤ Three different Vice Presidents served under four-time electoral victor Franklin Roosevelt:

1. John Garner IV     elected in 1932 and 1936
2. Henry Wallace     elected in 1940
3. Harry Truman     elected in 1944

# The Vice Presidents' Tenure

➤ More than one-third of the Vice Presidents did not serve one full term.

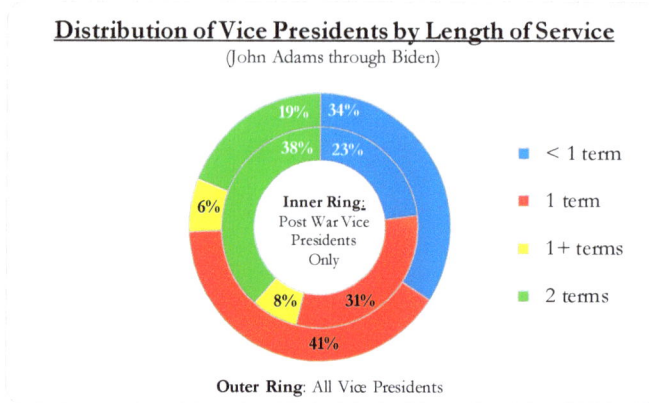

## Distribution of Vice Presidents by Length of Service
(John Adams through Biden)

Inner Ring:
Post War Vice Presidents Only

- ■ < 1 term
- ■ 1 term
- ■ 1+ terms
- ■ 2 terms

Inner ring: 34%, 23%, 31%, 8%, 6%, 38%, 19%
Outer ring: 41%

**Outer Ring**: All Vice Presidents

➤ Of the 16 Vice Presidents who served less than one term, . . .

❖ Six died in office:

| | | | |
|---|---|---|---|
| 1. | Elbridge Gerry | Served under James Madison | 1813-1814 |
| 2. | William King | Served under Franklin Pierce | 1853 |
| 3. | Henry Wilson | Served under Ulysses Grant | 1873-1875 |
| 4. | Thomas Hendricks | Served under Grover Cleveland | 1885 |
| 5. | Garret Hobart | Served under William McKinley | 1897-1899 |
| 6. | James Sherman | Served under William Taft | 1909-1912 |

❖ Nine ascended to the Presidency:

| | | | |
|---|---|---|---|
| 1. | John Tyler | Served under William Harrison | 1841 |
| 2. | Millard Fillmore | Served under Zachary Taylor | 1849-1850 |
| 3. | Andrew Johnson | Served under Abraham Lincoln | 1865 |
| 4. | Chester Arthur | Served under James Garfield | 1881 |
| 5. | Theodore Roosevelt | Served under William McKinley | 1901 |
| 6. | Calvin Coolidge | Served under Warren Harding | 1921-1923 |
| 7. | Harry Truman | Served under Franklin Roosevelt | 1945 |
| 8. | Lyndon Johnson | Served under John Kennedy | 1961-1963 |
| 9. | Gerald Ford | Served under Richard Nixon | 1973-1974 |

❖ One completed someone else's term:

| | | | |
|---|---|---|---|
| 1. | Nelson Rockefeller | Served under Gerald Ford | 1974-1977 |

- ➤ Nineteen Vice Presidents served one-term:

  | | | | |
  |---|---|---|---|
  | 1. | Thomas Jefferson | Served under John Adams | 1797-1801 |
  | 2. | Aaron Burr | Served under Thomas Jefferson | 1801-1805 |
  | 3. | Martin Van Buren | Served under Andrew Jackson | 1833-1837 |
  | 4. | Richard Johnson | Served under Martin Van Buren | 1837-1841 |
  | 5. | George Dallas | Served under James Polk | 1845-1849 |
  | 6. | John Breckinridge | Served under James Buchanan | 1857-1861 |
  | 7. | Hannibal Hamlin | Served under Abraham Lincoln | 1861-1865 |
  | 8. | Schuyler Colfax | Served under Ulysses Grant | 1869-1873 |
  | 9. | William Wheeler | Served under Rutherford Hayes | 1877-1881 |
  | 10. | Levi Morton | Served under Benjamin Harrison | 1889-1893 |
  | 11. | Adlai Stevenson | Served under Grover Cleveland | 1893-1897 |
  | 12. | Charles Fairbanks | Served under Theodore Roosevelt | 1905-1909 |
  | 13. | Charles Dawes | Served under Calvin Coolidge | 1925-1929 |
  | 14. | Charles Curtis | Served under Herbert Hoover | 1929-1933 |
  | 15. | Henry Wallace | Served under Franklin Roosevelt | 1941-1945 |
  | 16 | Alben Barkley | Served under Harry Truman | 1949-1953 |
  | 17. | Hubert Humphrey | Served under Lyndon Johnson | 1965-1969 |
  | 18. | Walter Mondale | Served under James Carter | 1977-1981 |
  | 19. | Danforth Quayle | Served under George H.W. Bush | 1989-1993 |

- ➤ Three Vice Presidents served more than one term but less than two terms, and two of the three served two different Presidents:

  | | | | |
  |---|---|---|---|
  | 1. | George Clinton | Served under Thomas Jefferson | 1805-1809 |
  | | | Served under James Madison | 1809-1812 |
  | | | • Clinton died in office. | |
  | 2. | John Calhoun | Served under John Quincy Adams | 1825-1829 |
  | | | Served under Andrew Jackson | 1829-1832 |
  | | | • Calhoun resigned. | |
  | 3. | Spiro Agnew | Served under Richard Nixon | 1969-1973 |
  | | | • Agnew resigned. | |

- Nine Vice Presidents served two full terms, and each served one President:

  1. John Adams           Served under George Washington    1793 - 1801
  2. Daniel Tompkins      Served under James Monroe        1817 - 1825
  3. Thomas Marshall      Served under Woodrow Wilson     1913 - 1921
  4. John Garner           Served under Franklin Roosevelt    1933 - 1941
  5. Richard Nixon        Served under Dwight Eisenhower   1953 - 1961
  6. George H.W. Bush    Served under Ronald Reagan      1981 - 1989
  7. Albert Gore           Served under William Clinton      1993 - 2001
  8. Richard Cheney       Served under George W. Bush     2001 - 2009
  9. Joseph Biden         Served under Barack Obama      2009 - 2017

- Prior to passage of the 25th Amendment there was no mechanism for filling a vacant Vice Presidency and consequently that office was often empty.

- The Vice Presidency has been vacant 18 times.
  - Seven of the 18 vacancies lasted almost a full term (*i.e.*, more than three years).
  - The longest vacancy was 31 days short of a full term and began when John Tyler ascended to the Presidency upon the death of William Harrison.
  - Five of the vacancies were shorter than one year; the shortest was 57 days.

- In the aggregate, the Vice Presidency has been vacant for 13,808 days, which is almost 38 years, and is 17% of the total of nearly 228 years from 30th April 1789 to 20th January 2017.

- Most of the vacancies in the Vice Presidency arose as a result of the death of the Vice President or his President:
  - Eight vacancies were created when the President died and these men ascended:

    1. John Tyler             5. Theodore Roosevelt
    2. Millard Fillmore      6. Calvin Coolidge
    3. Andrew Johnson     7. Harry Truman
    4. Chester Arthur       8. Lyndon Johnson

  - Seven vacancies arose when these Vice Presidents died:

    1. George Clinton       5. Thomas Hendricks
    2. Elbridge Gerry       6. Garret Hobart
    3. William King         7. James Sherman
    4. Henry Wilson

  - One vacancy was created when President Richard Nixon resigned and Vice President Gerald Ford ascended.

  - Two vacancies were created when the Vice President resigned:

    1. John Calhoun          2. Spiro Agnew

## Vacancies in the Office of Vice President

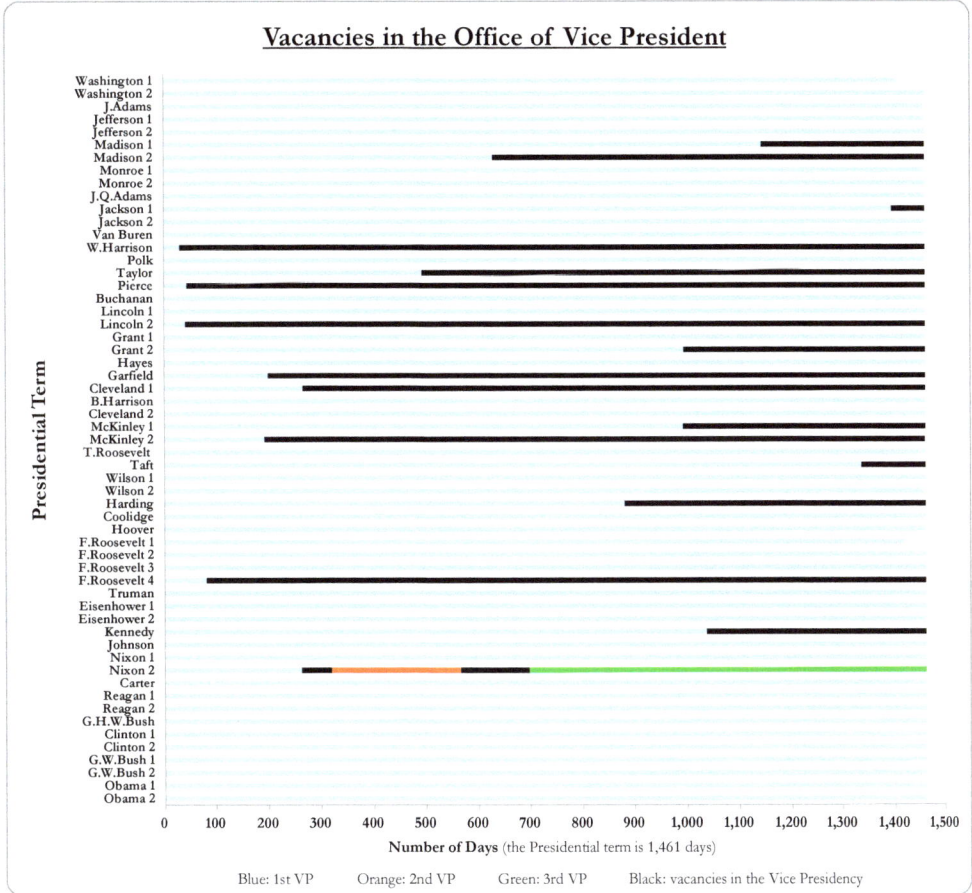

Blue: 1st VP    Orange: 2nd VP    Green: 3rd VP    Black: vacancies in the Vice Presidency

> The five shortest Vice Presidencies:

1. John Tyler            31 days      (vacated the office to become President)
2. Andrew Johnson        42 days      (vacated the office to become President)
3. William King          45 days      (died in office)
4. Harry Truman          82 days      (vacated the office to become President)
5. Theodore Roosevelt    194 days     (vacated the office to become President)

# The Vice Presidents' Education

➢ Thirty-seven Vice Presidents graduated from college; almost one-quarter did not.

➢ Only two Vice Presidents who served after 1893 did not have a college degree:
   1. Charles Curtis      Herbert Hoover's Vice President
   2. Harry Truman      Franklin Roosevelt's third Vice President

➢ Twenty-nine colleges boast a Vice Presidential alumnus; six colleges produced multiple Vice Presidents:
   1. Harvard produced four
   2. Princeton produced three
   3. Yale produced two
   4. William and Mary produced two
   5. University of Minnesota produced two
   6. Hanover College produced two

## The Vice Presidents' Undergraduate Education

| | Vice President | College | | | Vice President | College |
|---|---|---|---|---|---|---|
| 1 | John Adams | Harvard | | 26 | Charles Fairbanks | Ohio Wesleyan |
| 2 | Thomas Jefferson | William and Mary | | 27 | James Sherman | Hamilton |
| 3 | Aaron Burr | Princeton | | 28 | Thomas Marshall | Wabash |
| 4 | George Clinton | none | | 29 | Calvin Coolidge | Amherst |
| 5 | Elbridge Gerry | Harvard | | 30 | Charles Dawes | Marietta |
| 6 | Daniel Tompkins | Columbia | | 31 | Charles Curtis | none |
| 7 | John Calhoun | Yale | | 32 | John Garner | Vanderbilt * |
| 8 | Martin Van Buren | none | | 33 | Henry Wallace | Iowa State |
| 9 | Richard Johnson | Transylvania | | 34 | Harry Truman | none |
| 10 | John Tyler | William and Mary | | 35 | Alben Barkley | Emory |
| 11 | George Dallas | Princeton | | 36 | Richard Nixon | Whittier |
| 12 | Millard Fillmore | none | | 37 | Lyndon Johnson | Southwest Texas State Teachers |
| 13 | William King | UNC Chapel Hill | | | | |
| 14 | John Breckinridge | Princeton | | 38 | Hubert Humphrey | Minnesota |
| 15 | Hannibal Hamlin | none | | 39 | Spiro Agnew | Johns Hopkins |
| 16 | Andrew Johnson | none | | 40 | Gerald Ford | Michigan |
| 17 | Schuyler Colfax | none | | 41 | Nelson Rockefeller | Dartmouth |
| 18 | Henry Wilson | none | | 42 | Walter Mondale | Minnesota |
| 19 | William Wheeler | Vermont | | 43 | George H.W. Bush | Yale |
| 20 | Chester Arthur | Union | | 44 | Danforth Quayle | DePauw |
| 21 | Thomas Hendricks | Hanover | | 45 | Albert Gore | Harvard |
| 22 | Levi Morton | none | | 46 | Richard Cheney | Wyoming |
| 23 | Adlai Stevenson | Centre | | 47 | Joseph Biden | Delaware |
| 24 | Garret Hobart | Rutgers | | 48 | Michael Pence | Hanover |
| 25 | Theodore Roosevelt | Harvard | | | | * dropped out |

# The Vice Presidents . . . Personally

➤ The Vice Presidents varied widely in age. Thirty-five years separated the youngest Vice President from the oldest.

### Distribution of Vice Presidents' Ages at 1st Inauguration
(John Adams through Pence)

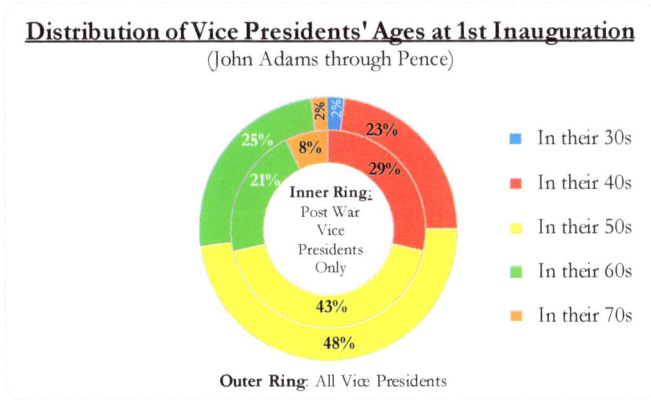

Inner Ring: Post War Vice Presidents Only

- In their 30s
- In their 40s
- In their 50s
- In their 60s
- In their 70s

Outer Ring: All Vice Presidents

➤ The five youngest Vice Presidents:
1. John Breckinridge — 36.1 years of age when first sworn in
2. Richard Nixon — 40.0 years of age when first sworn in
3. Danforth Quayle — 42.0 years of age when first sworn in
4. Theodore Roosevelt — 42.4 years of age when first sworn in
5. Daniel Tompkins — 42.7 years of age when first sworn in

➤ The five oldest Vice Presidents:
1. Alben Barkley — 71.2 years of age when first sworn in
2. Charles Curtis — 69.1 years of age when first sworn in
3. Elbridge Gerry — 68.6 years of age when first sworn in
4. William King — 66.9 years of age when first sworn in
5. Nelson Rockefeller — 66.4 years of age when first sworn in

➤ Age of the Vice Presidents as a group on the date of their first inauguration:

| All Vice Presidents | | Post War Vice Presidents | |
|---|---|---|---|
| ❖ Average: | 53.9 years of age | ❖ Average: | 53.6 years of age |
| ❖ Median: | 52.8 years of age | ❖ Median: | 53.0 years of age |

➤ The five longest-lived Vice Presidents:
1. John Garner                         Died when 99.0 years of age
2. Levi Morton                        Died when 96.0 years of age
3. Gerald Ford                        Died when 93.5 years of age
4. John Adams                        Died when 90.4 years of age
5. Harry Truman                    Died when 88.6 years of age

➤ The five shortest-lived Vice Presidents:
1. Daniel Tompkins               Died when 51.0 years of age
2. John Breckinridge            Died when 54.3 years of age
3. Garret Hobart                  Died when 55.5 years of age
4. James Sherman                Died when 57.0 years of age
5. Chester Arthur                Died when 57.1 years of age

➤ Life span of the Vice Presidents as a group (excluding those still living):

| All Vice Presidents | | Post War Vice Presidents | |
|---|---|---|---|
| ❖ Average: | 72.6 years of age | ❖ Average: | 76.1 years of age |
| ❖ Median: | 71.2 years of age | ❖ Median: | 77.9 years of age |

➤ The 48 Vice Presidents hailed from 22 different states.
   ❖ Almost one-quarter of the Vice Presidents came from New York.
   ❖ Five states account for more than half of the Vice Presidents:
1. Indiana                   4. Kentucky
2. Massachusetts        5. New York
3. Texas

**Home States of the Vice Presidents**
(John Adams through Pence)

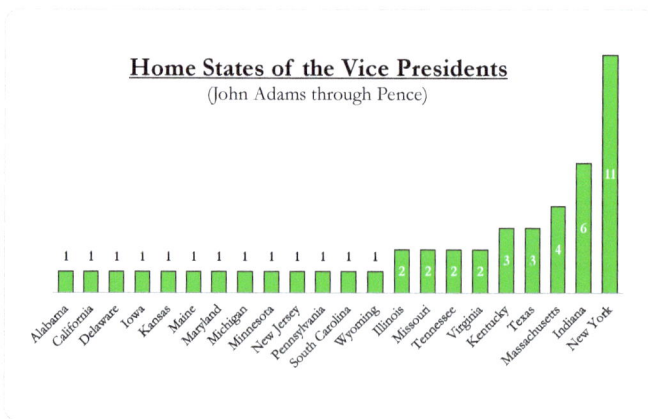

*See the Appendices for a listing of each Vice President's home state.*

➤ The 14 post war Vice Presidents hailed from 12 different states.
Only Texas and Indiana produced more than one post war Vice President.

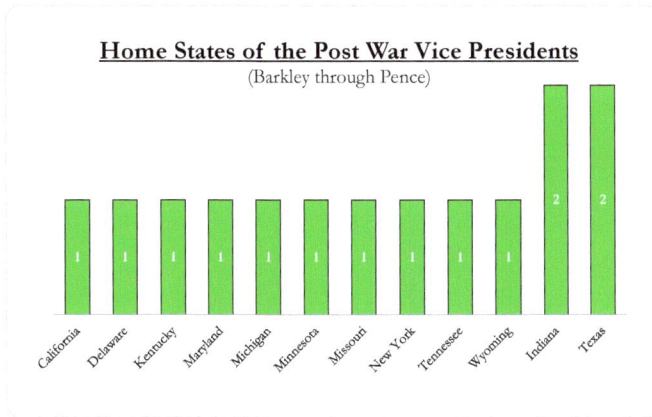

### Home States of the Post War Vice Presidents
(Barkley through Pence)

| California | Delaware | Kentucky | Maryland | Michigan | Minnesota | Missouri | New York | Tennessee | Wyoming | Indiana | Texas |
|---|---|---|---|---|---|---|---|---|---|---|---|
| 1 | 1 | 1 | 1 | 1 | 1 | 1 | 1 | 1 | 1 | 2 | 2 |

*See the Appendices for additional "dates and places" information about the Vice Presidents.*

# IV.  Party Control of the Presidency

➢ In the two-party era, Republicans have occupied the White House more than Democrats.

**Party Control of the White House in the Two-Party Era**

|  | Republicans | Democrats |
|---|---|---|
| 1860 to 2020 | 92 years<br>58% | 68 years<br>43% |
| Post war period | 40 years<br>56% | 32 years<br>44% |
| 538-electoral-vote era | 32 years<br>57% | 24 years<br>43% |
| 19th century | 27 years<br>69% | 12 years<br>31% |
| 20th century | 53 years<br>53% | 47 years<br>47% |
| 21st century | 12 years<br>57% | 9 years<br>43% |

➢ The Democrats own the longest single stay in the White House: Franklin Roosevelt and then Harry Truman sat in the Oval Office for 20 years, from 1933 to 1953.

➢ If Abraham Lincoln had completed his second term – or if he had had a Republican Vice President who ascended when Lincoln was assassinated – the Republicans would have owned the *Longest Stay* accolade, as they would have served for 24 consecutive years, from 1861 until 1885.

➢ The Republicans' two 16-year periods of control:
   1. 1869 - 1885:  Ulysses Grant, Rutherford Hayes, James Garfield, Chester Arthur
   2. 1897 - 1913:  William McKinley, Theodore Roosevelt, William Taft

➢ The Republicans' two 12-year periods of control:
   1. 1921 – 1933:   Warren Harding, Calvin Coolidge, Herbert Hoover
   2. 1981 – 1993:   Ronald Reagan, George H.W. Bush

> ➤ Overall, the Republicans have occupied the White House for more multi-term periods than have the Democrats.

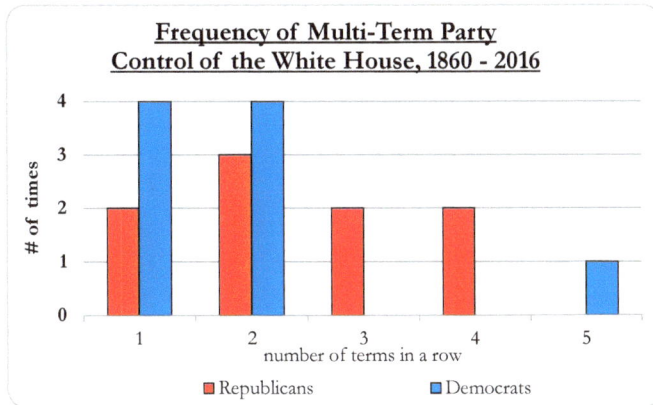

**Frequency of Multi-Term Party Control of the White House, 1860 - 2016**

(bar chart: # of times vs number of terms in a row)

Republicans ■ Democrats ■

## The Ebb and Flow of Party Control of the White House

| Nineteenth Century | Twentieth Century | 21st C. |
|---|---|---|
| 26 Republican Years<br>12 Democrat Years | 53 Republican Years<br>47 Democrat Years | 12 Rep. Years<br>9 Dem. Years |

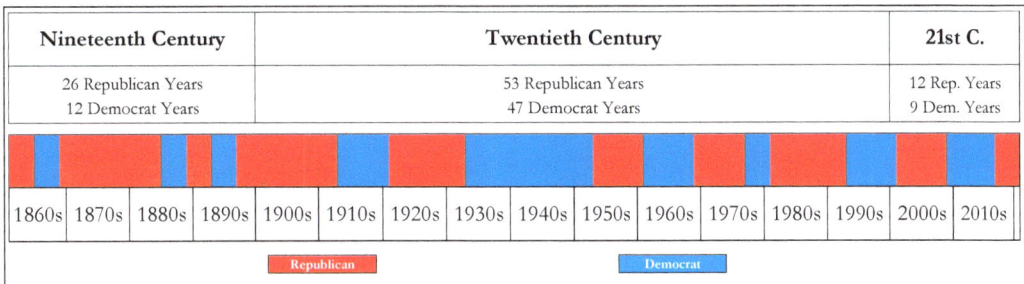

1860s 1870s 1880s 1890s 1900s 1910s 1920s 1930s 1940s 1950s 1960s 1970s 1980s 1990s 2000s 2010s

Republican ■   Democrat ■

# V.    Presidential Elections

## Election Mechanics

Contrary to popular belief in some quarters, Presidents are not chosen by the direct vote of the people. Instead, the choice is made indirectly via the popular election of "electors" in each state who, in turn, vote separately for President and for Vice President. In most states (*i.e.,* all but Arizona, Idaho, Kansas, North and South Dakota, Oklahoma, Tennessee, and Virginia) the names of the electors do not appear along with their candidates' names on the ballot. So voters rarely know the names of the electors.

In order to make any showing in the Electoral College voting, a candidate must have concentrated support in at least one state. A candidate who has significant support throughout the country but does not win a plurality in any one state will emerge from the Electoral College empty-handed. A prominent example of this occurred in 1992 when Ross Perot won almost 19% of the national popular vote but did not win a plurality in any state. Hence, he received not a single electoral vote.

Because the Electoral College is based largely on a state-by-state, winner-take-all system, the winner's margin of victory is amplified and the apparent performance of the loser is understated. In addition, the performance of third-party candidates tends to be minimized.

The Electoral Count Act of 1887 provides that state law governs the actions of Electoral College members and is the basis for resolving disputes that arise in counting votes.

In all but two states – Maine and Nebraska – the electors' mandate is based on the winner of the *plurality* of the state-wide popular vote. A candidate who wins the most popular votes would (should) receive 100% of the state's electoral votes.

Maine and Nebraska allocate electoral votes according to the "congressional district method": two electoral votes go to the winner of the state-wide popular vote and one electoral vote is earned for winning the popular vote in each Congressional district (Maine has two districts and Nebraska three).

In 29 states and the District of Columbia the electors are bound *by law* to vote for a specific candidate:

| | | |
|---|---|---|
| 1. Alabama | 11. Massachusetts | 21. Oregon |
| 2. Alaska | 12. Michigan | 22. South Carolina |
| 3. California | 13. Mississippi | 23. Tennessee |
| 4. Colorado | 14. Montana | 24. Utah |
| 5. Connecticut | 15. Nebraska | 25. Vermont |
| 6. Delaware | 16. Nevada | 26. Virginia |
| 7. Florida | 17. New Mexico | 27. Washington |
| 8. Hawaii | 18. North Carolina | 28. Wisconsin |
| 9. Maine | 19. Ohio | 29. Wyoming |
| 10. Maryland | 20. Oklahoma | |

Few of these states penalize "faithless electors"; *i.e.,* electors who do not vote in accordance with the law. In some states it is a criminal offense but in many cases there is just a small fine ($500 or $1,000). A number of state laws provide that, by not voting or voting for a candidate other than the one who won the state's popular vote, a faithless elector is, *ipso facto*, removed from her/his position and a replacement elector is installed.

In 21 states the electors are not bound *by law* to vote for a specific candidate:

| | | |
|---|---|---|
| 1. Arizona | 8. Kansas | 15. New York |
| 2. Arkansas | 9. Kentucky | 16. North Dakota |
| 3. Georgia | 10. Louisiana | 17. Pennsylvania |
| 4. Idaho | 11. Minnesota | 18. Rhode Island |
| 5. Illinois | 12. Missouri | 19. South Dakota |
| 6. Indiana | 13. New Hampshire | 20. Texas |
| 7. Iowa | 14. New Jersey | 21. West Virginia |

➤ Legal obligation or not, penalty or not, there have been few faithless electors.
  ❖ 15 of the 58 elections for President featured at least one faithless elector, 10 of which were in the post war era.
    1. **1796**  **one** elector for the winning Federalist candidate (John Adams) voted for the losing Democratic-Republican candidate (Jefferson).
    2. **1808**  **six** electors for the winning Democratic-Republican candidate (Madison) voted for their Vice Presidential candidate (George Clinton); one other vote was not counted.
    3. **1820**  **one** elector for the winning Democratic-Republican candidate (Monroe) voted for a non-candidate in his party (John Quincy Adams); three other votes were not counted.
    4. **1832**  **two** electors for the losing National Republican candidate (Henry Clay) abstained.

5.  **1872**  None of the **66** electors pledged to Democrat loser Horace Greeley voted for him; 63 electors spread their votes amongst four men and three votes were not counted.

6.  **1948**  **one** elector for the winning Democrat (Truman) voted for a third-party candidate (States Rights Party's Strom Thurmond).

7.  **1956**  **one** elector for the losing Democrat candidate (Adlai Stevenson) voted for a non-politician.

8.  **1960**  **one** elector for the losing Republican candidate (Nixon) voted for a third-party candidate (Harry F. Byrd).

9.  **1968**  **one** elector for the winning Republican candidate (Nixon) voted for a third-party candidate (George Wallace).

10. **1972**  **one** elector for the winning Republican candidate (Nixon) voted for a third-party candidate (Libertarian John Hospers).

11. **1976**  **one** elector for the losing Republican candidate (Ford) voted for a non-candidate in the same party (Reagan).

12. **1988**  **one** elector for the losing Democrat candidate (Michael Dukakis) voted for his party's Vice Presidential candidate (Lloyd Bentsen).

13. **2000**  **one** elector for the losing Democrat candidate (Al Gore) abstained in protest over the lack of Congressional representation for Washington, DC.

14. **2004**  **one** elector for the losing Democrat candidate (John Kerry) voted for his party's Vice Presidential candidate (John Edwards).

15. **2016**  **seven** electors were faithless: five pledged to the losing Democrat candidate (Hillary Clinton) and two pledged to the winning Republican candidate (Trump).

    - Republican electors voted for two non-candidates in their party (John Kasich and Ron Paul).
    - Three Democrat electors voted for a non-candidate in the Republican Party (Colin Powell).
    - One Democrat elector voted for a non-candidate in their party (Bernie Sanders).
    - One Democrat elector voted for a non-politician.

➢ Of the nearly 24,000 electoral votes cast from 1789 to 2016, only 30 – or about one-eighth of one percent – were faithless (excluding the 66 votes pledged to losing Democrat candidate Horace Greeley who died after election day and before the Electoral College voted in 1872).

   ❖ 16 of the 30 faithless votes were in post war elections.

- Of the 10 post war elections with faithless electors, only one – 2016 – had more than one faithless elector.

- In most cases, the faithless elector voted for someone else in his/her own party.

- Faithless electors have never affected the outcome of an election.

## Election Timetable

The election of electors takes place on the first Tuesday after the first Monday in November of Presidential election years. (This date is a matter of Federal law; see Title 3, Chapter 1, §1 of the United States Code.) Presidential election day is no earlier than 2$^{nd}$ November and no later than 8$^{th}$ November. In 2020 it will be 3$^{rd}$ November.

Electors meet in their respective states to cast their votes on the first Monday after the second Wednesday in December; *i.e.*, depending on the year, on a day from the 13$^{th}$ to 19$^{th}$ of December. In 2020 it will be 14$^{th}$ December. The results are then formally conveyed to Congress to be tallied at 1:00 pm on 6$^{th}$ January.

## Electoral College "Tie Breaker"

To be elected, a candidate must receive a simple majority of the electoral votes (*i.e.*, 270 out of 538 total votes). If the Electoral College voting does not result in a candidate receiving a majority of the votes, the winner is chosen by the houses of Congress: The 12$^{th}$ Amendment provides that the House of Representatives selects the President from amongst the three candidates who received the most electoral votes for President, and that the Senate chooses the Vice President from amongst the two candidates who received the most electoral votes for Vice President.

In the House, meetings for this purpose require a quorum of at least one member from two-thirds of the state delegations. Each state delegation gets one vote, and a majority vote within the delegation determines how that one vote is cast. If a delegation cannot reach a majority decision about which candidate to choose, that state does not vote. The favorable vote of a majority of the delegations carries the day. When voting for Vice President, the Senate must have a quorum of two-thirds of the Senators. Each Senator gets one vote, and the majority rules.

Congressional action to select a President and/or Vice President commences immediately after the electoral votes are counted; *i.e.*, on the afternoon of 6$^{th}$ January. Since the new Congress is seated on 3$^{rd}$ January, it is the *new* Representatives – meeting in the House chambers and presided over by the President of the Senate – that decide Presidential elections. The *new and returning* Senators decide Vice Presidential elections when the Electoral College voting does not produce a majority winner.

If a President has not been chosen by Inauguration Day and a Vice President has been, the Vice President becomes Acting President until a President is chosen. If neither a President nor a Vice President has been chosen by 20$^{th}$ January (or if the President-elect and Vice President-elect die after being chosen but before being inaugurated), then the Presidential Succession Act of 1948 governs. (*See Chapter II, "Succession."*)

## Electoral College Votes

➢ The number of Electoral College electors equals the sum of the number of Representatives (currently 435), plus the number of Senators (currently 100), plus 3 for the District of Columbia.

➢ There have been 538 electors since 1964 when the District of Columbia was enfranchised.

➢ The number of Representatives from each state – and hence the number of electoral votes – is reviewed and, if necessary, revised every ten years based on shifts in population as reflected in the decennial census.

➢ While the total number of electors has not changed in half a century, the geographic distribution of electoral votes has changed significantly as population has migrated from the north and mid-west to the south and west.

➢ From 1980 to 2010…
   ❖ 12 states gained electoral votes, and 19 states lost electoral votes.
   ❖ 19 states and the District of Columbia neither gained nor lost electoral votes.
   ❖ States in the west and southwest out-gained all other regions by posting a net increase of 26 electoral votes, including +9 for Texas and +8 for California.
   ❖ States in the south and southeast enjoyed a net increase of 11 electoral votes, including a +8 change for Florida.
   ❖ States in the mid-west suffered a net loss of 20 electoral votes, including -5 for Ohio and -4 each for Illinois and Michigan.
   ❖ States in the northeast and mid-Atlantic region lost a net of 17 electoral votes, including -7 for New York and -5 for Pennsylvania.

# Electoral Votes by State, Changing Over Time

| | 1980s | +/- | 1990s | +/- | 2000s | +/- | 2010s | 2010 v. 1980 |
|---|---|---|---|---|---|---|---|---|
| Alabama | 9 | 0 | 9 | 0 | 9 | 0 | 9 | 0 |
| Alaska | 3 | 0 | 3 | 0 | 3 | 0 | 3 | 0 |
| Arizona | 7 | 1 | 8 | 2 | 10 | 1 | 11 | 4 |
| Arkansas | 6 | 0 | 6 | 0 | 6 | 0 | 6 | 0 |
| California | 47 | 7 | 54 | 1 | 55 | 0 | 55 | 8 |
| Colorado | 8 | 0 | 8 | 1 | 9 | 0 | 9 | 1 |
| Connecticut | 8 | 0 | 8 | -1 | 7 | 0 | 7 | -1 |
| Delaware | 3 | 0 | 3 | 0 | 3 | 0 | 3 | 0 |
| Florida | 21 | 4 | 25 | 2 | 27 | 2 | 29 | 8 |
| Georgia | 12 | 1 | 13 | 2 | 15 | 1 | 16 | 4 |
| Hawaii | 4 | 0 | 4 | 0 | 4 | 0 | 4 | 0 |
| Idaho | 4 | 0 | 4 | 0 | 4 | 0 | 4 | 0 |
| Illinois | 24 | -2 | 22 | -1 | 21 | -1 | 20 | -4 |
| Indiana | 12 | 0 | 12 | -1 | 11 | 0 | 11 | -1 |
| Iowa | 8 | -1 | 7 | 0 | 7 | -1 | 6 | -2 |
| Kansas | 7 | -1 | 6 | 0 | 6 | 0 | 6 | -1 |
| Kentucky | 9 | -1 | 8 | 0 | 8 | 0 | 8 | -1 |
| Louisiana | 10 | -1 | 9 | 0 | 9 | -1 | 8 | -2 |
| Maine | 4 | 0 | 4 | 0 | 4 | 0 | 4 | 0 |
| Maryland | 10 | 0 | 10 | 0 | 10 | 0 | 10 | 0 |
| Massachusetts | 13 | -1 | 12 | 0 | 12 | -1 | 11 | -2 |
| Michigan | 20 | -2 | 18 | -1 | 17 | -1 | 16 | -4 |
| Minnesota | 10 | 0 | 10 | 0 | 10 | 0 | 10 | 0 |
| Mississippi | 7 | 0 | 7 | -1 | 6 | 0 | 6 | -1 |
| Missouri | 11 | 0 | 11 | 0 | 11 | -1 | 10 | -1 |
| Montana | 4 | -1 | 3 | 0 | 3 | 0 | 3 | -1 |
| Nebraska | 5 | 0 | 5 | 0 | 5 | 0 | 5 | 0 |
| Nevada | 4 | 0 | 4 | 1 | 5 | 1 | 6 | 2 |
| New Hampshire | 4 | 0 | 4 | 0 | 4 | 0 | 4 | 0 |
| New Jersey | 16 | -1 | 15 | 0 | 15 | -1 | 14 | -2 |
| New Mexico | 5 | 0 | 5 | 0 | 5 | 0 | 5 | 0 |
| New York | 36 | -3 | 33 | -2 | 31 | -2 | 29 | -7 |
| North Carolina | 13 | 1 | 14 | 1 | 15 | 0 | 15 | 2 |
| North Dakota | 3 | 0 | 3 | 0 | 3 | 0 | 3 | 0 |
| Ohio | 23 | -2 | 21 | -1 | 20 | -2 | 18 | -5 |
| Oklahoma | 8 | 0 | 8 | -1 | 7 | 0 | 7 | -1 |
| Oregon | 7 | 0 | 7 | 0 | 7 | 0 | 7 | 0 |
| Pennsylvania | 25 | -2 | 23 | -2 | 21 | -1 | 20 | -5 |
| Rhode Island | 4 | 0 | 4 | 0 | 4 | 0 | 4 | 0 |
| South Carolina | 8 | 0 | 8 | 0 | 8 | 1 | 9 | 1 |
| South Dakota | 3 | 0 | 3 | 0 | 3 | 0 | 3 | 0 |
| Tennessee | 11 | 0 | 11 | 0 | 11 | 0 | 11 | 0 |
| Texas | 29 | 3 | 32 | 2 | 34 | 4 | 38 | 9 |
| Utah | 5 | 0 | 5 | 0 | 5 | 1 | 6 | 1 |
| Vermont | 3 | 0 | 3 | 0 | 3 | 0 | 3 | 0 |
| Virginia | 12 | 1 | 13 | 0 | 13 | 0 | 13 | 1 |
| Washington | 10 | 1 | 11 | 0 | 11 | 1 | 12 | 2 |
| West Virginia | 6 | -1 | 5 | 0 | 5 | 0 | 5 | -1 |
| Wisconsin | 11 | 0 | 11 | -1 | 10 | 0 | 10 | -1 |
| Wyoming | 3 | 0 | 3 | 0 | 3 | 0 | 3 | 0 |
| District of Columbia | 3 | 0 | 3 | 0 | 3 | 0 | 3 | 0 |

➢ The Presidency can be won by taking just 11 states.

## The "Magic Eleven" of the Electoral College *

| | State | Electoral Votes | Cumu-lative | | State | Electoral Votes | Cumu-lative |
|---|---|---|---|---|---|---|---|
| 1. | California | 55 | 55 | 26. | Louisiana | 8 | 422 |
| 2. | Texas | 38 | 93 | 27. | Connecticut | 7 | 429 |
| 3. | Florida | 29 | 122 | 28. | Oklahoma | 7 | 436 |
| 4. | New York | 29 | 151 | 29. | Oregon | 7 | 443 |
| 5. | Illinois | 20 | 171 | 30. | Arkansas | 6 | 449 |
| 6. | Pennsylvania | 20 | 191 | 31. | Iowa | 6 | 455 |
| 7. | Ohio | 18 | 209 | 32. | Kansas | 6 | 461 |
| 8. | Georgia | 16 | 225 | 33. | Mississippi | 6 | 467 |
| 9. | Michigan | 16 | 241 | 34. | Nevada | 6 | 473 |
| 10. | North Carolina | 15 | 256 | 35. | Utah | 6 | 479 |
| 11. | New Jersey | 14 | 270 | 36. | Nebraska | 5 | 484 |
| 12. | Virginia | 13 | 283 | 37. | New Mexico | 5 | 489 |
| 13. | Washington | 12 | 295 | 38. | West Virginia | 5 | 494 |
| 14. | Arizona | 11 | 306 | 39. | Hawaii | 4 | 498 |
| 15. | Indiana | 11 | 317 | 40. | Idaho | 4 | 502 |
| 16. | Massachusetts | 11 | 328 | 41. | Maine | 4 | 506 |
| 17. | Tennessee | 11 | 339 | 42. | New Hampshire | 4 | 510 |
| 18. | Maryland | 10 | 349 | 43. | Rhode Island | 4 | 514 |
| 19. | Minnesota | 10 | 359 | 44. | Alaska | 3 | 517 |
| 20. | Missouri | 10 | 369 | 45. | Delaware | 3 | 520 |
| 21. | Wisconsin | 10 | 379 | 46. | Montana | 3 | 523 |
| 22. | Alabama | 9 | 388 | 47. | North Dakota | 3 | 526 |
| 23. | Colorado | 9 | 397 | 48. | South Dakota | 3 | 529 |
| 24. | South Carolina | 9 | 406 | 49. | Vermont | 3 | 532 |
| 25. | Kentucky | 8 | 414 | 50. | Wyoming | 3 | 535 |
| | | | | 51. | District of Columbia | 3 | 538 |

* The electoral votes shown are based on the 2010 census and will be in effect for the elections of 2012, 2016, and 2020.

➢ Since the *Magic Eleven* states are geographically and demographically diverse, it is rare that a candidate wins all of them. Two candidates have achieved this in the post war period:

❖ In 1972 Richard Nixon (R) won the *Magic Eleven* as well as 38 of the other 39 states.

❖ In 1984 Ronald Reagan (R) won the *Magic Eleven* as well as 38 of the other 39 states.

# The Candidates

➢ The Constitution sets forth several basic requirements for being President or Vice President of the United States of America. He/she must:

❖ be a "natural-born citizen" of the United States,

❖ be at least 35 years of age, and

❖ have lived in the United States for at least 14 years.

➢ Seventy-four different candidates (including one woman) have run for President (including winners and second-place losers only).

➢ Thirty-nine different candidates have won a Presidential election.

➢ Two candidates ran unopposed:

1. George Washington, in both 1789 and 1792
2. James Monroe, in his 1820 re-election.

➢ Until the 1940 election, party leaders chose the Vice Presidential candidate. In 1940, Franklin Roosevelt parted with convention and named his own Vice Presidential candidate. (Roosevelt's two-term Vice President, John Garner, had publicly opposed Roosevelt's policies, prompting Roosevelt to jettison Garner.) This precedent has been followed since then.

➢ The 1968 contest between Richard Nixon (R) and Hubert Humphrey (D) was the only one in history in which both candidates had been Vice President.

➢ The 2008 campaign between John McCain (R) and Barack Obama (D) was the only one in history in which both candidates were sitting Senators.

➢ The 2008 election was the first since 1952 in which neither candidate was an incumbent President or Vice President.

> Six pairs of candidates ran against each other twice:

   1.   John Quincy Adams (D-R)   In 1824:   Adams prevailed in an election decided
       vs. Andrew Jackson (D)                by the House of Representatives.
                              In 1828:   Jackson won.

   2.   Andrew Jackson (D)       In 1824:   Neither was victorious.
       vs. Henry Clay (N)        In 1832:   Jackson won.

   3.   Martin Van Buren (D)     In 1836:   Van Buren won.
       vs. William Harrison (W)   In 1840:   Harrison won.

   4.   Benjamin Harrison (R)    In 1888:   Harrison won.
       vs. Grover Cleveland (D)   In 1892:   Cleveland won.
                                     Both lost as the incumbent.

   5.   William McKinley (R)     In 1900:   McKinley won.
       vs. William Bryan (D)     In 1904:   McKinley won.

   6.   Dwight Eisenhower (R)    In 1952:   Eisenhower won.
       vs. Adlai Stevenson (D)    In 1956:   Eisenhower won.

> The winner and his principal opponent hailed from the same state four times:

   1.   New Yorkers       Theodore Roosevelt vs. Alton Parker     in 1904
   2.   Ohioans           Warren Harding vs. James Cox         in 1920
   3.   New Yorkers       Franklin Roosevelt vs. Wendell Wilkie   in 1940
   4.   New Yorkers       Franklin Roosevelt vs. Thomas Dewey   in 1944

> Thirty-four candidates stood for election more than once; 13 of them never lost and seven never won.

   ❖   Twenty-three men tried twice
   ❖   Nine men tried three times
   ❖   Two men tried four times

- Twelve men tried twice and won twice:
  1. George Washington     Won in 1789 and 1792    (incumbent)
  2. James Madison     Won in 1808 and 1812    (incumbent)
  3. James Monroe     Won in 1816 and 1820    (incumbent)
  4. Abraham Lincoln     Won in 1860 and 1864    (incumbent)
  5. Ulysses Grant     Won in 1868 and 1872    (incumbent)
  6. William McKinley     Won in 1896 and 1900    (incumbent)
  7. Woodrow Wilson     Won in 1912 and 1916    (incumbent)
  8. Dwight Eisenhower     Won in 1952 and 1956    (incumbent)
  9. Ronald Reagan     Won in 1980 and 1984    (incumbent)
  10. William Clinton     Won in 1992 and 1996    (incumbent)
  11. George W. Bush     Won in 2000 and 2004    (incumbent)
  12. Barack Obama     Won in 2008 and 2012    (incumbent)

- Eight men tried twice and won once:
  1. William Harrison     Lost in 1836, won in 1840
  2. Martin Van Buren     Won in 1836, lost in 1840   (incumbent)
  3. Benjamin Harrison     Won in 1888, lost in 1892   (incumbent)
  4. Theodore Roosevelt     Won in 1904 (incumbent), lost in 1912
  5. William Taft     Won in 1908, lost in 1912   (incumbent)
  6. Herbert Hoover     Won in 1928, lost in 1932   (incumbent)
  7. James Carter     Won in 1976, lost in 1980   (incumbent)
  8. George H.W. Bush     Won in 1988, lost in 1992   (incumbent)

- Three men tried twice and lost twice:
  1. Aaron Burr     Lost in 1796 and 1800
  2. Thomas Dewey     Lost in 1944 and 1948
  3. Adlai Stevenson     Lost in 1952 and 1956

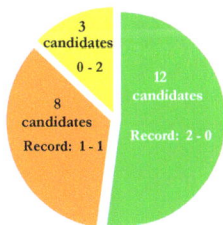

**23 Candidates Ran for President Twice**

3 candidates 0 - 2

8 candidates Record: 1 - 1

12 candidates Record: 2 - 0

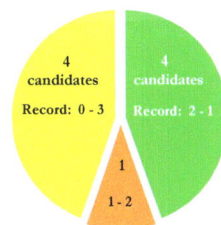

**Nine Candidates Ran for President Thrice**

4 candidates Record: 0 - 3

4 candidates Record: 2 - 1

1 1 - 2

➤ Four men tried thrice and won twice:

    1. Thomas Jefferson       Lost in 1796, won in 1800 and 1804 (incumbent)

    2. Andrew Jackson        Lost in 1824, won in 1828 and 1832 (incumbent)

    3. Grover Cleveland      Won in 1884, lost in 1888 (incumbent), won in 1892

    4. Richard Nixon         Lost in 1960, won in 1968 and 1972 (incumbent)

➤ One man tried thrice and won once:

    1. John Quincy Adams    Lost in 1820, won in 1824, lost in 1828 (incumbent)

➤ Four men tried thrice and lost all three times:

    1. George Clinton         Lost in 1792, 1796, and 1808

    2. Charles Pinckney      Lost in 1800 (4th place), 1804, 1808

    3. Henry Clay            Lost in 1824 (4th place), 1832, and 1844

    4. William Bryan         Lost in 1896, 1900, and 1908

➤ Two men tried four times; one won all four times and one won only once:

    1. John Adams            Lost in 1789 and 1792; won in 1796,
                                    lost in 1800 (incumbent)

    2. Franklin Roosevelt    Won in 1932, 1936, 1940, and 1944
                                      (incumbent in 1936, 1940, and 1944)

➤ Perseverance paid off for the six men who lost when they first ran and won later:

    1. John Adams            Lost in 1789 and 1792, won in 1796

    2. Thomas Jefferson      Lost in 1796, won in 1800

    3. John Quincy Adams    Lost in 1820, won in 1824

    4. Andrew Jackson        Lost in 1824, won in 1828

    5. William Harrison      Lost in 1836, won in 1840

    6. Richard Nixon         Lost in 1960, won in 1968

*See the Appendices for additional information about the candidates.*

# Curious Facts about Elections

➢ The Electoral College did not decide the Presidential election in three instances:
  1. Exercising its duties under the 12th Amendment, the House of Representatives decided in favor of Thomas Jefferson (D-R) in 1800.
  2. Exercising its duties under the 12th Amendment, the House decided in favor of John Quincy Adams (D-R) in 1824.
  3. A Congressional commission decided in favor of Rutherford Hayes (R) in 1876.

➢ One Vice Presidential election was decided by the Senate exercising its duties under the 12th Amendment. The Senate chose Richard Johnson (D) in 1836 after no Vice Presidential candidate received a majority of the electoral vote.

➢ Were it not for the actions of one faithless elector, James Monroe would have scored the only unanimous Electoral College victory in history (excluding George Washington's victories, which were earned prior to passage of the 12th Amendment).

➢ Two Presidents – both incumbents – came close to unanimous Electoral College victories, each falling short by just one state (and the District of Columbia):
  ❖ In 1972 Richard Nixon (R) lost Massachusetts by nine percentage points.
  ❖ By a margin of only 0.18%, Ronald Reagan (R) barely lost Minnesota in 1984.

➢ Since 1860 the winner has always been either a Democrat or Republican.

➢ Since 1860, the second-place finisher has been a Democrat or Republican in every election save three:
  1. Democrat-Populist William Bryan in 1896 and 1900
  2. Theodore Roosevelt of the Bull Moose Party in 1912

➢ The election of 1912 was the first in which the United States consisted of all 48 continental states.

➢ George H.W. Bush's victory in 1988 was the first time in 152 years (*i.e.*, since Martin Van Buren won in 1836) that a sitting Vice President won the Presidency.

- Only one of the three multi-President families had a winning record.
  - ❖ The Adams family went 2 - 5, and one win was controversial.
  - ❖ The Harrison family went 2 - 2.
  - ❖ The Bush family went 3 - 1, and one win was controversial.
  - ❖ As a group, the families had a losing record of seven wins and eight losses.

- Only two third-party candidates have won at least one state in the modern era:
  1. Strom Thurmond of the States Rights Party won four states in 1948.
  2. George Wallace of the American Independent Party won five states in 1968.

- Most Presidents were elected only once . . . or not at all.

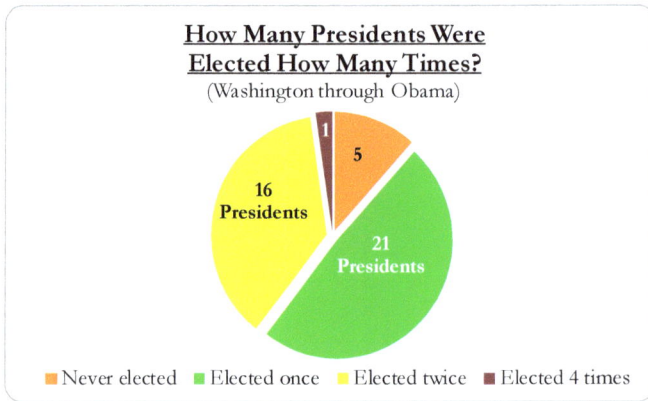

**How Many Presidents Were Elected How Many Times?**
(Washington through Obama)

■ Never elected  ■ Elected once  ■ Elected twice  ■ Elected 4 times

**Presidents Were Elected Once, Twice, Four Times . . . Or Never**

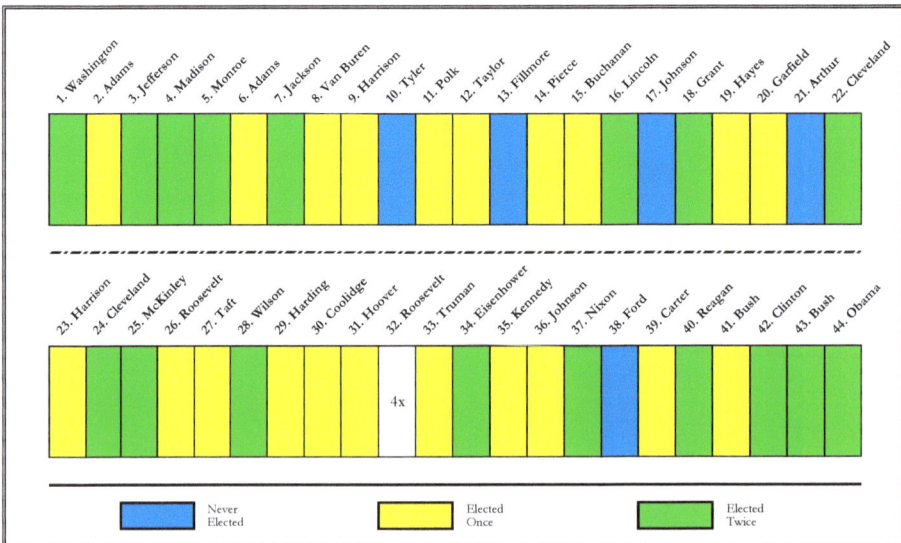

# Election Results:  The Electoral College

➢ Half of winning Presidential candidates received at least 70% of the electoral vote.

➢ In the post war period elections have tended to be closer.

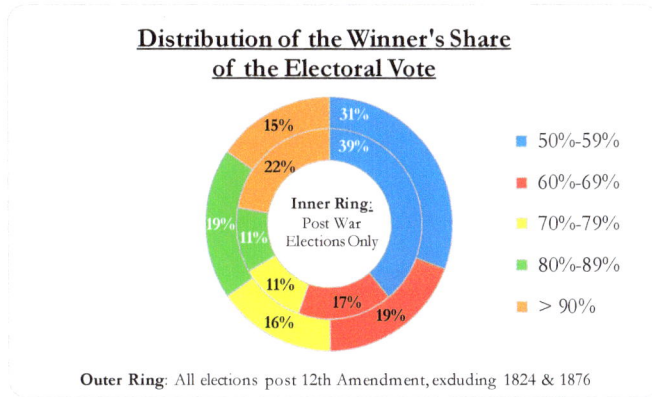

### Distribution of the Winner's Share of the Electoral Vote

**Inner Ring:** Post War Elections Only

Legend:
- 50%-59%
- 60%-69%
- 70%-79%
- 80%-89%
- > 90%

Inner Ring values: 31%, 39%, 19%, 17%, 11%, 11%, 19%, 22%, 15%
Outer Ring values: 31%, 39%, 19%, 17%, 16%, 11%, 19%, 22%, 15%

**Outer Ring:** All elections post 12th Amendment, excluding 1824 & 1876

➢ About four in ten victories were narrow (*i.e.*, the winner garnered less than 60%).

➢ Seven men – in eight elections – won more than 90% of the electoral vote:
   1. Thomas Jefferson (D-R)      in 1804      (incumbent)
   2. James Monroe (D-R)          in 1820      (incumbent; ran unopposed)
   3. Abraham Lincoln (R)         in 1864      (incumbent)
   4. Franklin Roosevelt (D)      in 1936      (incumbent)
   5. Lyndon Johnson (D)          in 1964      (incumbent)
   6. Richard Nixon (R)           in 1972      (incumbent)
   7. Ronald Reagan (R)           in 1980
   8. Ronald Reagan (R)           in 1984      (incumbent)

   ❖ Reagan is the only candidate who achieved this mark when *not* an incumbent.

➤ Seven men – in ten elections – won 80% - 90% of the electoral vote:

1. James Monroe (D-R)           in 1816     (incumbent)
2. Franklin Pierce (D)          in 1852
3. Ulysses Grant (R)            in 1872     (incumbent)
4. Woodrow Wilson (D)           in 1912
5. Herbert Hoover (R)           in 1928
6. Franklin Roosevelt (D)       in 1932
7. Franklin Roosevelt (D)       in 1940     (incumbent)
8. Franklin Roosevelt (D)       in 1944     (incumbent)
9. Dwight D. Eisenhower (R)     in 1952
10. Dwight D. Eisenhower (R)    in 1956     (incumbent)

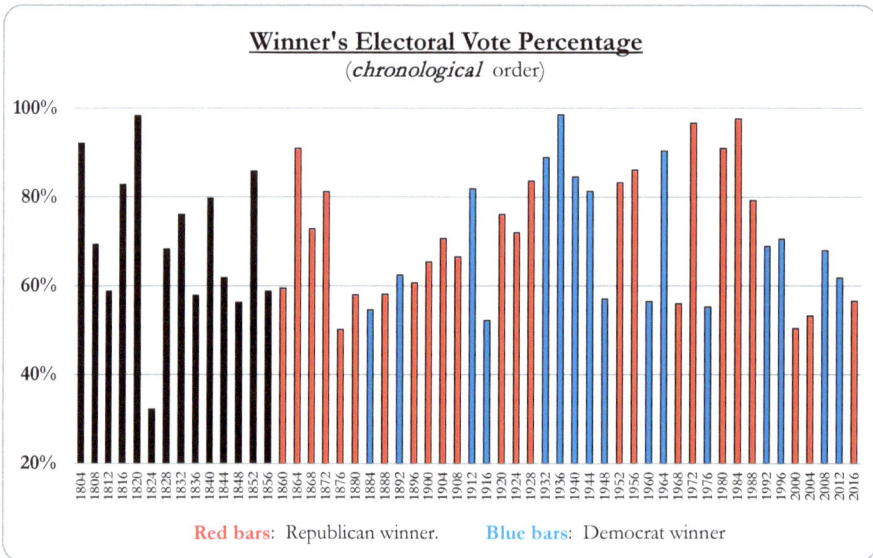

**Winner's Electoral Vote Percentage**
(*chronological* order)

Red bars: Republican winner.      Blue bars: Democrat winner

➤ Eight men won 70% - 80% of the electoral vote:

1. Andrew Jackson (D)           in 1832     (incumbent)
2. William Harrison (W)         in 1840
3. Ulysses Grant (R)            in 1868
4. Theodore Roosevelt (R)       in 1904     (incumbent)
5. Warren Harding (R)           in 1920
6. Calvin Coolidge (R)          in 1924     (incumbent)
7. George H. W. Bush (R)        in 1988
8. William Clinton (D)          in 1996     (incumbent)

➢ Eight men – in ten elections – won 60% - 70% of the electoral vote:

1. James Madison (D-R)        in 1808
2. Andrew Jackson (D)         in 1828
3. James Polk (D)             in 1844
4. Grover Cleveland (D)       in 1892
5. William McKinley (R)       in 1896
6. William McKinley (R)       in 1900      (incumbent)
7. William Taft (R)           in 1908
8. William Clinton (D)        in 1992
9. Barack Obama (D)           in 2008
10. Barack Obama (D)          in 2012      (incumbent)

➢ Five post war losers garnered more than 40% of the electoral vote.

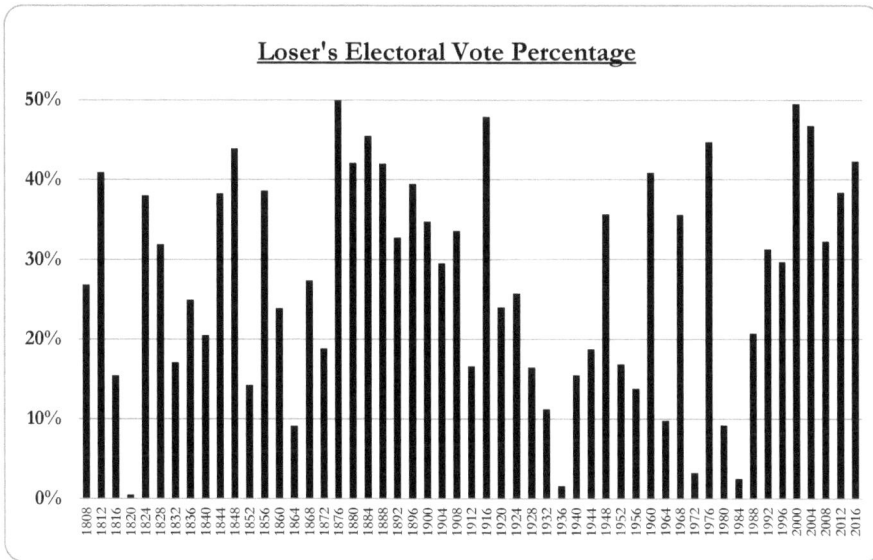

**Loser's Electoral Vote Percentage**

➢ In the modern era, the loser's share of the electoral vote has averaged 27.9%.

➢ Fifteen men – in 16 elections – won less than 60% of the electoral vote:

1. James Madison (D-R)        in 1812      (incumbent)
2. Martin Van Buren (D)       in 1836
3. Zachary Taylor (W)         in 1848
4. James Buchanan (D)         in 1856
5. Abraham Lincoln (R)        in 1860
6. James Garfield (R)         in 1880
7. Grover Cleveland (D)       in 1884
8. Benjamin Harrison (R)      in 1888
9. Woodrow Wilson (D)         in 1916      (incumbent)
10. Harry Truman (D)          in 1948      (incumbent)
11. John Kennedy (D)          in 1960
12. Richard Nixon (R)         in 1968
13. Jimmy Carter (D)          in 1976
14. George W. Bush (R)        in 2000
15. George W. Bush (R)        in 2004      (incumbent)
16. Donald J. Trump (R)       in 2016

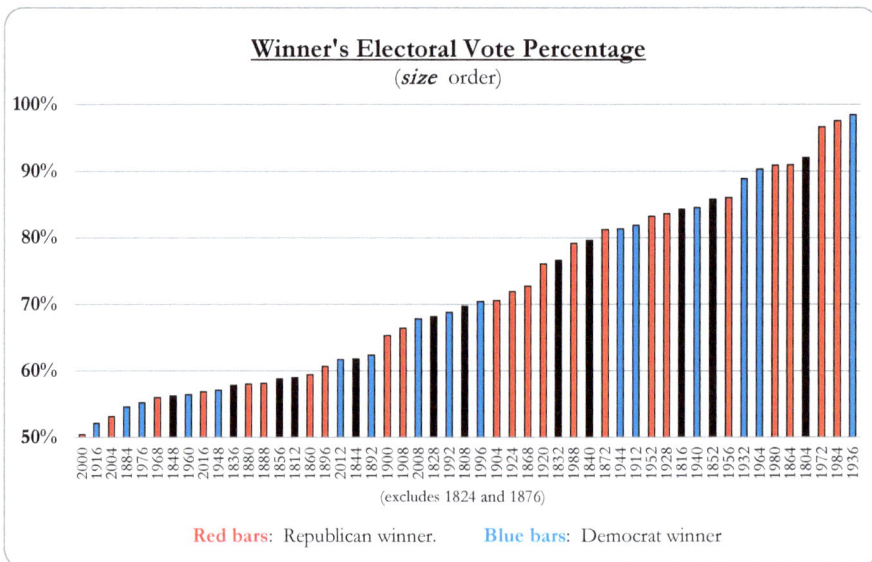

**Winner's Electoral Vote Percentage**
(*size* order)

(excludes 1824 and 1876)

**Red bars**: Republican winner.    **Blue bars**: Democrat winner

➢ In 1824, John Quincy Adams (D-R) received only 32.2% of the electoral vote but nonetheless won the Presidency when no one garnered a majority of the electoral votes and the election was decided by the House of Representatives.

> Winners have been sent to the White House with near-unanimous victories …
> and with the slimmest of margins … and with no margin at all.

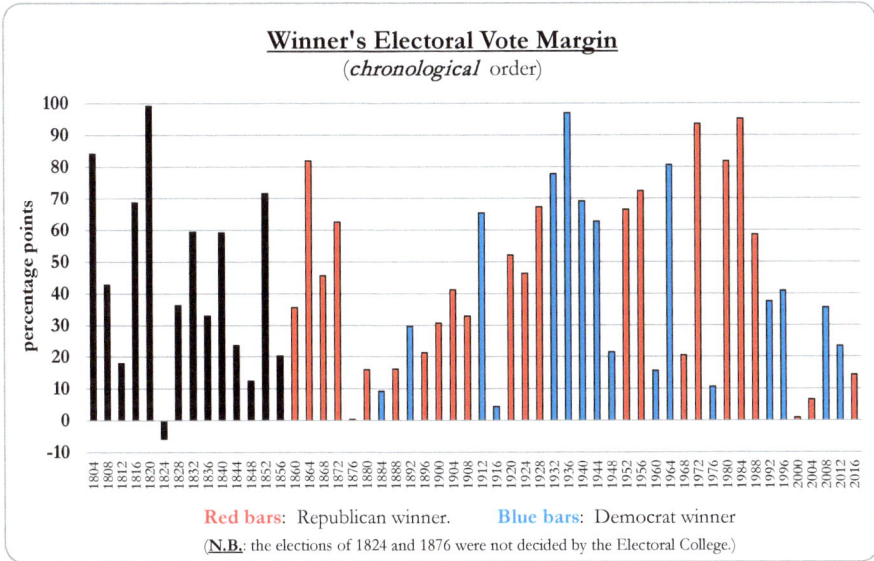

**Winner's Electoral Vote Margin**
(*chronological* order)

Red bars: Republican winner.     Blue bars: Democrat winner
(**N.B.**: the elections of 1824 and 1876 were not decided by the Electoral College.)

> George W. Bush (R) scored history's narrowest electoral-vote victory when he
> garnered just 50.5% in 2000.

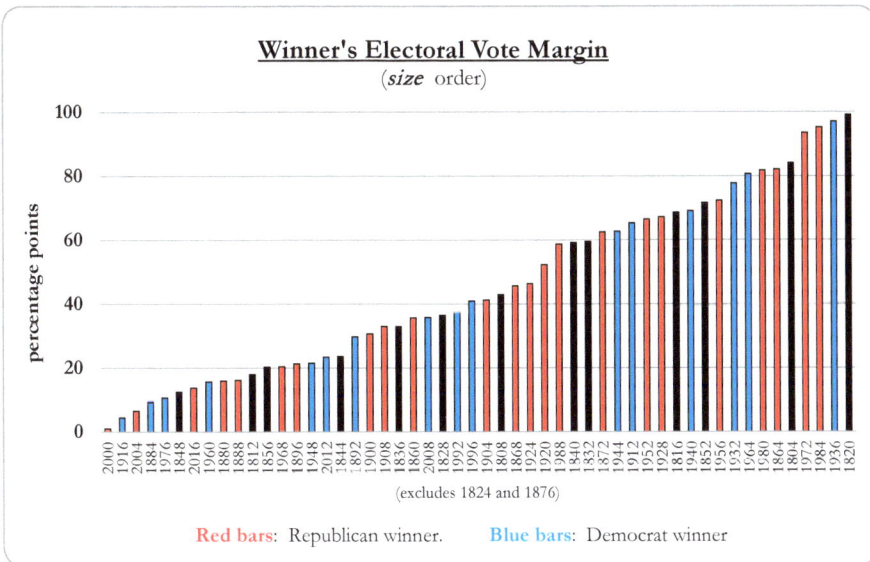

**Winner's Electoral Vote Margin**
(*size* order)

(excludes 1824 and 1876)

Red bars: Republican winner.     Blue bars: Democrat winner

- The average electoral-vote margin is 45.6 percentage points in all elections since 1804 (excluding 1824 and 1876).
  - In post war elections the average margin is 43.1 percentage points.

- Republicans have recorded the four highest electoral-vote tallies in the 538 era.
  - Two candidates won more than 500 votes, each having taken 49 states:
    1. Richard Nixon (R) won 520 votes in 1972.
    2. Ronald Reagan (R) won 525 votes in 1984.

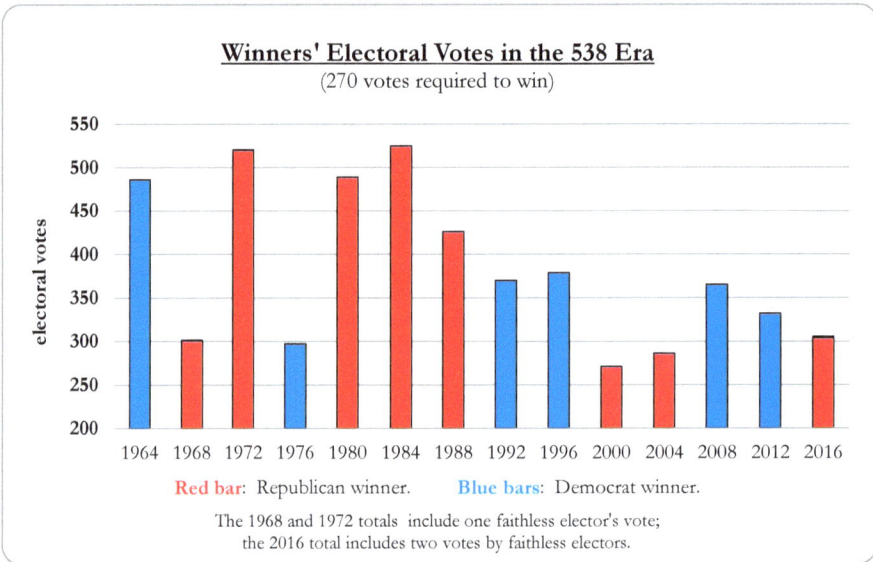

**Winners' Electoral Votes in the 538 Era**
(270 votes required to win)

Red bar: Republican winner.    Blue bars: Democrat winner.

The 1968 and 1972 totals include one faithless elector's vote;
the 2016 total includes two votes by faithless electors.

- In 2000 and 2004 Republican George W. Bush scored the two lowest electoral-vote totals in the 538 era.

*See the Appendices for detailed results of all Presidential elections, 1789 to 2016.*

# Election Results:  The Popular Vote

➢ The winning candidate's share of the national popular vote has ranged from under 40% to over 60%.

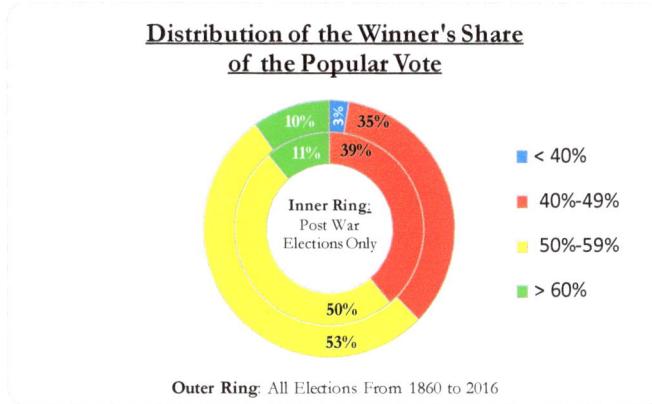

### Distribution of the Winner's Share of the Popular Vote

10%  3%  35%

11%  39%

Inner Ring:
Post War
Elections Only

■ < 40%

■ 40%-49%

50%-59%

■ > 60%

50%

53%

**Outer Ring**: All Elections From 1860 to 2016

➢ Four winning candidates won more than 60% of the popular vote:
1. Warren Harding (R)          won 61.7%      in 1920
2. Lyndon Johnson (D)          won 60.8%      in 1964
3. Richard Nixon (R)           won 60.2%      in 1972
4. Franklin Roosevelt (D)      won 60.2%      in 1936

❖ Warren Harding is the only candidate in history who won more than 60% of the popular vote when *not* an incumbent.

➤ Twenty-one winning candidates received 50% - 60% of the popular vote:

1.  Abraham Lincoln (R)         in 1864      (incumbent)
2.  Ulysses Grant (R)           in 1868
3.  Ulysses Grant (R)           in 1872      (incumbent)
4.  William McKinley (R)        in 1896
5.  William McKinley (R)        in 1900      (incumbent)
6.  Theodore Roosevelt (R)      in 1904      (incumbent)
7.  William Taft (R)            in 1908
8.  Calvin Coolidge (R)         in 1924      (incumbent)
9.  Herbert Hoover (R)          in 1928
10. Franklin Roosevelt (D)      in 1932
11. Franklin Roosevelt (D)      in 1940      (incumbent)
12. Franklin Roosevelt (D)      in 1944      (incumbent)
13. Dwight Eisenhower (R)       in 1952
14. Dwight Eisenhower (R)       in 1956      (incumbent)
15. James Carter (D)            in 1976
16. Ronald Reagan (R)           in 1980
17. Ronald Reagan (R)           in 1984      (incumbent)
18. George H.W. Bush (R)        in 1988
19. George W. Bush (R)          in 2004      (incumbent)
20. Barack Obama (D)            in 2008
21. Barack Obama (D)            in 2012      (incumbent)

➤ In 15 of the 40 Presidential elections since 1860 the winner did not receive a simple majority of the national popular vote.

1.  Abraham Lincoln (R)         in 1860
2.  Rutherford Hayes (R)        in 1876
3.  James Garfield (R)          in 1880
4.  Grover Cleveland (D)        in 1884
5.  Benjamin Harrison (R)       in 1888
6.  Grover Cleveland (D)        in 1892
7.  Woodrow Wilson (D)          in 1912
8.  Woodrow Wilson (D)          in 1916      (incumbent)
9.  Harry Truman (D)            in 1948      (incumbent)
10. John Kennedy (D)            in 1960
11. Richard Nixon (R)           in 1968
12. William Clinton (D)         in 1992
13. William Clinton (D)         in 1996      (incumbent)
14. George W. Bush (R)          in 2000
15. Donald Trump (R)            in 2016

➢ Eleven of the 15 won a plurality, and four of the 15 won even less.

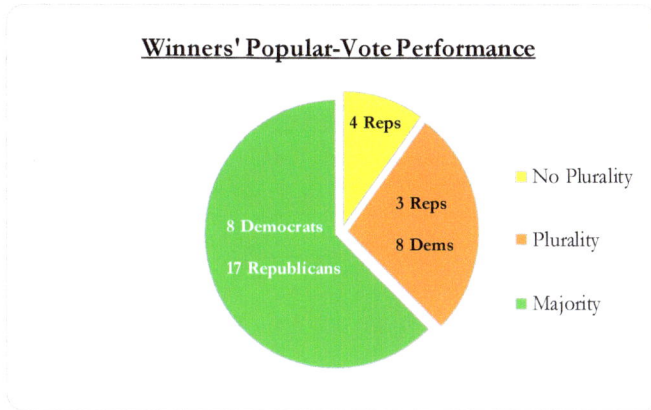

**Winners' Popular-Vote Performance**

4 Reps — No Plurality

3 Reps
8 Dems — Plurality

8 Democrats
17 Republicans — Majority

➢ All candidates who won the Electoral College vote without having garnered at least a plurality of the national popular vote were Republicans:

1. Benjamin Harrison (R)      in 1888
2. George W. Bush (R)         in 2000
3. Donald Trump (R)           in 2016

❖ Rutherford Hayes (R), who was selected to be President by a special electoral commission in 1876, also did not win a plurality of the national popular vote.

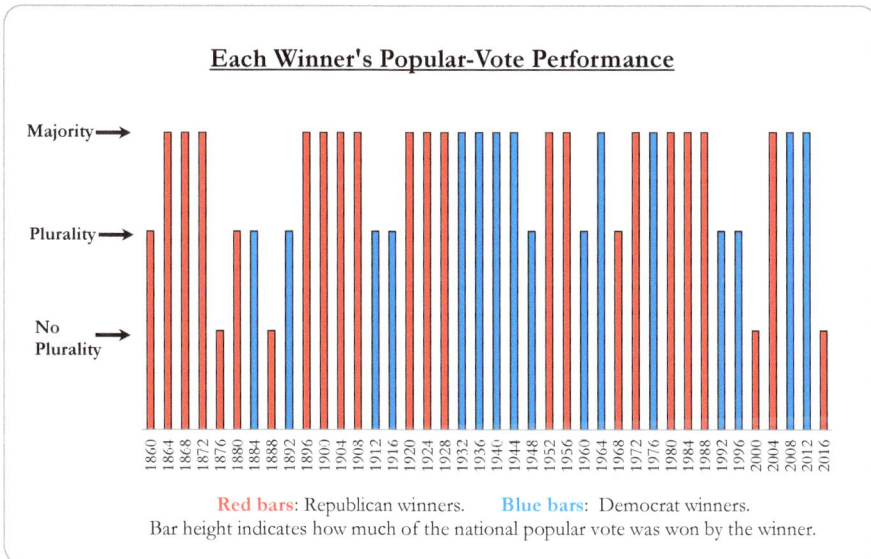

**Each Winner's Popular-Vote Performance**

Majority ➡

Plurality ➡

No
Plurality ➡

1860 1864 1868 1872 1876 1880 1884 1888 1892 1896 1900 1904 1908 1912 1916 1920 1924 1928 1932 1936 1940 1944 1948 1952 1956 1960 1964 1968 1972 1976 1980 1984 1988 1992 1996 2000 2004 2008 2012 2016

**Red bars**: Republican winners.      **Blue bars**: Democrat winners.
Bar height indicates how much of the national popular vote was won by the winner.

➤ In 1860's four-way race, Abraham Lincoln (R) received only 39.6% of the popular vote, which was the plurality but also the smallest share of the popular vote of any winning candidate in history.

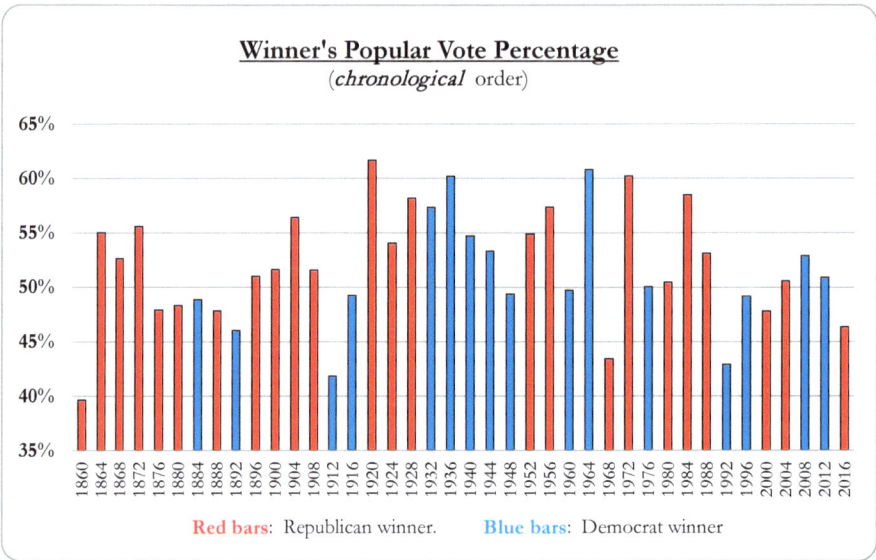

**Winner's Popular Vote Percentage**
(*chronological* order)

Red bars: Republican winner.    Blue bars: Democrat winner

➤ Samuel Tilden (D) is the only candidate in Presidential election history to win an *absolute majority* of the popular vote but *not* win the election. He lost in the controversial election of 1876 that was decided by a special electoral commission established by Congress.

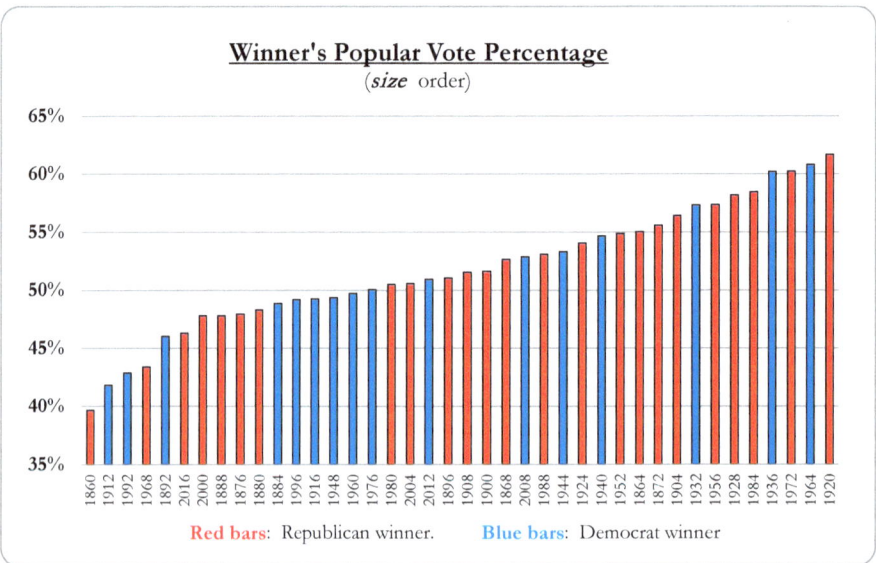

**Winner's Popular Vote Percentage**
(*size* order)

Red bars: Republican winner.    Blue bars: Democrat winner

> Four candidates received a plurality of the national popular vote but did not win.

1. Samuel Tilden (D)       in 1876       (decided by special electoral commission)
2. Grover Cleveland (D)    in 1888
3. Albert Gore (D)         in 2000
4. Hillary Clinton (D)     in 2016

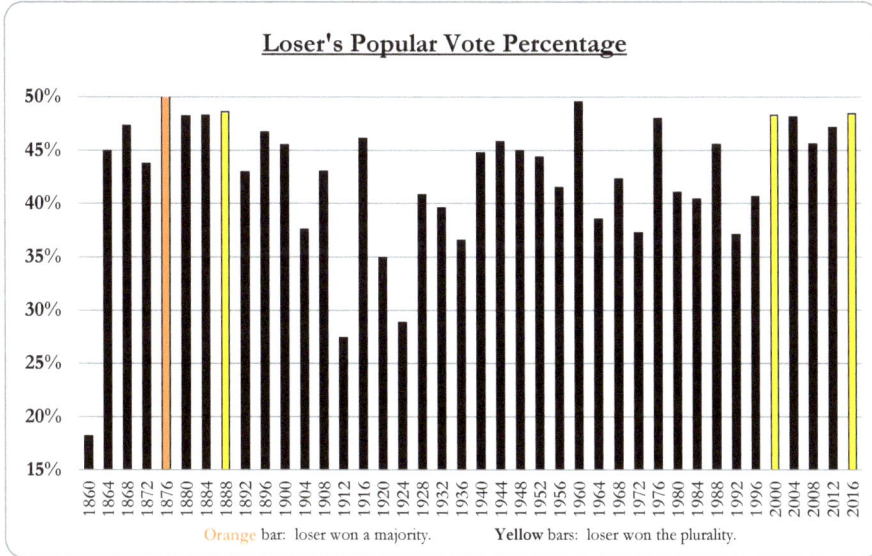

**Loser's Popular Vote Percentage**

Orange bar: loser won a majority.       Yellow bars: loser won the plurality.

> Winning popular-vote margins range from negative to razor thin to "landslide positive."

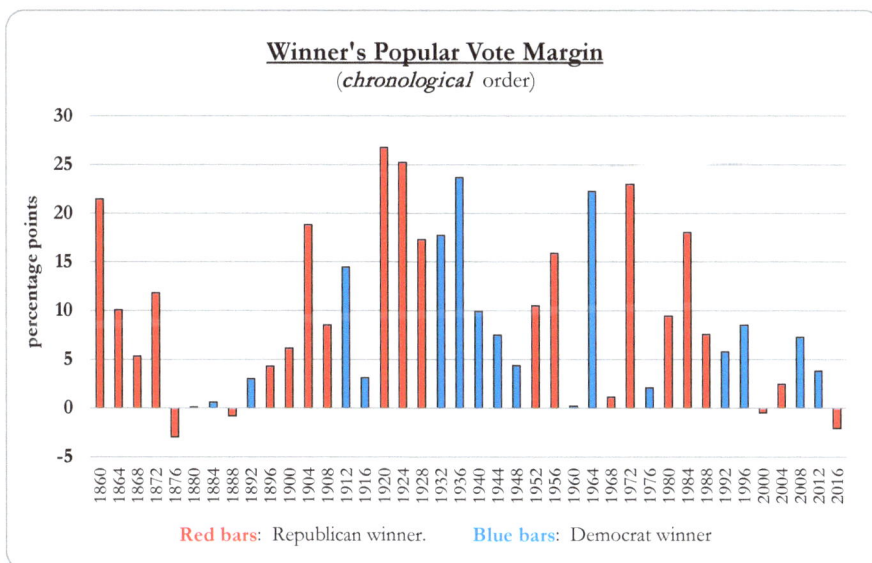

**Winner's Popular Vote Margin**
(*chronological* order)

Red bars: Republican winner.       Blue bars: Democrat winner

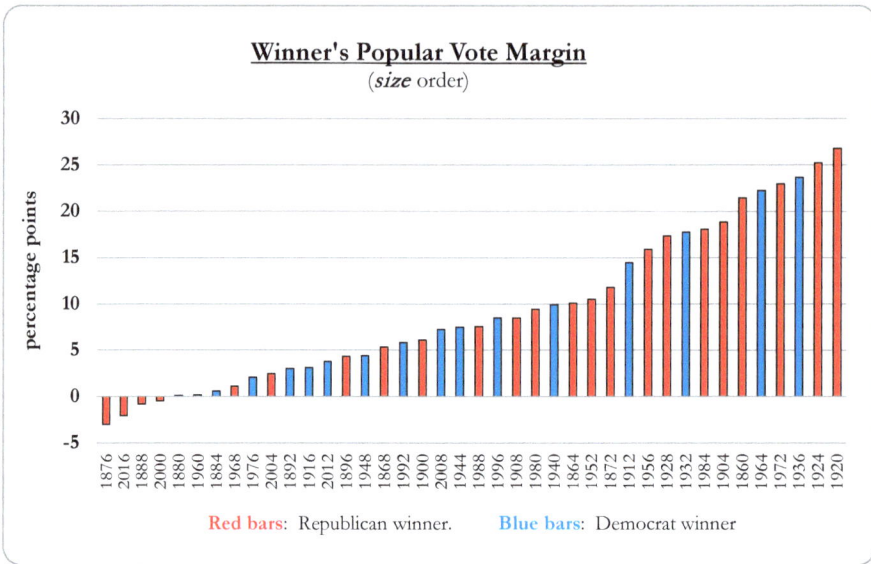

**Winner's Popular Vote Margin**
(*size* order)

Red bars: Republican winner.    Blue bars: Democrat winner

➢ Strong third-party candidates have had a significant impact on the national popular vote from time to time – including preventing a winner from garnering a majority or even a plurality of the national popular vote – but they rarely affect the electoral vote and have never affected the outcome of an election.

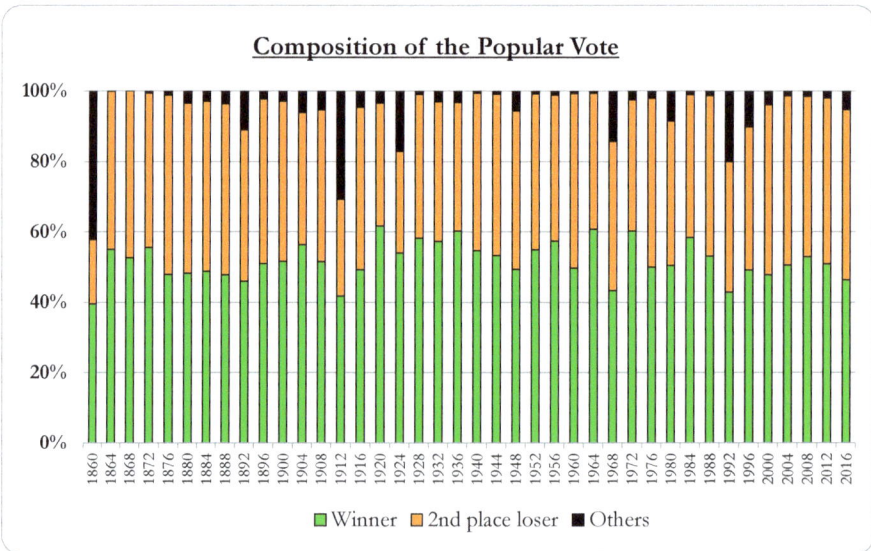

**Composition of the Popular Vote**

■ Winner   ■ 2nd place loser   ■ Others

➢ Since 1860, third- and fourth-place finishers have won a significant portion of the popular vote five times:

1. **1860**: In this four-way race, winner Abraham Lincoln (R) and second-place John Breckinridge (D) *combined* did not even win 60% of the popular vote.

   ❖ John Bell (C) won 12.6% of the popular vote and 12.9% of the electoral vote.

   ❖ Stephen Douglas (D) won 29.5% of the popular vote but only 4.0% of the electoral vote.

2. **1912**: Theodore Roosevelt split with his fellow Republicans to run as the candidate of his own Bull Moose Party. This allowed Woodrow Wilson (D) to win 81.9% of the electoral vote with only 41.8% of the popular vote. Incumbent William Taft (R) took 23.2% of the popular vote but only 1.5% of the electoral vote.

3. **1924**: Robert LaFollette (P) won 16.6% of the popular vote but only 2.4% of the electoral vote.

4. **1968**: George Wallace (AI) won 12.9% of the popular vote and took five states to win 8.6% of the electoral votes.

5. **1992**: Ross Perot (I) won 18.9% of the popular vote but no electoral votes.

*See the Appendices for detailed results of all Presidential elections, 1789 to 2016.*

# Election Results: Electoral Vote versus Popular Vote

➢ Given the way Electoral College voting works, winning candidates garner a higher percentage of the electoral vote than the popular vote (sometimes referred to as the winning-margin "amplification"):

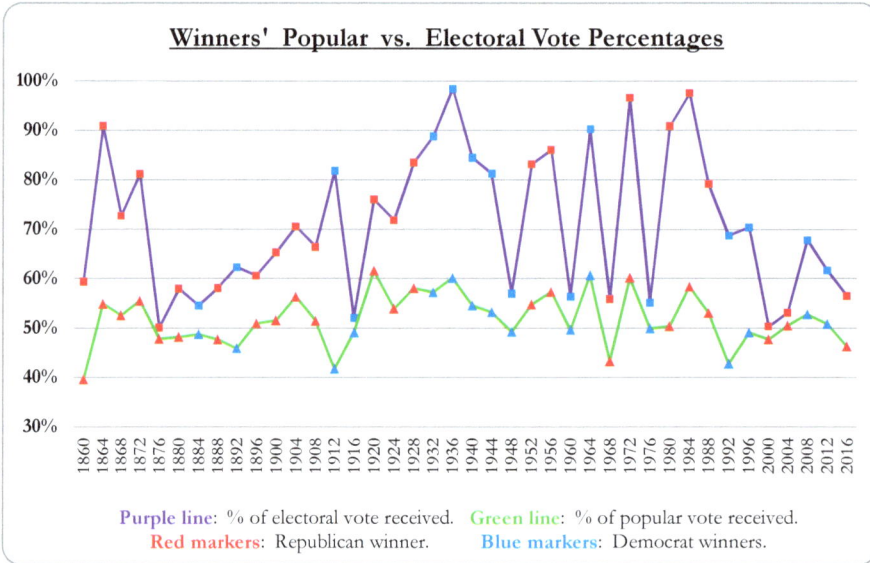

**Winners' Popular vs. Electoral Vote Percentages**

Purple line: % of electoral vote received.    Green line: % of popular vote received.
Red markers: Republican winner.    Blue markers: Democrat winners.

➢ The amplification has been large (as much as 40 percentage points) and very small:

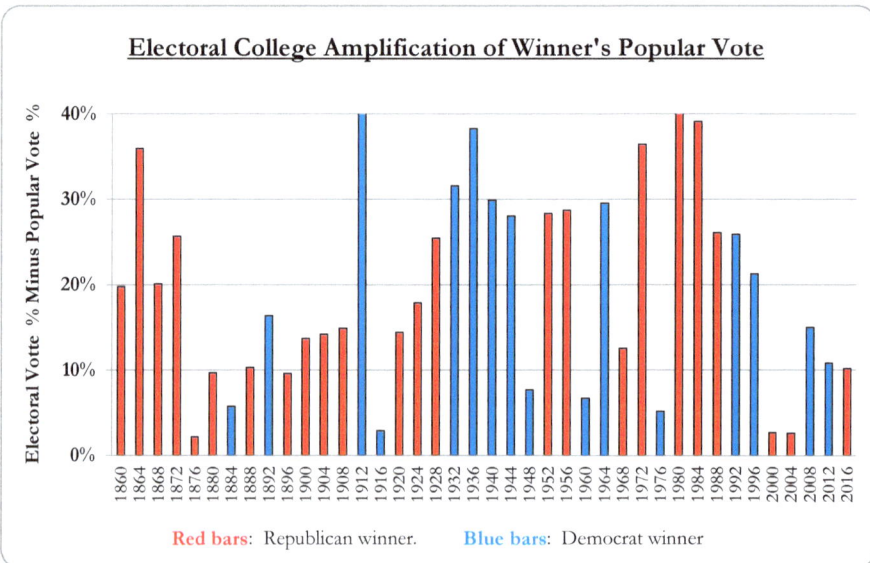

**Electoral College Amplification of Winner's Popular Vote**

Red bars: Republican winner.    Blue bars: Democrat winner

➤ The loser's electoral vote percentage can make his performance appear much worse:

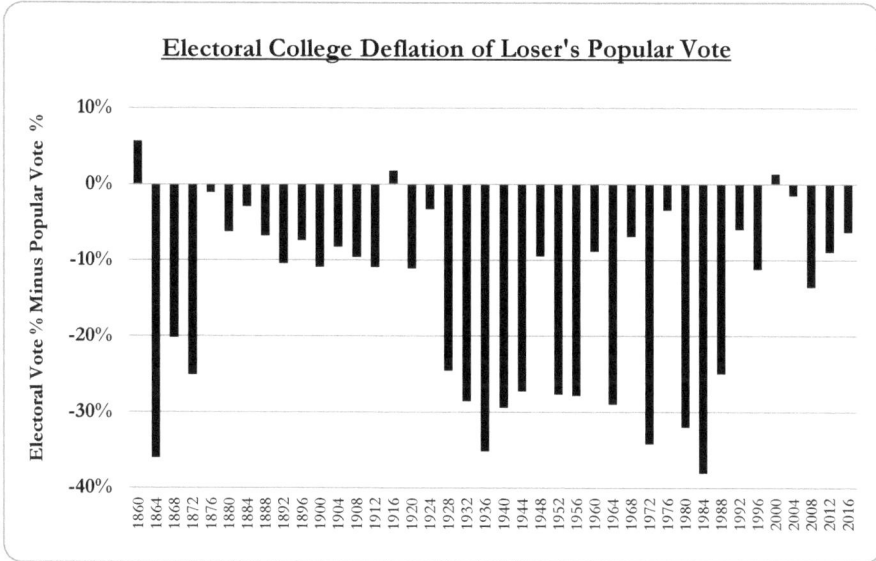

**Electoral College Deflation of Loser's Popular Vote**

y-axis: Electoral Vote % Minus Popular Vote %
(10%, 0%, -10%, -20%, -30%, -40%)

x-axis: 1860, 1864, 1868, 1872, 1876, 1880, 1884, 1888, 1892, 1896, 1900, 1904, 1908, 1912, 1916, 1920, 1924, 1928, 1932, 1936, 1940, 1944, 1948, 1952, 1956, 1960, 1964, 1968, 1972, 1976, 1980, 1984, 1988, 1992, 1996, 2000, 2004, 2008, 2012, 2016

# Election Results:  The Electoral Fate of Incumbents

➢ Having held 58 Presidential elections, there have been 57 incumbents as election day approached.

➢ Incumbent Presidents ran and won, ran and lost, were not re-nominated, were term limited, retired, resigned, died, and were assassinated.

## Incumbent Presidents' Next Move

| Term | Presidency | Election | President | Disposition at the End of (or During) Each Term | Term | Presidency | Election | President | Disposition at the End of (or During) Each Term |
|---|---|---|---|---|---|---|---|---|---|
| 1 | 1 | 1789 | Washington | ran for re-election and won | 30 | | 1904 | T. Roosevelt | retired; ran and lost in 1912 |
| 2 | | 1792 | Washington | retired | 31 | 27 | 1908 | Taft | ran for re-election and lost |
| 3 | 2 | 1796 | J. Adams | ran for re-election and lost | 32 | 28 | 1912 | Wilson | ran for re-election and won |
| 4 | 3 | 1800 | Jefferson | ran for re-election and won | 33 | | 1916 | Wilson | retired |
| 5 | | 1804 | Jefferson | retired | 34 | 29 | 1920 | Harding | died in his first term |
| 6 | 4 | 1808 | Madison | ran for re-election and won | | 30 | | Coolidge | ran and won |
| 7 | | 1812 | Madison | retired | 35 | | 1924 | Coolidge | retired |
| 8 | 5 | 1816 | Monroe | ran for re-election and won | 36 | 31 | 1928 | Hoover | ran for re-election and lost |
| 9 | | 1820 | Monroe | retired | 37 | 32 | 1932 | F. Roosevelt | ran for re-election and won |
| 10 | 6 | 1824 | J.Q. Adams | ran for re-election and lost | 38 | | 1936 | F. Roosevelt | ran for re-election and won |
| 11 | 7 | 1828 | Jackson | ran for re-election and won | 39 | | 1940 | F. Roosevelt | ran for re-election and won |
| 12 | | 1832 | Jackson | retired | 40 | | 1944 | F. Roosevelt | died in his fourth term |
| 13 | 8 | 1836 | Van Buren | ran for re-election and lost | | 33 | | Truman | ran and won |
| 14 | 9 | 1840 | W. Harrison | died in his first term | 41 | | 1948 | Truman | retired |
| | 10 | | Tyler | was not nominated | 42 | 34 | 1952 | Eisenhower | ran for re-election and won |
| 15 | 11 | 1844 | Polk | retired | 43 | | 1956 | Eisenhower | term limited |
| 16 | 12 | 1848 | Taylor | died in his first term | 44 | 35 | 1960 | Kennedy | assassinated in first term |
| | 13 | | Fillmore | was not nominated | | 36 | | L. Johnson | ran and won |
| 17 | 14 | 1852 | Pierce | was not re-nominated | 45 | | 1964 | L. Johnson | retired |
| 18 | 15 | 1856 | Buchanan | was not re-nominated | 46 | 37 | 1968 | Nixon | ran for re-election and won |
| 19 | 16 | 1860 | Lincoln | ran for re-election and won | 47 | | 1972 | Nixon | resigned in his second term |
| 20 | | 1864 | Lincoln | assassinated in second term | | 38 | | Ford | ran and lost |
| | 17 | | A. Johnson | was not nominated | 48 | 39 | 1976 | Carter | ran for re-election and lost |
| 21 | 18 | 1868 | Grant | ran for re-election and won | 49 | 40 | 1980 | Reagan | ran for re-election and won |
| 22 | | 1872 | Grant | was not re-nominated | 50 | | 1984 | Reagan | term limited |
| 23 | 19 | 1876 | Hayes | retired | 51 | 41 | 1988 | G.H.W. Bush | ran for re-election and lost |
| 24 | 20 | 1880 | Garfield | assassinated in first term | 52 | 42 | 1992 | Clinton | ran for re-election and won |
| | 21 | | Arthur | was not nominated | 53 | | 1996 | Clinton | term limited |
| 25 | 22 | 1884 | Cleveland | ran for re-election and lost | 54 | 43 | 2000 | G.W. Bush | ran for re-election and won |
| 26 | 23 | 1888 | B. Harrison | ran for re-election and lost | 55 | | 2004 | G.W. Bush | term limited |
| 27 | 24 | 1892 | Cleveland | was not re-nominated | 56 | 44 | 2008 | Obama | ran for re-election and won |
| 28 | 25 | 1896 | McKinley | ran for re-election and won | 57 | | 2012 | Obama | term limited |
| 29 | | 1900 | McKinley | assassinated in second term | 58 | 45 | 2016 | Trump | *current incumbent* |
| | 26 | | T. Roosevelt | ran and won | | | | | |

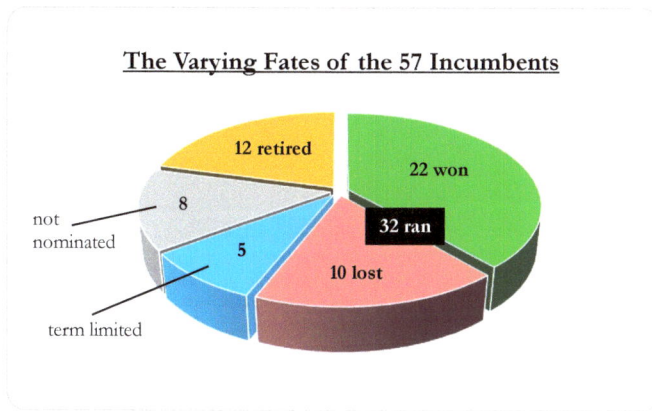

### The Varying Fates of the 57 Incumbents

12 retired

not nominated — 8

term limited — 5

22 won

32 ran

10 lost

➢ Thirty-two of the 58 Presidential elections featured an incumbent candidate.

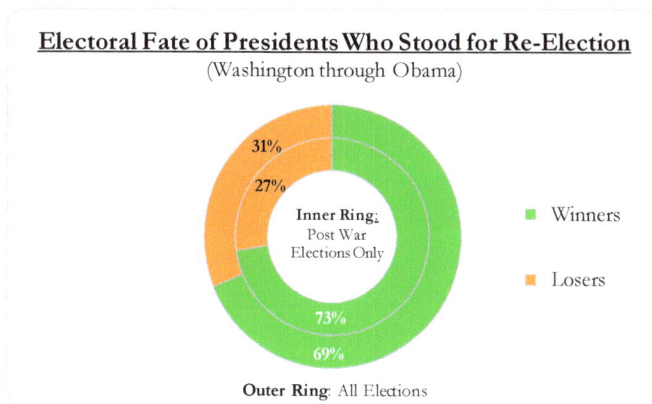

### Electoral Fate of Presidents Who Stood for Re-Election
(Washington through Obama)

31%

27%

**Inner Ring:** Post War Elections Only

73%

69%

■ Winners

■ Losers

**Outer Ring**: All Elections

➢ Twenty-two incumbents won:

| | | | |
|---|---|---|---|
| 1. George Washington | in 1792 | 12. Franklin Roosevelt | in 1936 |
| 2. Thomas Jefferson | in 1804 | 13. Franklin Roosevelt | in 1940 |
| 3. James Madison | in 1812 | 14. Franklin Roosevelt | in 1944 |
| 4. James Monroe | in 1820 | 15. **Harry Truman** | in 1948 |
| 5. Andrew Jackson | in 1832 | 16. Dwight Eisenhower | in 1956 |
| 6. Abraham Lincoln | in 1864 | 17. **Lyndon Johnson** | in 1964 |
| 7. Ulysses Grant | in 1872 | 18. Richard Nixon | in 1972 |
| 8. William McKinley | in 1900 | 19. Ronald Reagan | in 1984 |
| 9. **Theodore Roosevelt** | in 1904 | 20. William Clinton | in 1996 |
| 10. Woodrow Wilson | in 1916 | 21. George W. Bush | in 2004 |
| 11. **Calvin Coolidge** | in 1924 | 22. Barack Obama | in 2012 |

*Candidates whose names appear in bold-face type became incumbents by ascending to the Presidency.*

➤ Ten incumbents lost:

| | | | | | |
|---|---|---|---|---|---|
| 1. | John Adams | in 1800 | 6. | William Taft (3rd place) | in 1912 |
| 2. | John Quincy Adams | in 1828 | 7. | Herbert Hoover | in 1932 |
| 3. | Martin Van Buren | in 1840 | 8. | **Gerald Ford** | in 1976 |
| 4. | Grover Cleveland | in 1888 | 9. | James Carter | in 1980 |
| 5. | Benjamin Harrison | in 1892 | 10. | George H.W. Bush | in 1992 |

*Candidates whose names appear in bold-face type became incumbents by ascending to the Presidency.*

➤ In 36 of the 58 Presidential elections the winner was *not* an incumbent, although one of the 36 (Grover Cleveland) had previously been President.

➤ Theodore Roosevelt, who did not stand for re-election at the end of his full term, ran four years later, in 1912. He broke with the Republican Party and its incumbent, William Taft, and ran under the banner of his own Bull Moose Party. He and Taft split the Republican vote, allowing Woodrow Wilson (D) to win the Presidency.

➤ Sixteen Presidents were re-elected as elected incumbents, including the 13 two-term Presidents, and three Presidents whose second term was cut short by assassination (Abraham Lincoln and William McKinley) or by resignation (Richard Nixon).

➤ Most incumbent winners won more electoral votes in their re-election bid than they did in their initial outing; on average, a winning incumbent's percentage improved by 10 points.

➤ The largest improvement by an incumbent winner was Thomas Jefferson's 65.6 point rise in 1804 (but the voting system in 1804 was different than it was when Jefferson ran in 1800).

➤ Only three incumbent winners recorded a smaller percentage of the electoral vote in their re-election than they had garnered in their first election (excluding Franklin Roosevelt's third and fourth elections):
1. James Madison won 69.7% in 1808 but only 59.0% in 1812, a drop of 10.7 points.
2. Woodrow Wilson won 81.9% in 1912 and but only 52.2% in 1916, a decline of 29.8 points.
3. Barack Obama won 67.8% in 2008 but only 61.7% in 2012, a decline of 6.1 points.

- Franklin Roosevelt's electoral-vote percentage rose by 9.6 points – from 88.9% to 98.5% -- the first time he was an incumbent but it fell in his third and fourth elections, by 13.9 points in 1940 and 3.2 points in 1944. Thus, his electoral-vote percentages in his second and third races as an incumbent were lower than his initial run as a non-incumbent.

- On average, losing incumbents experienced a 34.4 percentage-point erosion in their electoral vote. The worst performance was recorded by Herbert Hoover – losing 72.5 points – and the "best" performance was owned by John Adams – losing only 2.1 points (excluding his son's 0.4 decline from the depressed level of 1824 when the House of Representatives – not the Electoral College – decided the election).

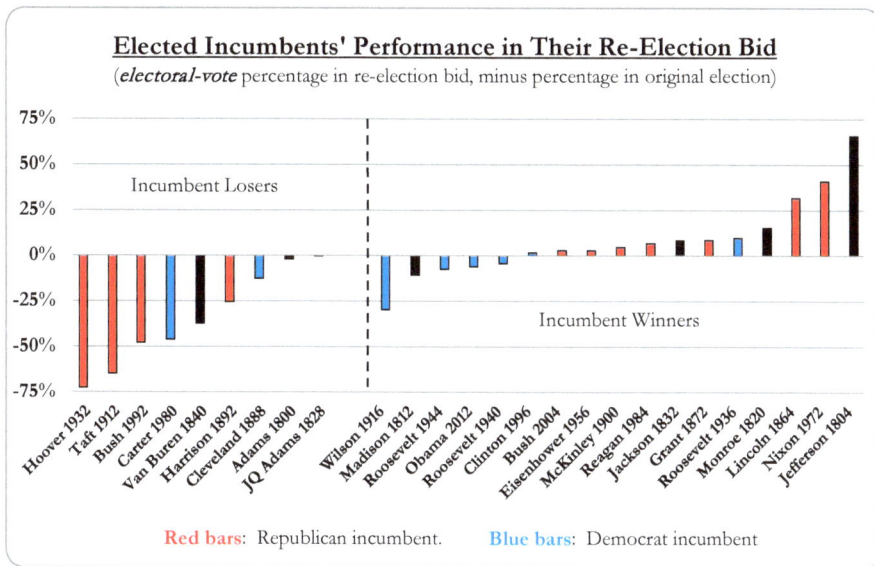

**Elected Incumbents' Performance in Their Re-Election Bid**
(*electoral-vote* percentage in re-election bid, minus percentage in original election)

Incumbent Losers

Incumbent Winners

**Red bars**: Republican incumbent.     **Blue bars**: Democrat incumbent

- Barack Obama is the only incumbent winner in history who won a smaller percentage of the popular vote in his re-election than achieved in the initial outing (excluding Franklin Roosevelt's third and fourth elections).

- On average, the popular-vote percentage of winning incumbents improved by 5.8 percentage points compared to their initial winning percentage (excluding Franklin Roosevelt's third and fourth elections). Leaving aside Barack Obama's two-percentage point *decline*, the smallest improvement was William McKinley's 0.6 percentage point gain in 1900. The largest improvement was Richard Nixon's 16.8 point rise in 1972.

➢ While his popular-vote percentage rose by 2.9 points – from 57.3% to 60.2% -- the first time he was an incumbent, Franklin Roosevelt's popular-vote percentage fell in his third and fourth elections, by 5.5 points in 1940 and 1.4 points in 1944. As a result, his popular-vote percentages in his second and third races as an incumbent were lower than his initial run as a non-incumbent.

➢ On average, losing incumbents experienced a 12.8 percentage-point erosion in their popular vote. The worst performance was recorded by William Taft in 1912 (losing 28.4 percentage points) and the "best" performance was owned by Grover Cleveland in 1888 (losing just 0.2 point).

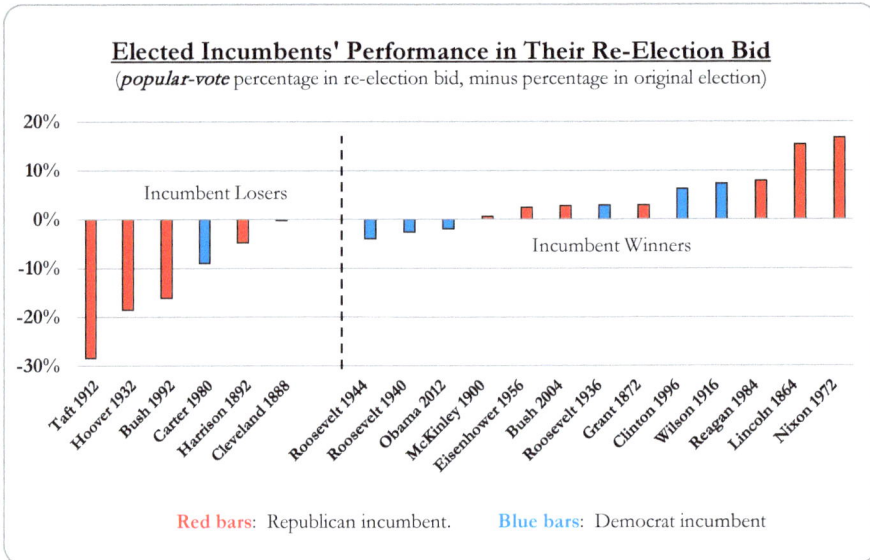

**Elected Incumbents' Performance in Their Re-Election Bid**
(*popular-vote* percentage in re-election bid, minus percentage in original election)

Red bars: Republican incumbent.      Blue bars: Democrat incumbent

# Election Results:  The Electoral Fate of the Incumbent Party

➢ It is relatively rare for the Presidency to change party in consecutive elections. This has happened only twice in the two-party era:

❖ 1884 / 1888 / 1892 / 1896:  Grover Cleveland (D) took the White House from the Republicans in 1884, was then defeated by Benjamin Harrison (R) in 1888 who, in turn, was defeated by Cleveland in 1892. Four years later, William McKinley won, putting a Republican back in the Oval Office.

❖ 1972 / 1976 / 1980:  James Carter (D) defeated the incumbent Gerald Ford (R) and was then beaten by Ronald Reagan (R).

### The Electoral Fate of the Incumbent Party, 1860 to 2016

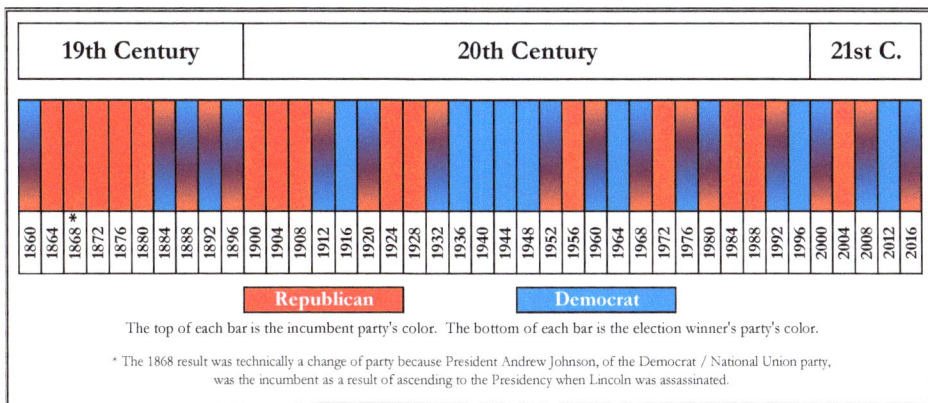

| 19th Century | 20th Century | 21st C. |

Republican          Democrat

The top of each bar is the incumbent party's color.  The bottom of each bar is the election winner's party's color.

\* The 1868 result was technically a change of party because President Andrew Johnson, of the Democrat / National Union party, was the incumbent as a result of ascending to the Presidency when Lincoln was assassinated.

➢ It has been extraordinarily difficult for a party to maintain control of the White House following a two-term Presidency. In only two of the seven two-term Presidencies from 1860 to 2016 did the incumbent party maintain control of the White House.

|  | All | Post War |
|---|---|---|
| ❖ Elections in which the party changed: | 7 | 4 |
| ❖ Elections resulting in no change of party: | 2 | 1 |

➢ In the 15 elections from 1860 to 2016 that did not feature an incumbent candidate, the incumbent party usually lost control of the White House. The result was particularly lopsided in the post war period:

|  | All | Post War |
|---|---|---|
| ❖ Elections in which the party changed: | 11 | 6 |
| ❖ Elections resulting in no change of party: | 4 | 1 |

➤ From 1900 through 2016, there were six two-term Presidents. In five out of the six cases, the election immediately following the end of the two terms was won by the other party. The one exception was George H.W. Bush's victory at the end of Reagan's two terms.

1. The Republicans (Warren Harding) took over from the Democrats in 1921 at the end of Woodrow Wilson's two terms.

2. The Democrats (John Kennedy) took over from the Republicans in 1961 at the end of Dwight Eisenhower's two terms.

3. The Republicans maintained control of the White House when George H.W. Bush won in 1988 at the end of Ronald Reagan's two terms.

4. The Republicans (George W. Bush) took over from the Democrats in 2001 at the end of William Clinton's two terms.

5. The Democrats (Barack Obama) took over from the Republicans in 2009 at the end of George W. Bush's two terms.

6. The Republicans (Donald Trump) took over from the Democrats in 2017 at the end of Barack Obama's two terms.

# Election Results:  The Ebb and Flow of Each Party's Victories

➤ In the two-party era, the Republican candidate has won more often than not.

## Presidential Election Wins in the Two-Party Era, by Party

|  | Republican Wins | Democrat Wins |
|---|---|---|
| 1860 to 2016 | 24<br>60% | 16<br>40% |
| Post war period | 10<br>56% | 8<br>44% |
| 538-electoral-vote era | 8<br>57% | 6<br>43% |
| 19th century | 8<br>80% | 2<br>20% |
| 20th century | 13<br>52% | 12<br>48% |
| 21st century | 3<br>60% | 2<br>40% |

➤ In winning the six Presidential elections from 1860 to 1880, the Republicans earned the accolade of *Most Victories in a Row*.

➤ The Democrats' longest winning streak was five, from 1932 to 1948.

## The Ebb and Flow of Party Presidential-Election Victories

| 19th Century | 20th Century | 21st C. |
|---|---|---|
| 8 Republican Wins<br>2 Democrat Wins | 13 Republican Wins<br>12 Democrat Wins | 3 Rep.<br>2 Dem. |

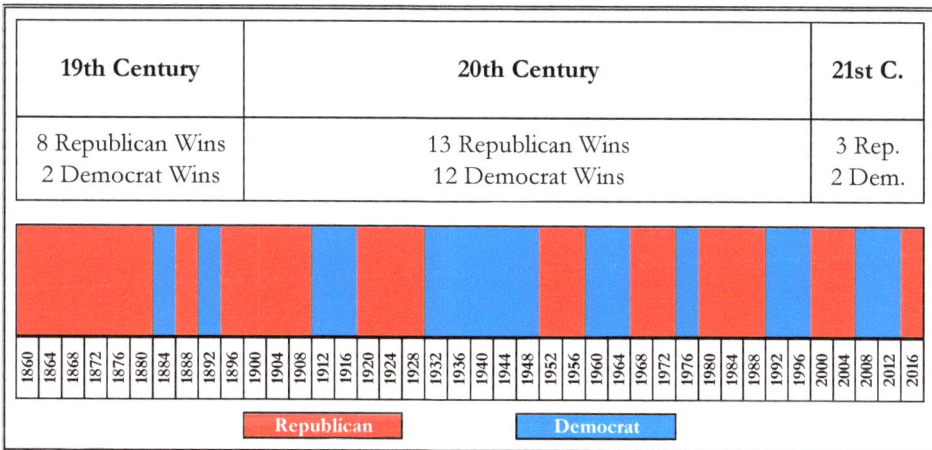

➤ Republicans have more winning streaks and longer streaks than do the Democrats.

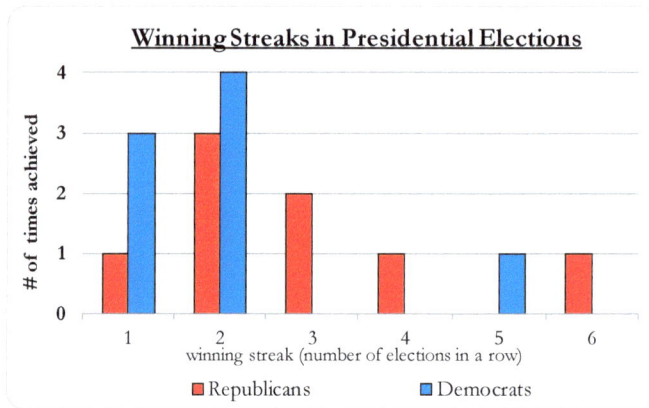

**Winning Streaks in Presidential Elections**

# Election Results:  State-by-State Outcomes

➢ In the post war period, no state has voted consistently for the same party.

&#10087; The District of Columbia has voted for the Democrat candidate in every election since it was enfranchised in 1964.

➢ In the post war period, only five states voted consistently for the same party in all elections save one, and they all voted Republican:

1. Alaska (1960 to present)
2. Kansas
3. Nebraska
4. North Dakota
5. South Dakota

&#10087; The exception in each case was Lyndon Johnson's 1964 defeat of Barry Goldwater.

➢ An additional four states voted for the same party – the Republican Party – in all but two elections:

1. Idaho
2. Oklahoma
3. Utah
4. Wyoming

&#10087; In addition to 1964, the exception in each case was Harry Truman's 1948 defeat of Thomas Dewey.

➢ In the 13 elections after 1964, every state has voted for a Republican candidate at least once. Three states voted Republican *only* once or twice:

&#10087; Minnesota's sole Republican vote was for Richard Nixon in 1972.

&#10087; Hawaii and Massachusetts each voted Republican only twice:

- Massachusetts voted for Ronald Reagan in 1980 and 1984.
- Hawaii voted for Richard Nixon in 1972 and for Ronald Reagan in 1984.

➢ In the 13 elections after 1964, nine states never voted for a Democrat candidate. An additional six states voted Democrat only once.

# Presidential Election Results by State, 1948 -2016

| | 2016 | 2012 | 2008 | 2004 | 2000 | 1996 | 1992 | 1988 | 1984 | 1980 | 1976 | 1972 | 1968 | 1964 | 1960 | 1956 | 1952 | 1948 |
|---|---|---|---|---|---|---|---|---|---|---|---|---|---|---|---|---|---|---|

Alabama
Alaska
Arizona
Arkansas
California
Colorado
Connecticut
Delaware
Florida
Georgia
Hawaii
Idaho
Illinois
Indiana
Iowa
Kansas
Kentucky
Louisiana
Maine
Maryland
Massachusetts
Michigan
Minnesota
Mississippi
Missouri
Montana
Nebraska
Nevada
New Hampshire
New Jersey
New Mexico
New York
North Carolina
North Dakota
Ohio
Oklahoma
Oregon
Pennsylvania
Rhode Island
South Carolina
South Dakota
Tennessee
Texas
Utah
Vermont
Virginia
Washington
West Virginia
Wisconsin
Wyoming
District of Columbia

| States Won (including District of Columbia) | 30 / 21 | 24 / 27 | 22 / 29 | 31 / 20 | 30 / 21 | 19 / 32 | 18 / 33 | 41 / 10 | 49 / 2 | 44 / 7 | 27 / 24 | 49 / 2 | 32 / 14 / 5 | 6 / 45 | 27 / 23 | 41 / 7 | 39 / 9 | 16 / 28 / 4 |
| Winner | Trump | Obama | Obama | Bush | Bush | Clinton | Clinton | Bush | Reagan | Reagan | Carter | Nixon | Nixon | Johnson | Kennedy | Eisenhower | Eisenhower | Truman |

Legend: Democrat — Republican — other — not a State or Electoral College participant

92

- In the post war era, the winning candidate twice carried fewer states than the loser, and in both cases the winner took 23 states and the loser 27:
  - ❖ John Kennedy (D) in 1960
  - ❖ James Carter (D) in 1976
    (Carter also carried Washington, DC, which had not yet been enfranchised in 1960.)

**States Carried by the Presidential Election Winner**

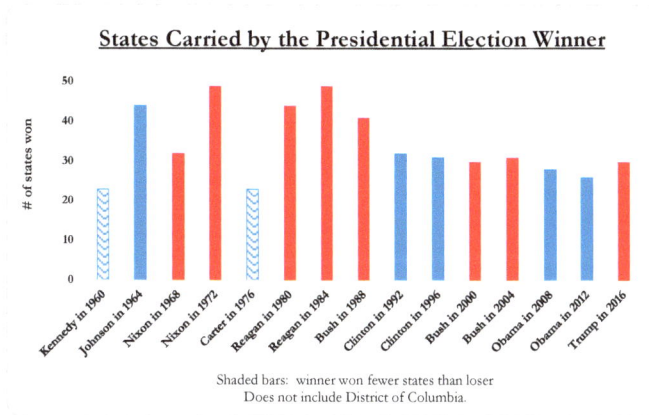

Shaded bars: winner won fewer states than loser
Does not include District of Columbia.

- Only one state – Ohio – has a perfect record of voting for the winning Presidential candidate in every election in the 538 era. If it were not for voting for Richard Nixon (R) in 1960, Ohio would have a perfect record throughout the post war period.

- Most states have sided with the winner more than 60% of the time, but few have gotten it right more than about three-quarters of the time.

**States' Record of Voting for the Winner**

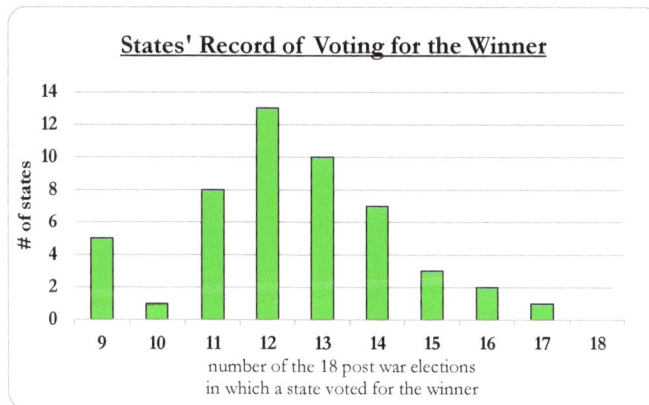

number of the 18 post war elections
in which a state voted for the winner

# States' Record of Voting for the Winning Presidential Candidate, 1948 - 2016

| | 2016 | 2012 | 2008 | 2004 | 2000 | 1996 | 1992 | 1988 | 1984 | 1980 | 1976 | 1972 | 1968 | 1964 | 1960 | 1956 | 1952 | 1948 |
|---|---|---|---|---|---|---|---|---|---|---|---|---|---|---|---|---|---|---|
| Alabama | | | | | | | | | | | | | | | | | | |
| Alaska | | | | | | | | | | | | | | | | | | |
| Arizona | | | | | | | | | | | | | | | | | | |
| Arkansas | | | | | | | | | | | | | | | | | | |
| California | | | | | | | | | | | | | | | | | | |
| Colorado | | | | | | | | | | | | | | | | | | |
| Connecticut | | | | | | | | | | | | | | | | | | |
| Delaware | | | | | | | | | | | | | | | | | | |
| Florida | | | | | | | | | | | | | | | | | | |
| Georgia | | | | | | | | | | | | | | | | | | |
| Hawaii | | | | | | | | | | | | | | | | | | |
| Idaho | | | | | | | | | | | | | | | | | | |
| Illinois | | | | | | | | | | | | | | | | | | |
| Indiana | | | | | | | | | | | | | | | | | | |
| Iowa | | | | | | | | | | | | | | | | | | |
| Kansas | | | | | | | | | | | | | | | | | | |
| Kentucky | | | | | | | | | | | | | | | | | | |
| Louisiana | | | | | | | | | | | | | | | | | | |
| Maine | | | | | | | | | | | | | | | | | | |
| Maryland | | | | | | | | | | | | | | | | | | |
| Massachusetts | | | | | | | | | | | | | | | | | | |
| Michigan | | | | | | | | | | | | | | | | | | |
| Minnesota | | | | | | | | | | | | | | | | | | |
| Mississippi | | | | | | | | | | | | | | | | | | |
| Missouri | | | | | | | | | | | | | | | | | | |
| Montana | | | | | | | | | | | | | | | | | | |
| Nebraska | | | | | | | | | | | | | | | | | | |
| Nevada | | | | | | | | | | | | | | | | | | |
| New Hampshire | | | | | | | | | | | | | | | | | | |
| New Jersey | | | | | | | | | | | | | | | | | | |
| New Mexico | | | | | | | | | | | | | | | | | | |
| New York | | | | | | | | | | | | | | | | | | |
| North Carolina | | | | | | | | | | | | | | | | | | |
| North Dakota | | | | | | | | | | | | | | | | | | |
| Ohio | | | | | | | | | | | | | | | | | | |
| Oklahoma | | | | | | | | | | | | | | | | | | |
| Oregon | | | | | | | | | | | | | | | | | | |
| Pennsylvania | | | | | | | | | | | | | | | | | | |
| Rhode Island | | | | | | | | | | | | | | | | | | |
| South Carolina | | | | | | | | | | | | | | | | | | |
| South Dakota | | | | | | | | | | | | | | | | | | |
| Tennessee | | | | | | | | | | | | | | | | | | |
| Texas | | | | | | | | | | | | | | | | | | |
| Utah | | | | | | | | | | | | | | | | | | |
| Vermont | | | | | | | | | | | | | | | | | | |
| Virginia | | | | | | | | | | | | | | | | | | |
| Washington | | | | | | | | | | | | | | | | | | |
| West Virginia | | | | | | | | | | | | | | | | | | |
| Wisconsin | | | | | | | | | | | | | | | | | | |
| Wyoming | | | | | | | | | | | | | | | | | | |
| District of Columbia | | | | | | | | | | | | | | | | | | |
| **Winner** | Trump | Obama | Obama | Bush | Bush | Clinton | Clinton | Bush | Reagan | Reagan | Carter | Nixon | Nixon | Johnson | Kennedy | Eisenhower | Eisenhower | Truman |

| Legend | voted for the winning candidate | voted for a losing candidate |
|---|---|---|

94

# Frequency With Which Each State Voted for the Winner

| State | How Many Times in the 18 Post War Elections? * | State | How Many Times in the 10 Elections from 1980 to 2016? |
|-------|-----------------------------------------------|-------|------------------------------------------------------|
| District of Columbia ** | 6 times; i.e., 43% of the time | District of Columbia<br>Minnesota | 4 times; i.e., 40% of the time |
| Alabama<br>Alaska ***<br>Hawaii ***<br>Mississippi<br>South Carolina | 9 times; i.e., 50% of the time | Hawaii | 5 times; i.e., 50% of the time |
| Georgia | 10 times; i.e., 56% of the time | Alabama<br>Alaska<br>Georgia<br>Idaho<br>Kansas<br>Maryland<br>Massachusetts<br>Mississippi<br>Nebraska<br>New York<br>North Dakota<br>Oklahoma<br>Oregon<br>Rhode Island<br>South Carolina<br>South Dakota<br>Texas<br>Utah<br>Washington<br>West Virginia<br>Wyoming | 6 times; i.e., 60% of the time |
| Kansas<br>Maine<br>Minnesota<br>Nebraska<br>North Dakota<br>Oregon<br>South Dakota<br>Washington | 11 times; i.e., 61% of the time | | |
| Arizona<br>Connecticut<br>Idaho<br>Indiana<br>Louisiana<br>Maryland<br>Massachusetts<br>New York<br>Oklahoma<br>Utah<br>Vermont<br>West Virginia<br>Wyoming | 12 times; i.e., 67% of the time | | |
| Arkansas<br>California<br>Michigan<br>Montana<br>New Hampshire<br>New Jersey<br>North Carolina<br>Rhode Island<br>Texas<br>Virginia | 13 times; i.e., 72% of the time | Arizona<br>California<br>Connecticut<br>Delaware<br>Illinois<br>Indiana<br>Maine<br>Montana<br>New Jersey<br>North Carolina<br>Vermont<br>Virginia<br>Wisconsin | 7 times; i.e., 70% of the time |
| Colorado<br>Delaware<br>Illinois<br>Iowa<br>Kentucky<br>Pennsylvania<br>Wisconsin | 14 times; i.e., 78% of the time | Arkansas<br>Colorado<br>Iowa<br>Kentucky<br>Louisiana<br>Michigan<br>Missouri<br>New Hampshire<br>New Mexico<br>Pennsylvania<br>Tennessee | 8 times; i.e., 80% of the time |
| Missouri<br>New Mexico<br>Tennessee | 15 times; i.e., 83% of the time | | |
| Florida<br>Nevada | 16 times; i.e., 89% of the time | Florida<br>Nevada | 9 times; i.e., 90% of the time |
| Ohio | 17 times; i.e., 94% of the time | Ohio | 10 times; i.e., 100% of the time |

\*   Alaska, Hawaii, and DC did not participate in all 18 elections.

\*\*   DC voted for the winner 6 of 14 times (from 1964 -- when it first participated in the Electoral College -- to 2016).

\*\*\*  Alaska and Hawaii's percentage is 60% because they only voted in 15 elections (from 1960 to 2016).

# Oh Say Can You See . . .
## How Long It's Been Since Your Party Won Your State?

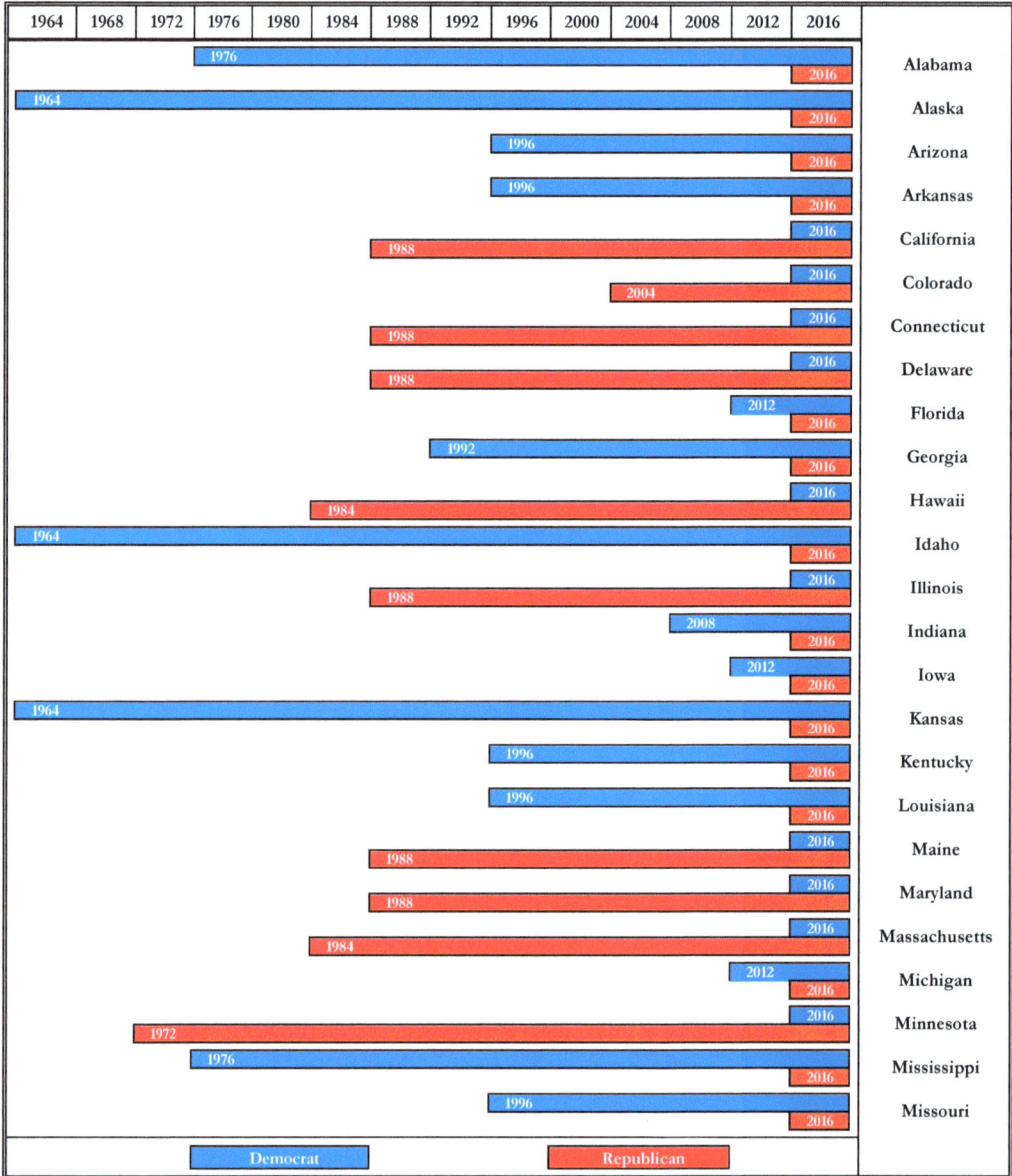

| 1964 | 1968 | 1972 | 1976 | 1980 | 1984 | 1988 | 1992 | 1996 | 2000 | 2004 | 2008 | 2012 | 2016 | |
|------|------|------|------|------|------|------|------|------|------|------|------|------|------|---|
| | | | 1976 | | | | | | | | | | | Alabama |
| | | | | | | | | | | | | | 2016 | |
| 1964 | | | | | | | | | | | | | | Alaska |
| | | | | | | | | | | | | | 2016 | |
| | | | | | | | | 1996 | | | | | | Arizona |
| | | | | | | | | | | | | | 2016 | |
| | | | | | | | | 1996 | | | | | | Arkansas |
| | | | | | | | | | | | | | 2016 | |
| | | | | | | | | | | | | | 2016 | California |
| | | | | | | 1988 | | | | | | | | |
| | | | | | | | | | | | | | 2016 | Colorado |
| | | | | | | | | | | 2004 | | | | |
| | | | | | | | | | | | | | 2016 | Connecticut |
| | | | | | | 1988 | | | | | | | | |
| | | | | | | | | | | | | | 2016 | Delaware |
| | | | | | | 1988 | | | | | | | | |
| | | | | | | | | | | | | 2012 | | Florida |
| | | | | | | | | | | | | | 2016 | |
| | | | | | | | 1992 | | | | | | | Georgia |
| | | | | | | | | | | | | | 2016 | |
| | | | | | | | | | | | | | 2016 | Hawaii |
| | | | | | 1984 | | | | | | | | | |
| 1964 | | | | | | | | | | | | | | Idaho |
| | | | | | | | | | | | | | 2016 | |
| | | | | | | | | | | | | | 2016 | Illinois |
| | | | | | | 1988 | | | | | | | | |
| | | | | | | | | | | | 2008 | | | Indiana |
| | | | | | | | | | | | | | 2016 | |
| | | | | | | | | | | | | 2012 | | Iowa |
| | | | | | | | | | | | | | 2016 | |
| 1964 | | | | | | | | | | | | | | Kansas |
| | | | | | | | | | | | | | 2016 | |
| | | | | | | | | 1996 | | | | | | Kentucky |
| | | | | | | | | | | | | | 2016 | |
| | | | | | | | | 1996 | | | | | | Louisiana |
| | | | | | | | | | | | | | 2016 | |
| | | | | | | | | | | | | | 2016 | Maine |
| | | | | | | 1988 | | | | | | | | |
| | | | | | | | | | | | | | 2016 | Maryland |
| | | | | | | 1988 | | | | | | | | |
| | | | | | | | | | | | | | 2016 | Massachusetts |
| | | | | | 1984 | | | | | | | | | |
| | | | | | | | | | | | | 2012 | | Michigan |
| | | | | | | | | | | | | | 2016 | |
| | | | | | | | | | | | | | 2016 | Minnesota |
| | | 1972 | | | | | | | | | | | | |
| | | | 1976 | | | | | | | | | | | Mississippi |
| | | | | | | | | | | | | | 2016 | |
| | | | | | | | | 1996 | | | | | | Missouri |
| | | | | | | | | | | | | | 2016 | |

| | | | | | | | |
|---|---|---|---|---|---|---|---|
| | | Democrat | | | Republican | | |

96

**Oh Say Can You See . . .**

## How Long It's Been Since Your Party Won Your State?

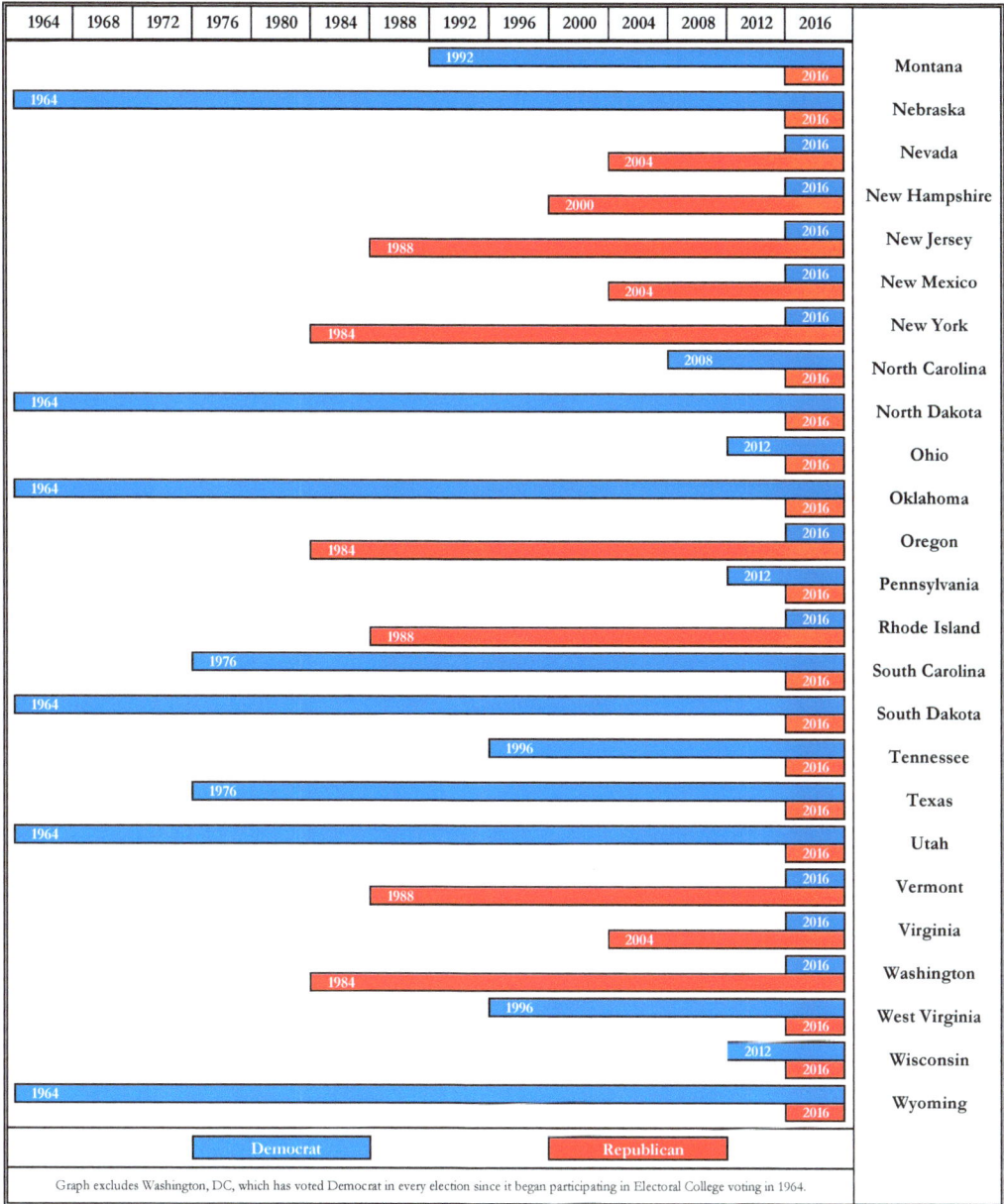

| 1964 | 1968 | 1972 | 1976 | 1980 | 1984 | 1988 | 1992 | 1996 | 2000 | 2004 | 2008 | 2012 | 2016 |
|------|------|------|------|------|------|------|------|------|------|------|------|------|------|

| State | Democrat | Republican |
|-------|----------|------------|
| Montana | 1992 | 2016 |
| Nebraska | 1964 | 2016 |
| Nevada | 2016 | 2004 |
| New Hampshire | 2016 | 2000 |
| New Jersey | 2016 | 1988 |
| New Mexico | 2016 | 2004 |
| New York | 2016 | 1984 |
| North Carolina | 2008 | 2016 |
| North Dakota | 1964 | 2016 |
| Ohio | 2012 | 2016 |
| Oklahoma | 1964 | 2016 |
| Oregon | 2016 | 1984 |
| Pennsylvania | 2012 | 2016 |
| Rhode Island | 2016 | 1988 |
| South Carolina | 1976 | 2016 |
| South Dakota | 1964 | 2016 |
| Tennessee | 1996 | 2016 |
| Texas | 1976 | 2016 |
| Utah | 1964 | 2016 |
| Vermont | 2016 | 1988 |
| Virginia | 2016 | 2004 |
| Washington | 2016 | 1984 |
| West Virginia | 1996 | 2016 |
| Wisconsin | 2012 | 2016 |
| Wyoming | 1964 | 2016 |

| Democrat | Republican |
|----------|------------|

Graph excludes Washington, DC, which has voted Democrat in every election since it began participating in Electoral College voting in 1964.

# Election Results:  Voter Participation

➢ In 1824, which was the first Presidential election in which most states chose Electoral College electors by a popular vote, about 367,000 American men voted.

➢ In 1860, which was the first Presidential election in which all states had made the switch to popular voting for electors, approximately 4.7 million American men voted.

➢ Women did not have the right to vote until the ratification of the 19th Amendment in the summer of 1920. This partly explains the jump in the popular vote starting with the 1920 Presidential election.

➢ The number of Americans who voted in Presidential elections rose – more or less steadily – from 1920 to 2016. The major deviations from the trend include:
  ❖ 1944 and 1948, reflecting the effects of World War II
  ❖ 1992, when the number of voters surged as a result of the presence of a strong third-party candidate – Ross Perot – who won 18.9% of the popular vote.

➢ The number of Americans who voted in the 2016 Presidential elections rose by more than seven million compared to 2012's level of only 128.6 million.

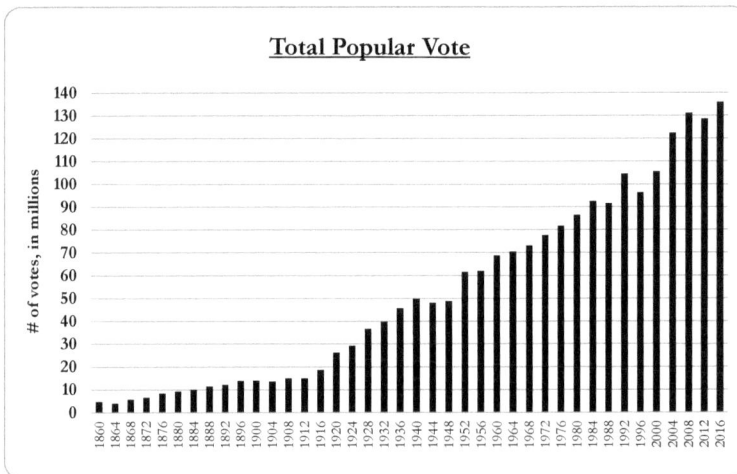

**Total Popular Vote**

➢ After declining sharply in the 1960s, 1970s, and the 1980s, voter turn-out rates seesawed in the mid 50 percent range in the 1990s, and have since risen to the +/- 60% range.

➤ The voter turn-out rate in 2012 was about two percentage points below the levels recorded in the previous two elections but returned to those levels in 2016.

➤ The 2016 rate of 60.2% was above the modern-era average of 57.9%.

### Voter Turn-Out in Presidential Elections
(as % of total voting-*eligible* population)

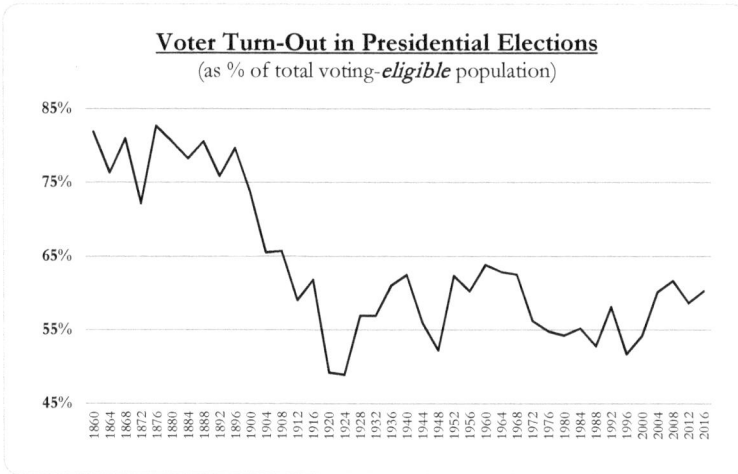

➤ Turn-out rates tend to be lower in elections that feature an incumbent candidate, although the difference has been less marked in the modern era.

### Voter Turn-Out by Category of Election

| Type of Election | Elections Held . . . | |
|---|---|---|
| | 1860 - 2016 | 1948 - 2016 |
| | Average Voter Turn-out | |
| No incumbent candidate | 67.1% | 59.6% |
| The incumbent was on the ballot | 61.4% | 56.7% |
| An incumbent ran and won | 60.9% | 57.1% |
| An incumbent ran and lost | 62.8% | 55.7% |
| The Republican candidate won | 65.5% | 57.5% |
| The Democrat candidate won | 60.9% | 58.0% |

➢ Given the extent to which Americans do (not) go to the polls and the election results themselves, most winners since 1900 have attracted the votes of only about one-quarter to one-third of the voters who were eligible to vote.

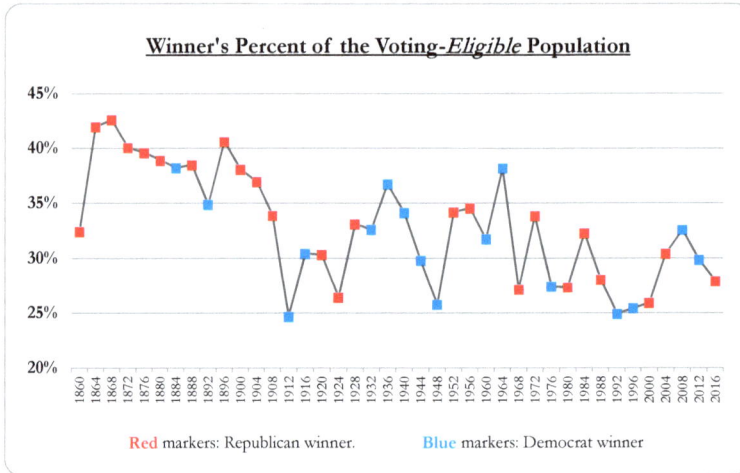

**Winner's Percent of the Voting-*Eligible* Population**

Red markers: Republican winner.          Blue markers: Democrat winner

# Five Controversial Elections

## The Election of 1800

The Federalists nominated incumbent President John Adams as their candidate for President and Charles Pinckney as their candidate for Vice President. The Democratic-Republicans nominated incumbent Vice President Thomas Jefferson as their candidate for President and Aaron Burr as their candidate for Vice President.

Under the voting system in effect at the time, each elector cast two votes. The candidate with the most votes became President and the Vice Presidency went to the second-place finisher. Jefferson and Burr received the same number of electoral votes, and no candidate won an electoral-vote majority. In accordance with the Constitution, the election was thrown into the House of Representatives.

With intense political maneuvering in the background, the House deliberated from 11th February to 17th February. On the 36th ballot Jefferson was selected; 10 delegations voted for Jefferson, four for Burr, and two state delegations were deadlocked and therefore ineligible to vote.

In the aftermath of the election of 1800, there was widespread recognition of the perils of the double-balloting system and the need for a Constitutional amendment to change it. The eventual passage of the 12th Amendment, which was approved by Congress in December 1803 and ratified in time for the election of 1804, eliminated double balloting for President and Vice President and established procedures for separate voting for each office.

## The Election of 1824

The election of 1824 was the second and only other election decided by the House of Representatives. The four major candidates – John Quincy Adams, Henry Clay, William Crawford, and Andrew Jackson – were all members of the Democratic-Republican party, which was, effectively, the only national political party at that time. Jackson won a plurality of the electoral and popular vote. He had 99 electoral votes, Adams received 84, Crawford 41, and Clay 37. Jackson won the national popular vote by more than 10 percentage points. However, none of the candidates garnered a majority of the electoral votes and the election was therefore thrown into the House of Representatives, which, in accordance with the 12th Amendment, could only choose from amongst the three leading candidates. Clay was relegated to the role of possible "king maker," and the other candidates vied for his support. Adams won on the first ballot in the House of Representatives. Thirteen state delegations voted for Adams, seven for Jackson, and four for Crawford.

There was some suspicion that Adams and Clay had made a back-room deal. Before the House voted, a scandal erupted when a Philadelphia newspaper published an anonymous letter claiming that Clay would support Adams in return for an appointment as Secretary of State. Clay vigorously denied this but was, in fact, later appointed Secretary of State in the Adams administration.

## The Election of 1876

The Democrats nominated Samuel Tilden and the Republicans nominated Rutherford Hayes. Tilden won an absolute majority of the popular vote by a margin of three percentage points, but he lost in the Electoral College by a single vote (out of 369).

In three southern states – South Carolina, Florida, and Louisiana – the results were hotly contested. All three were strongly divided between Whites and newly enfranchised Blacks, between supporters of Reconstruction and those who wished to bring it to an end. Each of the three states put forth two slates of electors.

At the time, there were no state laws dealing with contested or controversial slates of electors, and the Constitution is silent on the subject. So Congress passed a special law to decide the disputed vote. That law created a 15-member commission made up of five Senators, five members of the House, and five Supreme Court Justices. Initially the swing, or fifteenth, member of the Commission was a Justice who was widely considered to be independent. However, before the Commission could do its work, that Justice was appointed to the Senate, requiring him to resign from the Commission. A Republican Justice replaced him. When the Commission met they voted along party lines in each case, accepting the Republican slates from each of the three southern states in question.

Under the law that governed the workings of the Commission, its decisions could be overturned by a vote of both houses of Congress. While the House rejected the Commission's findings, the Senate accepted them. Thus, the Commission's decision stood, and Rutherford Hayes became President.

The turmoil surrounding this controversial election subsided when the Compromise of 1877 was reached: Southern Democrats accepted the decision of the Electoral Commission, and Hayes and the Republicans agreed to end Reconstruction and withdraw the carpetbag governments from southern states.

The legislative denouement finally came a decade later, with the passage of the Electoral Count Act of 1887, which endowed the states with final authority to resolve controversies about the election of electors.

## The Election of 2000

In 2000 incumbent Vice President Al Gore (D) ran against Texas Governor George W. Bush (R) in a closely contested race. As the results rolled in, it became clear that voters in Florida would decide the election. The initial call gave Bush that state by a few hundred votes (out of a total of almost six million). Given the very close vote and reports of problems with ballots, Gore's supporters called for a recount and went to court to force the State of Florida to conduct the recount. Bush's side sued to prevent the recount. This issue was further complicated by the fact that Florida's election laws set forth a deadline for announcing the final election results, so any recount had to be completed quickly if at all.

The Florida Supreme Court decided in favor of Gore and directed election officials to conduct a recount. Bush appealed that decision to the U.S. Supreme Court, which reversed the decision of the Florida Supreme Court. In a 5 - 4 decision the U.S. Supreme Court stated that the Supreme Court of Florida had violated the equal-protection guarantees of the Fourteenth Amendment because the Florida court required the recount only in certain election districts and because the recount had already been tainted. The U.S. Supreme Court also found that it would be impossible to conduct a Constitutionally acceptable recount by the deadline set forth in Florida law. Based on this finding, it ordered the recounts abandoned. Thus, the Bush victory in Florida stood and, in turn, Bush won the Presidency.

The U.S. Supreme Court's decision was and is still considered controversial. Even the Justices themselves did not agree on a number of points. The five Justices in the majority wrote two separate opinions and the four Justices in the minority each wrote an opinion, and each opinion cited different grounds for its decision. Some observers argued that the U.S. Supreme Court should not have taken the case but rather simply let the Florida Supreme Court's decision stand. Others pointed to the party-line decision of the Justices – Republicans sided with Bush and Democrats sided with Gore – to suggest that the case was decided by politics rather than by law.

## The Election of 2016

The 2016 election was not controversial in the senses that the other four elections were. Nonetheless, 2016 bears comment because the candidates, campaigns, and outcome were all noteworthy. Both major parties ran highly polarizing candidates: Donald Trump for the Republicans and Hillary Clinton for the Democrats. Donald Trump, the ultimate winner, became the first person in U.S. history to win the White House who had never been elected to political office, been a Cabinet Secretary, or been a war-time military hero. Hillary Clinton was the first female Presidential candidate for a major party. And many observers considered the election campaigns to be amongst the most acrimonious in U.S. history.

Much attention has been drawn to the election results themselves. Donald Trump won the Electoral College. While the tally of the national popular vote is irrelevant to determining the outcome of a Presidential election, some observers nonetheless cited that vote in advancing a partisan agenda.

Here are the facts:

➢ Donald Trump secured 56.5% of the Electoral College vote. Only eight winners from 1804 to 2016 tallied a lower percentage.

➢ Donald Trump won 30 states, which was more than his predecessor won in 2008 and 2012.

➢ Donald Trump's 30-state win was in line with the winner's performance in all elections since 1988.

- Neither candidate garnered a majority of the national popular vote, which is not rare: more than one-third of the election winners in the popular-vote era have not won a majority.

- Donald Trump did not win a plurality of the national popular vote, which had happened only twice previously (excluding the 1876 election that was decided by a special electoral commission); both of those winners were also Republicans.

- Donald Trump's winning margins ranged from a low of 0.2% (Michigan) to a high of 46.3% (Wyoming).

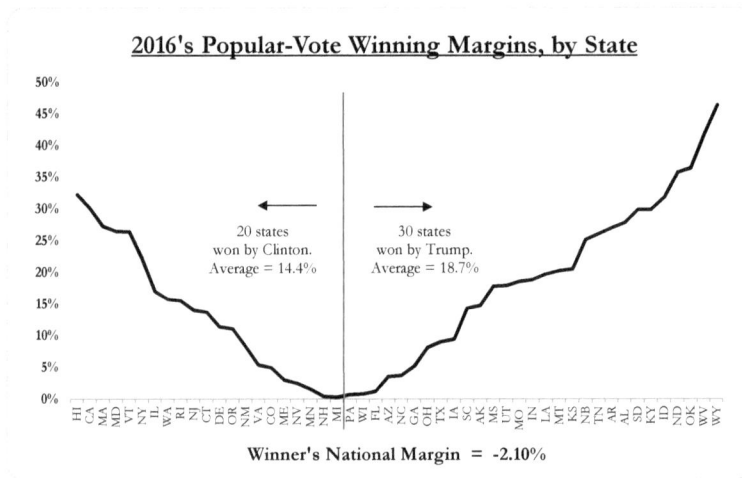

**2016's Popular-Vote Winning Margins, by State**

20 states won by Clinton. Average = 14.4%

30 states won by Trump. Average = 18.7%

**Winner's National Margin = -2.10%**

- Hillary Clinton's winning margins ranged from a low of 0.4% (New Hampshire) to a high of 32.2% (Hawaii).

# APPENDICES

# The Presidents of the United States of America

| | President | Party | Took Office | Age When First Sworn In | Left Office | Terms +days |
|---|---|---|---|---|---|---|
| 1 | George Washington | none | 30-Apr-1789 | 57.2 | 4-Mar-1797 | 2 |
| 2 | John Adams (1) | F | 4-Mar-1797 | 61.3 | 4-Mar-1801 | 1 |
| 3 | Thomas Jefferson (1) | D-R | 4-Mar-1801 | 57.9 | 4-Mar-1809 | 2 |
| 4 | James Madison | D-R | 4-Mar-1809 | 58.0 | 4-Mar-1817 | 2 |
| 5 | James Monroe | D-R | 4-Mar-1817 | 58.8 | 4-Mar-1825 | 2 |
| 6 | John Quincy Adams | D-R/N | 4-Mar-1825 | 57.6 | 4-Mar-1829 | 1 |
| 7 | Andrew Jackson | D | 4-Mar-1829 | 62.0 | 4-Mar-1837 | 2 |
| 8 | Martin Van Buren (1) | D | 4-Mar-1837 | 54.2 | 4-Mar-1841 | 1 |
| 9 | William Harrison | W | 4-Mar-1841 | 68.1 | 4-Apr-1841 | 0 +31 |
| 10 | John Tyler (2, 3) | W | 6-Apr-1841 | 51.0 | 4-Mar-1845 | 0 +1,428 |
| 11 | James Polk | D | 4-Mar-1845 | 49.3 | 4-Mar-1849 | 1 |
| 12 | Zachary Taylor | W | 4-Mar-1849 | 64.3 | 9-Jul-1850 | 0 +492 |
| 13 | Millard Fillmore (2, 3) | W | 10-Jul-1850 | 50.5 | 4-Mar-1853 | 0 +968 |
| 14 | Franklin Pierce | D | 4-Mar-1853 | 48.3 | 4-Mar-1857 | 1 |
| 15 | James Buchanan | D | 4-Mar-1857 | 65.9 | 4-Mar-1861 | 1 |
| 16 | Abraham Lincoln | R/NU | 4-Mar-1861 | 52.1 | 15-Apr-1865 | 1 +42 |
| 17 | Andrew Johnson (2, 3) | D/NU | 15-Apr-1865 | 56.3 | 4-Mar-1869 | 0 +1,419 |
| 18 | Ulysses Grant | R | 4-Mar-1869 | 46.9 | 4-Mar-1877 | 2 |
| 19 | Rutherford Hayes | R | 4-Mar-1877 | 54.4 | 4-Mar-1881 | 1 |
| 20 | James Garfield | R | 4-Mar-1881 | 49.3 | 19-Sep-1881 | 0 +199 |
| 21 | Chester Arthur (2, 3) | R | 29-Sep-1881 | 52.0 | 4-Mar-1885 | 0 +1,261 |
| 22 | Grover Cleveland | D | 4-Mar-1885 | 48.0 | 4-Mar-1889 | 2 |
| 23 | Benjamin Harrison | R | 4-Mar-1889 | 55.5 | 4-Mar-1893 | 1 |
| 24 | Grover Cleveland | D | 4-Mar-1893 | 56.0 | 4-Mar-1897 | 2 |
| 25 | William McKinley | R | 4-Mar-1897 | 54.1 | 14-Sep-1901 | 1 +194 |
| 26 | Theodore Roosevelt (2) | R | 14-Sep-1901 | 42.9 | 4-Mar-1909 | 1 +1,267 |
| 27 | William Taft | R | 4-Mar-1909 | 51.5 | 4-Mar-1913 | 1 |
| 28 | Woodrow Wilson | D | 4-Mar-1913 | 56.2 | 4-Mar-1921 | 2 |
| 29 | Warren Harding | R | 4-Mar-1921 | 55.3 | 2-Aug-1923 | 0 +882 |
| 30 | Calvin Coolidge (2) | R | 3-Aug-1923 | 51.1 | 4-Mar-1929 | 1 +579 |
| 31 | Herbert Hoover | R | 4-Mar-1929 | 54.6 | 4-Mar-1933 | 1 |
| 32 | Franklin Roosevelt | D | 4-Mar-1933 | 51.1 | 12-Apr-1945 | 3 +82 |
| 33 | Harry Truman (2) | D | 12-Apr-1945 | 60.9 | 20-Jan-1953 | 1 +1,379 |
| 34 | Dwight Eisenhower | R | 20-Jan-1953 | 62.3 | 20-Jan-1961 | 2 |
| 35 | John Kennedy | D | 20-Jan-1961 | 43.6 | 22-Nov-1963 | 0 +1,036 |
| 36 | Lyndon Johnson (2) | D | 22-Nov-1963 | 55.2 | 20-Jan-1969 | 1 +425 |
| 37 | Richard Nixon (1) | R | 20-Jan-1969 | 56.0 | 9-Aug-1974 | 1 +566 |
| 38 | Gerald Ford (2, 3) | R | 9-Aug-1974 | 61.1 | 20-Jan-1977 | 0 +895 |
| 39 | James Carter | D | 20-Jan-1977 | 52.3 | 20-Jan-1981 | 1 |
| 40 | Ronald Reagan | R | 20-Jan-1981 | 70.0 | 20-Jan-1989 | 2 |
| 41 | George H.W. Bush (1) | R | 20-Jan-1989 | 64.6 | 20-Jan-1993 | 1 |
| 42 | William Clinton | D | 20-Jan-1993 | 46.4 | 20-Jan-2001 | 2 |
| 43 | George W. Bush | R | 20-Jan-2001 | 54.5 | 20-Jan-2009 | 2 |
| 44 | Barack Obama | D | 20-Jan-2009 | 47.5 | 20-Jan-2017 | 2 |
| 45 | Donald Trump | R | 20-Jan-2017 | 70.6 | *incumbent* | |

1. Elected VP; then elected President.    2. Elected VP; then ascended to Presidency.    3. Never elected President

# Personal Data About the Presidents

| | Full Name | Birth Date | Death Date | Life Span |
|---|---|---|---|---|
| 1 | George Washington | 22-Feb-1732 | 14-Dec-1799 | 68 |
| 2 | John Adams | 30-Oct-1735 | 4-Jul-1826 | 90 |
| 3 | Thomas Jefferson | 13-Apr-1743 | 4-Jul-1826 | 83 |
| 4 | James Madison, Jr. | 16-Mar-1751 | 28-Jun-1836 | 85 |
| 5 | James Monroe | 28-Apr-1758 | 4-Apr-1831 | 74 |
| 6 | John Quincy Adams | 11-Jul-1767 | 23-Feb-1848 | 81 |
| 7 | Andrew Jackson | 15-Mar-1767 | 8-Jun-1845 | 78 |
| 8 | Martin Van Buren | 5-Dec-1782 | 24-Jul-1862 | 80 |
| 9 | William Henry Harrison | 9-Feb-1773 | 4-Apr-1841 | 68 |
| 10 | John Tyler | 29-Mar-1790 | 18-Jan-1862 | 72 |
| 11 | James Knox Polk | 2-Nov-1795 | 15-Jun-1849 | 54 |
| 12 | Zachary Taylor | 24-Nov-1784 | 9-Jul-1850 | 66 |
| 13 | Millard Fillmore | 7-Jan-1800 | 8-Mar-1874 | 74 |
| 14 | Franklin Pierce | 23-Nov-1804 | 8-Oct-1869 | 65 |
| 15 | James Buchanan, Jr. | 23-Apr-1791 | 1-Jun-1868 | 77 |
| 16 | Abraham Lincoln | 12-Feb-1809 | 15-Apr-1865 | 56 |
| 17 | Andrew Johnson | 29-Dec-1808 | 31-Jul-1875 | 67 |
| 18 | Ulysses S. Grant * | 27-Apr-1822 | 23-Jul-1885 | 63 |
| 19 | Rutherford Birchard Hayes | 4-Oct-1822 | 17-Jan-1893 | 70 |
| 20 | James Abram Garfield | 19-Nov-1831 | 19-Sep-1881 | 50 |
| 21 | Chester Alan Arthur | 5-Oct-1829 | 18-Nov-1886 | 57 |
| 22 | Stephen Grover Cleveland | 18-Mar-1837 | 24-Jun-1908 | 71 |
| 23 | Benjamin Harrison | 20-Aug-1833 | 13-Mar-1901 | 68 |
| 24 | Stephen Grover Cleveland | 18-Mar-1837 | 24-Jun-1908 | 71 |
| 25 | William McKinley, Jr. | 29-Jan-1843 | 14-Sep-1901 | 59 |
| 26 | Theodore Roosevelt | 27-Oct-1858 | 6-Jan-1919 | 60 |
| 27 | William Howard Taft | 15-Sep-1857 | 8-Mar-1930 | 72 |
| 28 | Thomas Woodrow Wilson | 28-Dec-1856 | 3-Feb-1924 | 67 |
| 29 | Warren Gamaliel Harding | 2-Nov-1865 | 2-Aug-1923 | 58 |
| 30 | John Calvin Coolidge, Jr. | 4-Jul-1872 | 5-Jan-1933 | 61 |
| 31 | Herbert Clark Hoover | 10-Aug-1874 | 20-Oct-1964 | 90 |
| 32 | Franklin Delano Roosevelt | 30-Jan-1882 | 12-Apr-1945 | 63 |
| 33 | Harry S. Truman | 8-May-1884 | 26-Dec-1972 | 89 |
| 34 | Dwight David Eisenhower | 14-Oct-1890 | 28-Mar-1969 | 78 |
| 35 | John Fitzgerald Kennedy | 29-May-1917 | 22-Nov-1963 | 46 |
| 36 | Lyndon Baines Johnson | 27-Aug-1908 | 22-Jan-1973 | 64 |
| 37 | Richard Milhous Nixon | 9-Jan-1913 | 22-Apr-1994 | 81 |
| 38 | Gerald Rudolph Ford, Jr.** | 14-Jul-1913 | 26-Dec-2006 | 93 |
| 39 | James Earl Carter, Jr. | 1-Oct-1924 | *living* | --- |
| 40 | Ronald Wilson Reagan | 6-Feb-1911 | 5-Jun-2004 | 93 |
| 41 | George Herbert Walker Bush | 12-Jun-1924 | *living* | --- |
| 42 | William Jefferson Clinton *** | 19-Aug-1946 | *living* | --- |
| 43 | George Walker Bush | 6-Jul-1946 | *living* | --- |
| 44 | Barack Hussein Obama | 4-Aug-1961 | *living* | --- |
| 45 | Donald John Trump | 14-Jun-1946 | *living* | --- |

Birth names:  * Hiram Ulysses Grant.  ** Leslie Lynch King, Jr.  *** William Jefferson Blythe III

# Personal Data About the Presidents, Part II

| | President | Home State | Birth Place | Death Place |
|---|---|---|---|---|
| 1 | George Washington | Virginia | Westmoreland Cty, VA | Mount Vernon, VA |
| 2 | John Adams | Massachusetts | Quincy, MA | Quincy, MA |
| 3 | Thomas Jefferson | Virginia | Shadwell, VA | Charlottesville, VA |
| 4 | James Madison | Virginia | Port Conway, VA | Montpelier, VA |
| 5 | James Monroe | Virginia | Westmoreland County, VA | New York, NY |
| 6 | John Quincy Adams | Massachusetts | Quincy, MA | Washington, DC |
| 7 | Andrew Jackson | Tennessee | Waxhaws area, NC/SC | Nashville, TN |
| 8 | Martin Van Buren | New York | Kinderhook, NY | Kinderhook, NY |
| 9 | William Harrison | Ohio | Charles City County, VA | Washington, DC |
| 10 | John Tyler | Virginia | Charles City County, VA | Richmond, VA |
| 11 | James Polk | Tennessee | Pineville, NC | Nashville, TN |
| 12 | Zachary Taylor | Louisiana | Barboursville, VA | Washington, DC |
| 13 | Millard Fillmore | New York | Summerhill, NY | Buffalo, NY |
| 14 | Franklin Pierce | New Hampshire | Hillsborough, NH | Concord, NH |
| 15 | James Buchanan | Pennsylvania | Mercersburg, PA | Lancaster, PA |
| 16 | Abraham Lincoln | Illinois | Hardin County, KY | Washington, DC |
| 17 | Andrew Johnson | Tennessee | Raleigh, NC | Elizabethton, TN |
| 18 | Ulysses Grant | Illinois | Point Pleasant, OH | Mount McGregor, NY |
| 19 | Rutherford Hayes | Ohio | Delaware, OH | Fremont, OH |
| 20 | James Garfield | Ohio | Moreland Hills, OH | Long Branch, NJ |
| 21 | Chester Arthur | New York | Fairfield, VT | New York, NY |
| 22 | Grover Cleveland | New York | Caldwell, NJ | Princeton, NJ |
| 23 | Benjamin Harrison | Indiana | North Bend, OH | Indianapolis, IN |
| 24 | Grover Cleveland | New York | Caldwell, NJ | Princeton, NJ |
| 25 | William McKinley | Ohio | Niles, OH | Buffalo, NY |
| 26 | Theodore Roosevelt | New York | New York, NY | Oyster Bay, NY |
| 27 | William Taft | Ohio | Cincinnati, OH | Washington, DC |
| 28 | Woodrow Wilson | New Jersey | Staunton, VA | Washington, DC |
| 29 | Warren Harding | Ohio | Blooming Grove, OH | San Francisco, CA |
| 30 | Calvin Coolidge | Massachusetts | Plymouth, VT | Northampton, MA |
| 31 | Herbert Hoover | California | West Branch, IA | New York, NY |
| 32 | Franklin Roosevelt | New York | Hyde Park, NY | Warm Springs, GA |
| 33 | Harry Truman | Missouri | Lamar, MO | Kansas City, MO |
| 34 | Dwight Eisenhower | New York | Denison, TX | Washington, DC |
| 35 | John Kennedy | Massachusetts | Brookline, MA | Dallas, TX |
| 36 | Lyndon Johnson | Texas | Stonewall, TX | Stonewall, TX |
| 37 | Richard Nixon | California | Yorba Linda, CA | New York, NY |
| 38 | Gerald Ford | Michigan | Omaha, NE | Rancho Mirage, CA |
| 39 | James Carter | Georgia | Plains, GA | *living* |
| 40 | Ronald Reagan | California | Tampico, IL | Bel Air, CA |
| 41 | George H.W. Bush | Texas | Milton, MA | *living* |
| 42 | William Clinton | Arkansas | Hope, AR | *living* |
| 43 | George W. Bush | Texas | New Haven, CT | *living* |
| 44 | Barack Obama | Illinois | Honolulu, HI | *living* |
| 45 | Donald Trump | New York | New York, NY | *living* |

# The Presidents' Wives

| | President | Wife | Birth Date | Wedding Date | Death Date |
|---|---|---|---|---|---|
| 1 | Washington | Martha Dandridge [Custis] (1) | 2-Jun-1731 | 6-Jan-1759 | 22-May-1802 |
| 2 | Adams | Abigail Smith | 11-Nov-1744 | 25-Oct-1764 | 28-Oct-1818 |
| 3 | Jefferson | Martha Wayles [Skelton] (1) | 19-Oct-1748 | 1-Jan-1772 | 6-Sep-1782 |
| 4 | Madison | Dolley Payne [Todd] (1) | 20-May-1768 | 14-Sep-1794 | 12-Jul-1849 |
| 5 | Monroe | Elizabeth Kortright | 30-Jun-1768 | 16-Feb-1786 | 23-Sep-1830 |
| 6 | J.Q. Adams | Louisa Catherine Johnson | 12-Feb-1775 | 26-Jul-1797 | 15-May-1852 |
| 7 | Jackson | Rachel Donelson [Robards] (2) | 15-Jun-1767 | 7-Jan-1794 | 22-Dec-1828 |
| 8 | Van Buren | Hannah Hoes | 8-Mar-1783 | 21-Feb-1807 | 5-Feb-1819 |
| 9 | W.H. Harrison | Anna Tuthill Symmes | 25-Jul-1775 | 22-Nov-1795 | 25-Feb-1864 |
| 10 | Tyler | Letitia Christian | 12-Nov-1790 | 29-Mar-1813 | 10-Sep-1842 |
| | | Julia Gardiner | 29-Jul-1820 | 26-Jun-1844 | 10-Jul-1889 |
| 11 | Polk | Sarah Childress | 4-Sep-1803 | 1-Jan-1824 | 14-Aug-1891 |
| 12 | Taylor | Margaret Mackall Smith | 21-Sep-1788 | 21-Jun-1810 | 14-Aug-1852 |
| 13 | Fillmore | Abigail Powers | 13-Mar-1798 | 5-Feb-1826 | 30-Mar-1853 |
| | | Caroline Carmichael [McIntosh] (1) | 21-Oct-1813 | 10-Feb-1858 | 11-Aug-1881 |
| 14 | Pierce | Jane Means Appleton | 12-Mar-1806 | 19-Nov-1834 | 2-Dec-1863 |
| 15 | Buchanan | *never married* | | | |
| 16 | Lincoln | Mary Todd | 13-Dec-1818 | 4-Nov-1842 | 16-Jul-1882 |
| 17 | A. Johnson | Eliza McCardle | 4-Oct-1810 | 17-May-1827 | 15-Jan-1876 |
| 18 | Grant | Julia Boggs Dent | 26-Jan-1826 | 22-Aug-1848 | 14-Dec-1902 |
| 19 | Hayes | Lucy Ware Webb | 28-Aug-1831 | 30-Dec-1852 | 25-Jun-1889 |
| 20 | Garfield | Lucretia Rudolph | 19-Apr-1832 | 11-Nov-1858 | 14-Mar-1918 |
| 21 | Arthur | Ellen Lewis Herndon | 30-Aug-1837 | 25-Oct-1859 | 12-Jan-1880 |
| 22 | Cleveland | Frances Clara Folsom | 21-Jul-1864 | 2-Jun-1886 | 29-Oct-1947 |
| 23 | B. Harrison | Caroline Lavinia Scott | 1-Oct-1832 | 20-Oct-1853 | 25-Oct-1892 |
| | | Mary Scott Lord [Dimmick] (1) | 30-Apr-1858 | 6-Apr-1896 | 5-Jan-1948 |
| 24 | Cleveland | Frances Clara Folsom | 21-Jul-1864 | 2-Jun-1886 | 29-Oct-1947 |
| 25 | McKinley | Ida Saxton | 8-Jun-1847 | 25-Jan-1871 | 26-May-1907 |
| 26 | Roosevelt | Edith Kermit Carow | 6-Aug1861 | 2-Dec-1886 | 30-Sep-1948 |
| 27 | Taft | Helen Louise Herron | 2-Jun-1861 | 19-Jun-1886 | 22-May-1943 |
| 28 | Wilson | Ellen Louise Axson | 15-May-1860 | 24-Jun-1885 | 6-Aug-1914 |
| | | Edith Bolling [Galt] (1) | 15-Oct-1872 | 18-Dec-1915 | 28-Dec-1961 |
| 29 | Harding | Florence Mabel Kling [deWolfe] (2) | 15-Aug-1860 | 8-Jul-1891 | 21-Nov-1924 |
| 30 | Coolidge | Grace Anna Goodhue | 3-Jan-1879 | 4-Oct-1905 | 8-Jul-1957 |
| 31 | Hoover | Lou Henry | 29-Mar-1874 | 10-Feb-1899 | 7-Jan-1944 |
| 32 | F.Roosevelt | Anna Eleanor Roosevelt | 11-Oct-1884 | 17-Mar-1905 | 7-Nov-1962 |
| 33 | Truman | Elizabeth "Bess" Virginia Wallace (3) | 13-Feb-1885 | 28-Jun-1919 | 18-Oct-1982 |
| 34 | Eisenhower | Mamie Geneva Doud | 14-Nov-1896 | 1-Jul-1916 | 1-Nov-1979 |
| 35 | Kennedy | Jacqueline Lee Bouvier | 28-Jul-1929 | 12-Sep-1953 | 19-May-1994 |
| 36 | L.B. Johnson | "Lady Bird" Claudia Alta Taylor | 22-Dec-1912 | 17-Nov-1934 | 11-Jul-2007 |
| 37 | Nixon | Thelma Catherine "Pat" Ryan | 16-Mar-1912 | 21-Jun-1940 | 22-Jun-1993 |
| 38 | Ford | Elizabeth Ann Bloomer [Warren] (2) | 8-Apr-1918 | 15-Oct-1948 | 8-Jul-2011 |
| 39 | Carter | Eleanor Rosalynn Smith | 18-Aug-1927 | 7-Jul-1946 | *living* |
| 40 | Reagan | Sarah Jane Mansfield, "Jane Wyman" | 5-Jan-1917 | 26-Jan-1940 | 10-Sep-2007 |
| | | Anne Frances "Nancy" Davis (3) | 6-Jul-1921 | 6-Mar-1952 | 6-Mar-2016 |
| 41 | G.H.W. Bush | Barbara Pierce | 8-Jun-1925 | 6-Jan-1945 | *living* |
| 42 | Clinton | Hillary Diane Rodham | 26-Oct-1947 | 11-Oct-1975 | *living* |
| 43 | GW Bush | Laura Lane Welch | 4-Nov-1946 | 5-Nov-1977 | *living* |
| 44 | Obama | Michelle LaVaughn Robinson | 17-Jan-1964 | 3-Oct-1992 | *living* |
| 45 | Trump | Melania (nee Melanija) Knavs | 26-Apr-1970 | 22-Jan-2005 | *living* |

1. The President was her second husband, the first having died.
2. The President was her second husband; she was divorced.
3. Born Robbins. Adopted by Davis, her stepfather.
**N.B.**: previous married names are shown in square brackets

# The Presidents' Wives' Education

| | President | Wife | Highest Formal Education | College |
|---|---|---|---|---|
| 1 | Washington | Martha Dandridge [Custis] | none | |
| 2 | J.Adams | Abigail Smith | none | |
| 3 | Jefferson | Martha Wayles [Skelton] | none | |
| 4 | Madison | Dolley Payne [Todd] | none | |
| 5 | Monroe | Elizabeth Kortright | none | |
| 6 | J.Q.Adams | Louisa Catherine Johnson | none | |
| 7 | Jackson | Rachel Donelson [Robards] | none | |
| 8 | Van Buren | Hannah Hoes | none | |
| 9 | W.Harrison | Anna Tuthill Symmes | secondary | |
| 10 | Tyler | Letitia Christian | none | |
| | | Julia Gardiner | secondary | |
| 11 | Polk | Sarah Childress | secondary | |
| 12 | Taylor | Margaret Mackall Smith | none | |
| 13 | Fillmore | Abigail Powers | secondary | |
| | | Caroline Carmichael [McIntosh] | none | |
| 14 | Pierce | Jane Means Appleton | none | |
| 15 | Buchanan | *never married* | | |
| 16 | Lincoln | Mary Todd | secondary | |
| 17 | A.Johnson | Eliza McCardle | none | |
| 18 | Grant | Julia Boggs Dent | secondary | |
| 19 | Hayes | Lucy Ware Webb | post secondary | Cincinnati Wesleyan |
| 20 | Garfield | Lucretia Rudolph | post secondary | |
| 21 | Arthur | Ellen Lewis Herndon | secondary | |
| 22 | Cleveland | Frances Clara Folsom | secondary | |
| 23 | B.Harrison | Caroline Lavinia Scott | post secondary | |
| | | Mary Scott Lord [Dimmick] | none | |
| 25 | McKinley | Ida Saxton | post secondary | |
| 26 | Roosevelt | Edith Kermit Carow | none | |
| 27 | Taft | Helen Louise Herron | some college | University of Cincinnati |
| 28 | Wilson | Ellen Louise Axson | secondary | |
| | | Edith Bolling [Galt] | secondary | |
| 29 | Harding | Florence Mabel Kling [deWolfe] | secondary | |
| 30 | Coolidge | Grace Anna Goodhue | college | University of Vermont |
| 31 | Hoover | Lou Henry | college | Stanford University |
| 32 | F.Roosevelt | Anna Eleanor Roosevelt | secondary | |
| 33 | Truman | Elizabeth Virginia Wallace | secondary | |
| 34 | Eisenhower | Mamie Geneva Doud | secondary | |
| 35 | Kennedy | Jacqueline Lee Bouvier | college | George Washington Univ. |
| 36 | L.Johnson | Claudia Alta Taylor | college | Univ. of Texas at Austin |
| 37 | Nixon | Thelma Catherine Ryan | Master's | Univ. of Southern Calif. |
| 38 | Ford | Elizabeth Ann Bloomer [Warren] | secondary | |
| 39 | Carter | Eleanor Rosalynn Smith | junior college | Georgia Southwestern |
| 40 | Reagan | Anne Frances Robbins Davis | college | Smith College |
| 41 | GHW Bush | Barbara Pierce | some college | Smith College |
| 42 | Clinton | Hillary Diane Rodham | law school | Wellesley College |
| 43 | G.W.Bush | Laura Lane Welch | Master's | Southern Methodist Univ. |
| 44 | Obama | Michelle LaVaughn Robinson | law school | Princeton University |
| 45 | Trump | Melania Knavs | some college | University of Ljubljana |

# The First Ladies

| | President | Wife | Wife's Term as First Lady | |
|---|---|---|---|---|
| | | | Began | Ended |
| 1 | Washington | Martha | 30-Apr-1789 | 4-Mar-1797 |
| 2 | Adams | Abigail | 4-Mar-1797 | 4-Mar-1801 |
| 3 | Jefferson | Martha | *deceased prior to Presidency* | (1) |
| 4 | Madison | Dolley | 4-Mar-1809 | 4-Mar-1817 |
| 5 | Monroe | Elizabeth | 4-Mar-1817 | 4-Mar-1825 |
| 6 | J.Q. Adams | Louisa | 4-Mar-1825 | 4-Mar-1829 |
| 7 | Jackson | Rachel | *deceased prior to Presidency* | (2) |
| 8 | Van Buren | Hannah | *deceased prior to Presidency* | (3) |
| 9 | W.H. Harrison | Anna | 4-Mar-1841 | 4-Apr-1841 (4) |
| 10 | Tyler | Letitia | 4-Apr-1841 | 10-Sep-1842 (5) |
| | | Julia | 26-Jun-1844 | 4-Mar-1845 |
| 11 | Polk | Sarah | 4-Mar-1845 | 4-Mar-1849 |
| 12 | Taylor | Margaret | 4-Mar-1849 | 9-Jul-1850 |
| 13 | Fillmore | Abigail | 9-Jul-1850 | 4-Mar-1853 |
| 14 | Pierce | Jane | 4-Mar-1853 | 4-Mar-1857 |
| 15 | Buchanan | *never married* | | (6) |
| 16 | Lincoln | Mary | 4-Mar-1861 | 15-Apr-1865 |
| 17 | A. Johnson | Eliza | 15-Apr-1865 | 4-Mar-1869 (7) |
| 18 | Grant | Julia | 4-Mar-1869 | 4-Mar-1877 |
| 19 | Hayes | Lucy | 4-Mar-1877 | 4-Mar-1881 |
| 20 | Garfield | Lucretia | 4-Mar-1881 | 19-Sep-1881 |
| 21 | Arthur | Ellen | *deceased prior to Presidency* | (8) |
| 22 | Cleveland | Frances | 2-Jun-1886 | 4-Mar-1889 (9) |
| 23 | B. Harrison | Caroline | 4-Mar-1889 | 25-Oct-1892 (10) |
| 24 | Cleveland | Frances | 4-Mar-1893 | 4-Mar-1897 |
| 25 | McKinley | Ida | 4-Mar-1897 | 14-Sep-1901 |
| 26 | Roosevelt | Edith | 14-Sep-1901 | 4-Mar-1909 |
| 27 | Taft | Helen | 4-Mar-1909 | 4-Mar-1913 |
| 28 | Wilson | Ellen | 4-Mar-1913 | 6-Aug-1914 (11) |
| | | Edith | 18-Dec-1915 | 4-Mar-1921 |
| 29 | Harding | Florence | 4-Mar-1921 | 2-Aug-1923 |
| 30 | Coolidge | Grace | 2-Aug-1923 | 4-Mar-1929 |
| 31 | Hoover | Lou | 4-Mar-1929 | 4-Mar-1933 |
| 32 | F.D. Roosevelt | Eleanor | 4-Mar-1933 | 12-Apr-1945 |
| 33 | Truman | Bess | 12-Apr-1945 | 20-Jan-1953 |
| 34 | Eisenhower | Mamie | 20-Jan-1953 | 20-Jan-1961 |
| 35 | Kennedy | Jacqueline | 20-Jan-1961 | 22-Nov-1963 |
| 36 | L. Johnson | Lady Bird | 22-Nov-1963 | 20-Jan-1969 |
| 37 | Nixon | Pat | 20-Jan-1969 | 9-Aug-1974 |
| 38 | Ford | Betty | 9-Aug-1974 | 20-Jan-1977 |
| 39 | Carter | Rosalynn | 20-Jan-1977 | 20-Jan-1981 |
| 40 | Reagan | Nancy | 20-Jan-1981 | 20-Jan-1989 |
| 41 | G.H.W. Bush | Barbara | 20-Jan-1989 | 20-Jan-1993 |
| 42 | Clinton | Hillary | 20-Jan-1993 | 20-Jan-2001 |
| 43 | G.W. Bush | Laura | 20-Jan-2001 | 20-Jan-2009 |
| 44 | Obama | Michelle | 20-Jan-2009 | 20-Jan-2017 |
| 45 | Trump | Melania | 20-Jan-2017 | *incumbent* |

See notes on following page.

# The First Ladies – Footnotes

1.      Jefferson's wife died in 1782, some 18 years before he became President. Dolley Madison served as part-time White House hostess, and the Jefferson's daughter Martha "Patsy" Washington Jefferson Randolph sometimes filled that role on her infrequent visits to Washington.

2.      Emily Donelson, the President's deceased wife's niece, served as White House hostess and unofficial First Lady until her death on 19th December 1836. Commencing 26th November 1834 and continuing until the end of Jackson's term, the President's daughter-in-law, Sarah Yorke Jackson, also served in those roles.

3.      Angelica Singleton Van Buren, the President's daughter-in-law, served as White House hostess.

4.      The President's wife was reportedly ill and unable to travel to Washington at the time of his inauguration. Jane Irwin Harrison, their daughter-in-law, served as White House hostess pending the arrival of the President's wife.  The President died before his wife could travel.

5.      John Tyler's first wife died in the second year of his Presidency. He remarried about 21 months later. In the interim, his daughter-in-law (Priscilla Cooper Tyler) and daughter (Letitia Tyler Semple) served as acting White House hostesses.

6.      James Buchanan never married. His niece, Harriet Rebecca Lane, served as White House hostess.

7.      Mrs. Johnson suffered bad health and was not disposed to public life. Their daughters, Martha and Mary, frequently served as White House hostess.

8.      The President's wife was deceased. His sister, Mary Arthur McElroy, served as White House hostess.

9.      The President entered office as a bachelor. His sister Rose served as White House hostess until he married a little more than one year later.

10.      The President's wife died late in his Presidency. Their daughter, Mary Harrison McKee, served as White House hostess for the remaining months of his term.

11.      Wilson's first wife died in the second year of his first term. He remarried about 16 months later. His daughter Margaret Woodrow Wilson served as acting White House hostess in the interim.

# The Presidents' Children

(Washington to William Harrison)

| | President | Wife | M | F | Total | Children *<br>Names |
|---|---|---|---|---|---|---|
| 1 | George Washington | Martha | 0 | 0 | 0 | |
| 2 | John Adams | Abigail | 3 | 2 | 5 | Abigail "Nabby" Amelia Adams [Smith] (1765–1813)<br>John Quincy Adams (1767–1848)<br>Susanna Adams (1768–1770)<br>Charles Adams (1770–1800)<br>Thomas Boylston Adams (1772–1832) |
| 3 | Thomas Jefferson | Martha | 1 | 5 | 6 | Martha "Patsy" Jefferson [Randolph] (1772–1836)<br>Jane Randolph Jefferson (1774–1775)<br>unnamed son died in infancy (1777-1777)<br>Maria "Polly" Jefferson [Eppes] (1778–1804)<br>Lucy Elizabeth Jefferson (1780-1781)<br>Lucy Elizabeth Jefferson (2nd so-named) (1782–1785) |
| 4 | James Madison | Dolley | 0 | 0 | 0 | |
| 5 | James Monroe | Elizabeth | 1 | 2 | 3 | Eliza Kortright Monroe [Hay] (1786-1840)<br>James Spence Monroe (1799-1801)<br>Maria Hester Monroe [Gouverneur] (1803–1850) |
| 6 | John Quincy Adams | Louisa | 3 | 1 | 4 | George Washington Adams (1801-1829)<br>John Adams II (1803-1834)<br>Charles Francis Adams (1807-1886)<br>Louisa Catherine Adams (1811-1812) |
| 7 | Andrew Jackson | Rachel | 2 | 0 | 2 | Andrew Jackson, Jr. (1808-1865, adopted)<br>Lyncoya Jackson (c.1811-1828, adopted) |
| 8 | Martin Van Buren | Hannah | 5 | 0 | 5 | Abraham Van Buren (1807-1873)<br>John Van Buren (1810-1866)<br>Martin Van Buren, Jr. (1812-1855)<br>Winfield Scott Van Buren (1814-1814)<br>Smith Thompson Van Buren (1817-1876) |
| 9 | William Harrison | Anna | 4 | 6 | 10 | Elizabeth Bassett Harrison [Short] (1796 - 1846)<br>John Cleves Symmes Harrison (1798 - 1830)<br>Lucy Singleton Harrison [Estes] (1800 – 1826)<br>William Henry Harrison II (1802 – 1838)<br>John Scott Harrison (1804-1878)<br>Benjamin Harrison (1806 – 1840)<br>Mary Symmes Harrison [Thornton] (1809 – 1842)<br>Carter Bassett Harrison (1811 – 1839)<br>Anna Tuthill Harrison [Taylor] (1813 – 1845)<br>James Findlay Harrison (1814 –1817) |

# The Presidents' Children

(Tyler to Grant)

| | President | Wife | M | F | Total | Children * Names |
|---|---|---|---|---|---|---|
| 10 | John Tyler | Letitia | 3 | 5 | 8 | Mary Tyler [Jones] (1815-1847)<br>Robert Tyler (1816-1877)<br>John Tyler, Jr. (1819-1896)<br>Letitia Christian Tyler [Semple] (1821-1907)<br>Elizabeth Tyler [Waller] (1823 - 1870)<br>Ann Contesse Tyler (1825-1825)<br>Alice Tyler [Denison] (1827-1854)<br>Tazewell Tyler (1830-1874) |
| | | Julia | 5 | 2 | 7 | David Gardiner Tyler (1846-1927)<br>John Alexander Tyler (1848-1883)<br>Julia Gardiner Tyler [Spencer] (1849-1871)<br>Lachlan Tyler (1851-1902)<br>Lyon Gardiner Tyler (1853-1935)<br>Robert Fitzwalter Tyler (1856-1927)<br>Pearl Tyler [Ellis] (1860-1947) |
| 11 | James Polk | Sarah | 0 | 0 | 0 | |
| 12 | Zachary Taylor | Margaret | 1 | 5 | 6 | Anne Margaret Mackall Taylor [Wood] (1811-1875)<br>Sarah Knox Taylor [Davis] (1814 - 1835)<br>Octavia Pannel Taylor (1816-1820)<br>Margaret Smith Taylor (1819-1820)<br>Mary Elizabeth "Betty" Taylor [Bliss Dandridge] (1824-1909)<br>Richard Taylor (1826-1879) |
| 13 | Millard Fillmore | Abigail | 1 | 1 | 2 | Millard Powers Fillmore (1828–1889)<br>Mary Abigail Fillmore (1832–1854) |
| | | Caroline | 0 | 0 | 0 | |
| 14 | Franklin Pierce | Jane | 3 | 0 | 3 | Franklin Pierce, Jr. (1836–1836)<br>Frank Robert Pierce (1839–1843)<br>Benjamin Pierce (1841-1853) |
| 15 | James Buchanan | | 0 | 0 | 0 | |
| 16 | Abraham Lincoln | Mary | 4 | 0 | 4 | Robert Todd Lincoln (1843-1926)<br>Edward Baker Lincoln (1846-1850)<br>William "Willie" Wallace Lincoln (1850-1862)<br>Thomas "Tad" Lincoln (1853-1871) |
| 17 | Andrew Johnson | Eliza | 3 | 2 | 5 | Martha Johnson [Patterson] (1828–1901)<br>Charles Johnson (1830 – 1863)<br>Mary Johnson [Stover] (1832–1883)<br>Robert Johnson (1834 – 1869)<br>Andrew Johnson, Jr. (1852–1879) |
| 18 | Ulysses Grant | Julia | 3 | 1 | 4 | Frederick Dent Grant (1850–1912)<br>Ulysses S. Grant (1852–1929)<br>Ellen "Nellie" Wrenshall Grant [Sartores Jones] (1855–1922)<br>Jesse Root Grant (1858–1934) |

# The Presidents' Children

(Hayes to Hoover)

| | President | Wife | M | F | Total | Children *<br>Names |
|---|---|---|---|---|---|---|
| 19 | Rutherford Hayes | Lucy | 7 | 1 | 8 | Birchard Austin Hayes (1853–1926)<br>Webb Cook Hayes (1856–1934)<br>Rutherford Platt Hayes (1858–1927)<br>Joseph Thompson Hayes (1861–1863)<br>George Crook Hayes (1864–1866)<br>Fanny Hayes [Smith] (1867–1950)<br>Scott Russell Hayes (1871–1923)<br>Manning Force Hayes (1873–1874) |
| 20 | James Garfield | Lucretia | 5 | 2 | 7 | Eliza Arabella "Trot" Garfield (1860-1863)<br>Harry Augustus "Hal" Garfield (1863-1942)<br>James "Jim" Rudolf Garfield (1865-1950)<br>Mary "Mollie" Garfield [Stanley-Brown] (1867-1947)<br>Irvin McDowell Garfield (1870-1951)<br>Abram Garfield (1872-1958)<br>Edward Garfield (1874-1876) |
| 21 | Chester Arthur | Ellen | 2 | 1 | 3 | William Lewis Arthur (1860–1863)<br>Chester Alan Arthur, Jr. (1864–1937)<br>Ellen "Nellie" Herndon Arthur [Pinkerton] (1871–1915) |
| 22 & 24 | Grover Cleveland | Frances | 2 | 3 | 5 | Ruth Cleveland (1891-1904)<br>Esther Cleveland [Bosanquet] (1893-1980)<br>Marion Cleveland [Dell Amen] (1895-1977)<br>Richard Folsom "Dick" Cleveland (1897-1974)<br>Francis Grover Cleveland (1903-1995) |
| 23 | Benjamin Harrison | Caroline | 1 | 1 | 2 | Russell Benjamin Harrison (1854-1936)<br>Mary "Mamie" Scott Harrison [McKee] (1858-1930) |
| | | Mary | 0 | 1 | 1 | Elizabeth Harrison [Walker] (1897-1955) |
| 25 | William McKinley | Ida | 0 | 2 | 2 | Katherine McKinley (1871-1875)<br>Ida McKinley (1873-1873) |
| 26 | Theodore Roosevelt | Edith | 4 | 1 | 5 | Theodore Roosevelt Jr. (1887-1944)<br>Kermit Roosevelt (1889-1943)<br>Ethel Carow Roosevelt [Derby] (1891-1977)<br>Archibald Bullock Roosevelt (1894-1979)<br>Quentin Roosevelt (1897-1918) |
| 27 | William Taft | Helen | 2 | 1 | 3 | Robert Taft (1889-1953)<br>Helen Taft [Manning] (1891-1987)<br>Charles Taft (1897-1983) |
| 28 | Woodrow Wilson | Ellen | 0 | 3 | 3 | Margaret Woodrow Wilson (1886-1944)<br>Jessie Woodrow Wilson [Sayre] (1887-1933)<br>Eleanor "Nell" Randolph Wilson [McAdoo] (1889-1967) |
| | | Edith | 0 | 0 | 0 | |
| 29 | Warren Harding | Florence | 0 | 0 | 0 | |
| 30 | Calvin Coolidge | Grace | 2 | 0 | 2 | John Coolidge (1906–2000)<br>Calvin Coolidge, Jr. (1908–1924) |
| 31 | Herbert Hoover | Lou | 2 | 0 | 2 | Herbert Charles Hoover (1903–1969)<br>Allan Henry Hoover (1907–1993) |

# The Presidents' Children

(Franklin Roosevelt to Trump)

| | President | Wife | M | F | Total | Children * Names |
|---|---|---|---|---|---|---|
| 32 | Franklin Roosevelt | Anna | 5 | 1 | 6 | Anna Eleanor Roosevelt [Dall Boeettiger Halstead] (1906-1975)<br>James Roosevelt (1907-1991)<br>Franklin Delano Roosevelt, Jr. (1909-1909)<br>Elliott Roosevelt (1910-1990)<br>Franklin Delano Roosevelt, Jr. (2nd so-named) (1914–1988)<br>John Aspinwall Roosevelt (1916-1981) |
| 33 | Harry Truman | Elizabeth | 0 | 1 | 1 | Mary Margaret Truman [Daniel] (1924-2008) |
| 34 | Dwight Eisenhower | Mamie | 2 | 0 | 2 | Doud Dwight ("Icky") Eisenhower (1917-1921)<br>John Sheldon Doud Eisenhower (1922-2013) |
| 35 | John Kennedy | Jacqueline | 2 | 1 | 3 | Caroline Bouvier Kennedy [Schlossberg] (1957- )<br>John F. Kennedy, Jr. (1960-1999)<br>Patrick Bouvier Kennedy (1963-1963) |
| 36 | Lyndon Johnson | "Lady Bird" | 0 | 2 | 2 | Lynda Bird Johnson [Robb] (1944- )<br>Luci Baines Johnson [Nugent Turpin] (1947- ) |
| 37 | Richard Nixon | "Pat" | 0 | 2 | 2 | Patricia "Tricia" Nixon [Cox] (1946- )<br>Julie Nixon [Eisenhower] (1948- ) |
| 38 | Gerald Ford | Elizabeth | 3 | 1 | 4 | Michael Gerald Ford (1950- )<br>John Gardner Ford (1952- )<br>Steven Meigs Ford (1956- )<br>Susan Elizabeth Ford [Vance Bales] (1957- ) |
| 39 | James Carter | Rosalynn | 3 | 1 | 4 | John "Jack" William Carter (1947- )<br>James Earl "Chip" Carter (1950- )<br>Donnel Jeffrey Carter (1952- )<br>Amy Lynn Carter [Wentzel] (1967- ) |
| 40 | Ronald Reagan | Jane | 1 | 2 | 3 | Maureen Elizabeth Reagan (1941-2001)<br>Michael Edward Reagan (1945- ; adopted)<br>Christine Reagan (1947-1947) |
| | | "Nancy" | 1 | 1 | 2 | Patricia Ann Reagan, a/k/a Patti Davis [Grilley] (1952- )<br>Ronald Prescott Reagan (1958- ) |
| 41 | George H.W. Bush | Barbara | 4 | 2 | 6 | George Walker Bush (1946- )<br>Pauline Robinson "Robin" Bush (1949-1953)<br>John Ellis "Jeb" Bush (1953- )<br>Neil Mallon Bush (1955- )<br>Marvin Pierce Bush (1956- )<br>Dorothy "Doro" Walker Bush [Koch] (1959- ) |
| 42 | William Clinton | Hillary | 0 | 1 | 1 | Chelsea Victoria Clinton [Mezvinsky] (1980- ) |
| 43 | George W. Bush | Laura | 0 | 2 | 2 | Barbara Pierce Welch Bush (twin) (1981- )<br>Jenna Welch Bush [Hager] (twin) (1981- ) |
| 44 | Barack Obama | Michelle | 0 | 2 | 2 | Malia Ann (1998- )<br>Natasha "Sasha" (2001- ) |
| 45 | Donald Trump | Ivana | 2 | 1 | 3 | Donald Jr. (1977- )<br>Ivanka (1981- )<br>Eric (1984- ) |
| | | Marla | 0 | 1 | 1 | Tiffany (1993- ) |
| | | Melania | 1 | 0 | 1 | Barron (2006- ) |
| | 44 presidents | 50 wives | 93 | 69 | 162 | |

* Includes legitimate, live-born, biological children and legally adopted children. Stillborn, foster, illegitimate, and step children are not included.

# The Vice Presidents of the United States of America

| | Vice President | Party | Took Office | Age When First Sworn In | Left Office | Terms +days | |
|---|---|---|---|---|---|---|---|
| 1 | John Adams (1,2) | F | 21-Apr-1789 | 53.5 | 4-Mar-1797 | 2 | |
| 2 | Thomas Jefferson (1, 2) | D-R | 4-Mar-1797 | 53.9 | 4-Mar-1801 | 1 | |
| 3 | Aaron Burr (1) | D-R | 4-Mar-1801 | 45.1 | 4-Mar-1805 | 1 | |
| 4 | George Clinton (1) | D-R | 4-Mar-1805 | 65.6 | 20-Apr-1812 | 1 | +1,143 |
| 5 | Elbridge Gerry | D-R | 4-Mar-1813 | 68.6 | 23-Nov-1814 | 0 | +629 |
| 6 | Daniel Tompkins | D-R | 4-Mar-1817 | 42.7 | 4-Mar-1825 | 2 | |
| 7 | John Calhoun (1) | D-R | 4-Mar-1825 | 43.0 | 28-Dec-1832 | 1 | +1,395 |
| 8 | Martin Van Buren (1) | D | 4-Mar-1833 | 50.2 | 4-Mar-1837 | 1 | |
| 9 | Richard Johnson | D | 4-Mar-1837 | 56.4 | 4-Mar-1841 | 1 | |
| 10 | John Tyler (3) | W | 4-Mar-1841 | 50.9 | 4-Apr-1841 | 0 | +31 |
| 11 | George Dallas | D | 4-Mar-1845 | 52.6 | 4-Mar-1849 | 1 | |
| 12 | Millard Fillmore (3) | W | 4-Mar-1849 | 49.2 | 9-Jul-1850 | 0 | +492 |
| 13 | William King | D | 4-Mar-1853 | 66.9 | 18-Apr-1853 | 0 | +45 |
| 14 | John Breckinridge (1) | D | 4-Mar-1857 | 36.1 | 4-Mar-1861 | 1 | |
| 15 | Hannibal Hamlin | R | 4-Mar-1861 | 51.5 | 4-Mar-1865 | 1 | |
| 16 | Andrew Johnson (3) | D/NU | 4-Mar-1865 | 56.2 | 15-Apr-1865 | 0 | +42 |
| 17 | Schuyler Colfax | R | 4-Mar-1869 | 45.9 | 4-Mar-1873 | 1 | |
| 18 | Henry Wilson | R | 4-Mar-1873 | 61.0 | 22-Nov-1875 | 0 | +993 |
| 19 | William Wheeler | R | 4-Mar-1877 | 57.7 | 4-Mar-1881 | 1 | |
| 20 | Chester Arthur (3) | R | 4-Mar-1881 | 51.4 | 19-Sep-1881 | 0 | +199 |
| 21 | Thomas Hendricks | D | 4-Mar-1885 | 65.5 | 25-Nov-1885 | 0 | +266 |
| 22 | Levi Morton | R | 4-Mar-1889 | 64.8 | 4-Mar-1893 | 1 | |
| 23 | Adlai Stevenson | D | 4-Mar-1893 | 57.4 | 4-Mar-1897 | 1 | |
| 24 | Garret Hobart | R | 4-Mar-1897 | 52.8 | 21-Nov-1899 | 0 | +992 |
| 25 | Theodore Roosevelt (1, 2, 3) | R | 4-Mar-1901 | 42.4 | 14-Sep-1901 | 0 | +194 |
| 26 | Charles Fairbanks | R | 4-Mar-1905 | 52.8 | 4-Mar-1909 | 1 | |
| 27 | James Sherman | R | 4-Mar-1909 | 53.4 | 30-Oct-1912 | 0 | +1,336 |
| 28 | Thomas Marshall | D | 4-Mar-1913 | 59.0 | 4-Mar-1921 | 2 | |
| 29 | Calvin Coolidge (1, 2, 3) | R | 4-Mar-1921 | 48.7 | 2-Aug-1923 | 0 | +881 |
| 30 | Charles Dawes | R | 4-Mar-1925 | 59.5 | 4-Mar-1929 | 1 | |
| 31 | Charles Curtis | R | 4-Mar-1929 | 69.1 | 4-Mar-1933 | 1 | |
| 32 | John Garner | D | 4-Mar-1933 | 64.3 | 20-Jan-1941 | 2 | |
| 33 | Henry Wallace | D | 20-Jan-1941 | 52.3 | 20-Jan-1945 | 1 | |
| 34 | Harry Truman (1, 2, 3) | D | 20-Jan-1945 | 60.7 | 12-Apr-1945 | 0 | +82 |
| 35 | Alben Barkley | D | 20-Jan-1949 | 71.2 | 20-Jan-1953 | 1 | |
| 36 | Richard Nixon (1, 2) | R | 20-Jan-1953 | 40.0 | 20-Jan-1961 | 2 | |
| 37 | Lyndon Johnson (1, 2, 3) | D | 20-Jan-1961 | 52.4 | 22-Nov-1963 | 0 | +1,036 |
| 38 | Hubert Humphrey (1) | D | 20-Jan-1965 | 53.7 | 20-Jan-1969 | 1 | |
| 39 | Spiro Agnew | R | 20-Jan-1969 | 50.2 | 10-Oct-1973 | 1 | +263 |
| 40 | Gerald Ford (1, 3) | R | 6-Dec-1973 | 60.4 | 9-Aug-1974 | 0 | +246 |
| 41 | Nelson Rockefeller | R | 19-Dec-1974 | 66.4 | 20-Jan-1977 | 0 | +763 |
| 42 | Walter Mondale (1) | D | 20-Jan-1977 | 49.0 | 20-Jan-1981 | 1 | |
| 43 | George H.W. Bush (1, 2) | R | 20-Jan-1981 | 56.6 | 20-Jan-1989 | 2 | |
| 44 | Danforth Quayle | R | 20-Jan-1989 | 42.0 | 20-Jan-1993 | 1 | |
| 45 | Albert Gore (1) | D | 20-Jan-1993 | 44.8 | 20-Jan-2001 | 2 | |
| 46 | Richard Cheney | R | 20-Jan-2001 | 60.0 | 20-Jan-2009 | 2 | |
| 47 | Joseph Biden | D | 20-Jan-2009 | 66.2 | 20-Jan-2017 | 2 | |
| 48 | Michael Pence | R | 20-Jan-2017 | 57.6 | *Incumbent* | | |

1. Ran for President.   2. Elected President.   3. Ascended to Presidency.

# Personal Data About the Vice Presidents

| | Full Name | Birth Date | Death Date | Life Span | Children | Married |
|---|---|---|---|---|---|---|
| 1 | John Adams | 30-Oct-1735 | 4-Jul-1826 | 90 | 5 | yes |
| 2 | Thomas Jefferson | 13-Apr-1743 | 4-Jul-1826 | 83 | 5 | yes |
| 3 | Aaron Burr, Jr. | 6-Feb-1756 | 14-Sep-1836 | 81 | 1 | twice |
| 4 | George Clinton | 26-Jul-1739 | 20-Apr-1812 | 73 | 6 | yes |
| 5 | Elbridge Thomas Gerry | 17-Jul-1744 | 23-Nov-1814 | 70 | 9 | yes |
| 6 | Daniel D. Tompkins | 21-Jun-1774 | 11-Jun-1825 | 51 | 8 | yes |
| 7 | John Caldwell Calhoun | 18-Mar-1782 | 31-Mar-1850 | 68 | 16 | yes |
| 8 | Martin Van Buren | 5-Dec-1782 | 24-Jul-1862 | 80 | 4 | yes |
| 9 | Richard Mentor Johnson | 17-Oct-1780 | 19-Nov-1850 | 70 | 2 | CL |
| 10 | John Tyler, Jr. | 29-Mar-1790 | 18-Jan-1862 | 72 | 15 | twice |
| 11 | George Mifflin Dallas | 10-Jul-1792 | 31-Dec-1864 | 72 | 8 | yes |
| 12 | Millard Fillmore | 7-Jan-1800 | 8-Mar-1874 | 74 | 2 | twice |
| 13 | William Rufus DeVane King | 7-Apr-1786 | 18-Apr-1853 | 67 | | no |
| 14 | John Cabell Breckinridge | 16-Jan-1821 | 17-May-1875 | 54 | 5 | yes |
| 15 | Hannibal Hamlin | 27-Aug-1809 | 4-Jul-1891 | 82 | 6 | twice |
| 16 | Andrew Johnson | 29-Dec-1808 | 31-Jul-1875 | 67 | 5 | yes |
| 17 | Schuyler Colfax, Jr. | 23-Mar-1823 | 13-Jan-1885 | 62 | 1 | twice |
| 18 | Henry Wilson | 16-Feb-1812 | 22-Nov-1875 | 64 | 1 + 1(a) | yes |
| 19 | William Almon Wheeler | 30-Jun-1819 | 4-Jun-1887 | 68 | 0 | yes |
| 20 | Chester Alan Arthur | 5-Oct-1829 | 18-Nov-1886 | 57 | 3 | yes |
| 21 | Thomas Andrews Hendricks | 7-Sep-1819 | 25-Nov-1885 | 66 | 1 | yes |
| 22 | Levi Parsons Morton | 16-May-1824 | 16-May-1920 | 96 | 6 | twice |
| 23 | Adlai Ewing Stevenson I | 23-Oct-1835 | 14-Jun-1914 | 79 | 1 | yes |
| 24 | Garret Augustus Hobart | 3-Jun-1844 | 21-Nov-1899 | 55 | 2 | yes |
| 25 | Theodore Roosevelt | 27-Oct-1858 | 6-Jan-1919 | 60 | 6 | yes |
| 26 | Charles Warren Fairbanks | 11-May-1852 | 4-Jun-1918 | 66 | 5 | yes |
| 27 | James Schoolcraft Sherman | 24-Oct-1855 | 30-Oct-1912 | 57 | 3 | yes |
| 28 | Thomas Riley Marshall | 14-Mar-1854 | 1-Jun-1925 | 71 | 1 (a) | yes |
| 29 | John Calvin Coolidge, Jr. | 4-Jul-1872 | 5-Jan-1933 | 61 | 2 | yes |
| 30 | Charles Gates Dawes | 27-Aug-1865 | 23-Apr-1951 | 86 | 2 + 2(a) | yes |
| 31 | Charles Curtis | 25-Jan-1860 | 8-Feb-1936 | 76 | 3 | yes |
| 32 | John Nance Garner IV | 22-Nov-1868 | 7-Nov-1967 | 99 | 1 | yes |
| 33 | Henry Agard Wallace | 7-Oct-1888 | 18-Nov-1965 | 77 | 3 | yes |
| 34 | Harry S. Truman | 8-May-1884 | 26-Dec-1972 | 89 | 1 | yes |
| 35 | Alben William Barkley | 24-Nov-1877 | 30-Apr-1956 | 78 | 3 | twice |
| 36 | Richard Milhous Nixon | 9-Jan-1913 | 22-Apr-1994 | 81 | 2 | yes |
| 37 | Lyndon Baines Johnson | 27-Aug-1908 | 22-Jan-1973 | 64 | 2 | yes |
| 38 | Hubert Horatio Humphrey, Jr. | 27-May-1911 | 13-Jan-1978 | 67 | 4 | yes |
| 39 | Spiro Theodore Agnew | 9-Nov-1918 | 17-Sep-1996 | 78 | 4 | yes |
| 40 | Gerald Rudolph Ford, Jr.* | 14-Jul-1913 | 26-Dec-2006 | 93 | 4 | yes |
| 41 | Nelson Aldrich Rockefeller | 8-Jul-1908 | 26-Jan-1979 | 71 | 7 | yes |
| 42 | Walter Frederick Mondale | 5-Jan-1928 | *living* | --- | 3 | yes |
| 43 | George Herbert Walker Bush | 12-Jun-1924 | *living* | --- | 6 | yes |
| 44 | James Danforth Quayle | 4-Feb-1947 | *living* | --- | 3 | yes |
| 45 | Albert Arnold Gore, Jr. | 31-Mar-1948 | *living* | --- | 4 | yes |
| 46 | Richard Bruce Cheney | 30-Jan-1941 | *living* | --- | 2 | yes |
| 47 | Joseph Robinette Biden, Jr. | 20-Nov-1942 | *living* | --- | 4 | twice |
| 48 | Michael Richard Pence | 7-Jun-1959 | *living* | --- | 3 | yes |

\* Birth name: Leslie Lynch King, Jr.  (a) = adopted  CL = common law wife

# Personal Data About the Vice Presidents, Part II

| | Name | Home State | Birthplace | Death Place |
|---|---|---|---|---|
| 1 | John Adams | Massachusetts | Quincy, MA | Quincy, MA |
| 2 | Thomas Jefferson | Virginia | Shadwell, VA | Charlottesville, VA |
| 3 | Aaron Burr, Jr. | New York | Newark, NJ | Staten Island, NY |
| 4 | George Clinton | New York | Little Britain, NY | Washington, DC |
| 5 | Elbridge Thomas Gerry | Massachusetts | Marblehead, MA | Washington, DC |
| 6 | Daniel D. Tompkins | New York | Scarsdale, NY | Staten Island, NY |
| 7 | John Caldwell Calhoun | South Carolina | Abbeville, SC | Washington, DC |
| 8 | Martin Van Buren | New York | Kinderhook, NY | Kinderhook, NY |
| 9 | Richard Mentor Johnson | Kentucky | Beargrass, KY | Frankfort, KY |
| 10 | John Tyler, Jr. | Virginia | Charles City Cty, VA | Richmond, VA |
| 11 | George Mifflin Dallas | Pennsylvania | Philadelphia, PA | Philadelphia, PA |
| 12 | Millard Fillmore | New York | Summerhill, NY | Buffalo, NY |
| 13 | William Rufus DeVane King | Alabama | Sampson County, NC | Selma, AL |
| 14 | John Cabell Breckinridge | Kentucky | Lexington, KY | Lexington, KY |
| 15 | Hannibal Hamlin | Maine | Paris, ME | Bangor, ME |
| 16 | Andrew Johnson | Tennessee | Raleigh, NC | Elizabethton, TN |
| 17 | Schuyler Colfax, Jr. | Indiana | New York, NY | Mankato, MN |
| 18 | Henry Wilson | Massachusetts | Farmington, NH | Washington, DC |
| 19 | William Almon Wheeler | New York | Malone, NY | Malone, NY |
| 20 | Chester Alan Arthur | New York | Fairfield, VT | New York, NY |
| 21 | Thomas Andrews Hendricks | Indiana | Fultonham, OH | Indianapoli, IN |
| 22 | Levi Parsons Morton | New York | Shoreham, VT | Rhinebeck, NY |
| 23 | Adlai Ewing Stevenson I | Illinois | Christian County, KY | Chicago, IL |
| 24 | Garret Augustus Hobart | New Jersey | Long Branch, NJ | Paterson, NJ |
| 25 | Theodore Roosevelt | New York | New York, NY | Oyster Bay, NY |
| 26 | Charles Warren Fairbanks | Indiana | Unionville Center, OH | Indianapoli, IN |
| 27 | James Schoolcraft Sherman | New York | Utica, NY | Utica, NY |
| 28 | Thomas Riley Marshall | Indiana | North Manchester, IN | Washington, DC |
| 29 | John Calvin Coolidge, Jr. | Massachusetts | Plymouth, VT | Northampton, MA |
| 30 | Charles Gates Dawes | Illinois | Marietta, OH | Evanston, IL |
| 31 | Charles Curtis | Kansas | Topeka, KS | Washington, DC |
| 32 | John Nance Garner IV | Texas | Detroit, TX | Uvalde, TX |
| 33 | Henry Agard Wallace | Iowa | Orient, IA | Danbury, CT |
| 34 | Harry S. Truman | Missouri | Lamar, MO | Kansas City, MO |
| 35 | Alben William Barkley | Kentucky | Graves County, KY | Lexington, VA |
| 36 | Richard Milhous Nixon | California | Yorba Linda, CA | New York, NY |
| 37 | Lyndon Baines Johnson | Texas | Stonewall, TX | Stonewall, TX |
| 38 | Hubert Horatio Humphrey, Jr. | Minnesota | Wallace, SD | Waverly, MN |
| 39 | Spiro Theodore Agnew | Maryland | Baltimore, MD | Berlin, MD |
| 40 | Gerald Rudolph Ford, Jr.* | Michigan | Omaha, NE | Rancho Mirage, CA |
| 41 | Nelson Aldrich Rockefeller | New York | Bar Harbor, ME | New York, NY |
| 42 | Walter Frederick Mondale | Minnesota | Ceylon, MN | *living* |
| 43 | George Herbert Walker Bush | Texas | Milton, MA | *living* |
| 44 | James Danforth Quayle | Indiana | Indianapolis, IN | *living* |
| 45 | Albert Arnold Gore, Jr. | Tennessee | Washington, DC | *living* |
| 46 | Richard Bruce Cheney | Wyoming | Lincoln, NE | *living* |
| 47 | Joseph Robinette Biden, Jr. | Delaware | Scranton, PA | *living* |
| 48 | Michael Richard Pence | Indiana | Columbus, IN | *living* |

# Flow of Presidents and Vice Presidents Into and Out of Office --18th and 19th Centuries

| Term | Presidency | Election Year | Party | President | | | Vice President | | |
|---|---|---|---|---|---|---|---|---|---|
| | | | | Name | Term Began | Term Ended | Name | Term Began | Term Ended |
| 1 | 1 | 1789 | F | George Washington [1] | 30-Apr-1789 | 4-Mar-1793 | John Adams [1] | 21-Apr-1789 | 4-Mar-1793 |
| 2 | | 1792 | F | George Washington [1] | 4-Mar-1793 | 4-Mar-1797 | John Adams [1] | 4-Mar-1793 | 4-Mar-1797 |
| 3 | 2 | 1796 | F | John Adams [1] | 4-Mar-1797 | 4-Mar-1801 | Thomas Jefferson [1] | 4-Mar-1797 | 4-Mar-1801 |
| 4 | 3 | 1800 | D-R | Thomas Jefferson [1] | 4-Mar-1801 | 4-Mar-1805 | Aaron Burr [1] | 4-Mar-1801 | 4-Mar-1805 |
| 5 | | 1804 | D-R | Thomas Jefferson | 4-Mar-1805 | 4-Mar-1809 | George Clinton | 4-Mar-1805 | 4-Mar-1809 |
| 6 | 4 | 1808 | D-R | James Madison | 4-Mar-1809 | | George Clinton [2] | 4-Mar-1809 | 20-Apr-1812 |
| | | | | | | 4-Mar-1813 | vacant | 20-Apr-1812 | 4-Mar-1813 |
| 7 | | 1812 | D-R | James Madison | 4-Mar-1813 | | Elbridge Gerry [2] | 4-Mar-1813 | 23-Nov-1814 |
| | | | | | | 4-Mar-1817 | vacant | 23-Nov-1814 | 4-Mar-1817 |
| 8 | 5 | 1816 | D-R | James Monroe | 4-Mar-1817 | 4-Mar-1821 | Daniel Tompkins | 4-Mar-1817 | 4-Mar-1821 |
| 9 | | 1820 | D-R | James Monroe | 4-Mar-1821 | 4-Mar-1825 | Daniel Tompkins | 4-Mar-1821 | 4-Mar-1825 |
| 10 | 6 | 1824 | D-R | John Quincy Adams | 4-Mar-1825 | 4-Mar-1829 | John Calhoun | 4-Mar-1825 | 4-Mar-1829 |
| 11 | 7 | 1828 | D | Andrew Jackson | 4-Mar-1829 | | John Calhoun [4] | 4-Mar-1829 | 28-Dec-1832 |
| | | | | | | 4-Mar-1833 | vacant | 28-Dec-1832 | 4-Mar-1833 |
| 12 | | 1832 | D | Andrew Jackson | 4-Mar-1833 | 4-Mar-1837 | Martin Van Buren | 4-Mar-1833 | 4-Mar-1837 |
| 13 | 8 | 1836 | D | Martin Van Buren | 4-Mar-1837 | 4-Mar-1841 | Richard Johnson | 4-Mar-1837 | 4-Mar-1841 |
| 14 | 9 | 1840 | W | William Harrison [2] | 4-Mar-1841 | 4-Apr-1841 | John Tyler | 4-Mar-1841 | 4-Apr-1841 |
| | 10 | | W | John Tyler | 6-Apr-1841 | 4-Mar-1845 | vacant | 4-Apr-1841 | 4-Mar-1845 |
| 15 | 11 | 1844 | D | James Polk | 4-Mar-1845 | 4-Mar-1849 | George Dallas | 4-Mar-1845 | 4-Mar-1849 |
| 16 | 12 | 1848 | W | Zachary Taylor [2] | 4-Mar-1849 | 9-Jul-1850 | Millard Fillmore | 4-Mar-1849 | 9-Jul-1850 |
| | 13 | | W | Millard Fillmore | 10-Jul-1850 | 4-Mar-1853 | vacant | 9-Jul-1850 | 4-Mar-1853 |
| 17 | 14 | 1852 | D | Franklin Pierce | 4-Mar-1853 | | William King [2] | 4-Mar-1853 | 18-Apr-1853 |
| | | | | | | 4-Mar-1857 | vacant | 18-Apr-1853 | 4-Mar-1857 |
| 18 | 15 | 1856 | D | James Buchanan | 4-Mar-1857 | 4-Mar-1861 | John Breckinridge | 4-Mar-1857 | 4-Mar-1861 |
| 19 | 16 | 1860 | R | Abraham Lincoln | 4-Mar-1861 | 4-Mar-1865 | Hannibal Hamlin | 4-Mar-1861 | 4-Mar-1865 |
| 20 | | 1864 | R | Abraham Lincoln [3] | 4-Mar-1865 | 15-Apr-1865 | Andrew Johnson | 4-Mar-1865 | 15-Apr-1865 |
| | 17 | | D | Andrew Johnson | 15-Apr-1865 | 4-Mar-1869 | vacant | 15-Apr-1865 | 4-Mar-1869 |
| 21 | 18 | 1868 | R | Ulysses Grant | 4-Mar-1869 | 4-Mar-1873 | Schuyler Colfax | 4-Mar-1869 | 4-Mar-1873 |
| 22 | | 1872 | R | Ulysses Grant | 4-Mar-1873 | | Henry Wilson [2] | 4-Mar-1873 | 22-Nov-1875 |
| | | | | | | 4-Mar-1877 | vacant | 22-Nov-1875 | 4-Mar-1877 |
| 23 | 19 | 1876 | R | Rutherford Hayes | 4-Mar-1877 | 4-Mar-1881 | William Wheeler | 4-Mar-1877 | 4-Mar-1881 |
| 24 | 20 | 1880 | R | James Garfield [3] | 4-Mar-1881 | 19-Sep-1881 | Chester Arthur | 4-Mar-1881 | 20-Sep-1881 |
| | 21 | | R | Chester Arthur | 20-Sep-1881 | 4-Mar-1885 | vacant | 20-Sep-1881 | 4-Mar-1885 |
| 25 | 22 | 1884 | D | Grover Cleveland | 4-Mar-1885 | | Thomas Hendricks [2] | 4-Mar-1885 | 25-Nov-1885 |
| | | | | | | 4-Mar-1889 | vacant | 25-Nov-1885 | 4-Mar-1889 |
| 26 | 23 | 1888 | R | Benjamin Harrison | 4-Mar-1889 | 4-Mar-1893 | Levi Morton | 4-Mar-1889 | 4-Mar-1893 |
| 27 | 24 | 1892 | D | Grover Cleveland | 4-Mar-1893 | 4-Mar-1897 | Adlai Stevenson | 4-Mar-1893 | 4-Mar-1897 |
| 28 | 25 | 1896 | R | William McKinley | 4-Mar-1897 | | Garret Hobart [2] | 4-Mar-1897 | 21-Nov-1899 |
| | | | | | | 4-Mar-1901 | vacant | 21-Nov-1899 | 4-Mar-1901 |

# Flow of Presidents and Vice Presidents Into and Out of Office --20th and 21st Centuries

| Term | Presidency | Election Year | Party | President | | | Vice President | | |
|---|---|---|---|---|---|---|---|---|---|
| | | | | Name | Term Began | Term Ended | Name | Term Began | Term Ended |
| 29 | | 1900 | R | William McKinley [3] | 4-Mar-1901 | 14-Sep-1901 | Theodore Roosevelt | 4-Mar-1901 | 14-Sep-1901 |
| | 26 | | R | Theodore Roosevelt | 14-Sep-1901 | 4-Mar-1905 | vacant | 14-Sep-1901 | 4-Mar-1905 |
| 30 | | 1904 | R | Theodore Roosevelt | 4-Mar-1905 | 4-Mar-1909 | Charles Fairbanks | 4-Mar-1905 | 4-Mar-1909 |
| 31 | 27 | 1908 | R | William Taft | 4-Mar-1909 | | James Sherman [2] | 4-Mar-1909 | 30-Oct-1912 |
| | | | | | | 4-Mar-1913 | vacant | 30-Oct-1912 | 4-Mar-1913 |
| 32 | 28 | 1912 | D | Woodrow Wilson | 4-Mar-1913 | 4-Mar-1917 | Thomas Marshall | 4-Mar-1913 | 4-Mar-1917 |
| 33 | | 1916 | D | Woodrow Wilson | 4-Mar-1917 | 4-Mar-1921 | Thomas Marshall | 4-Mar-1917 | 4-Mar-1921 |
| 34 | 29 | 1920 | R | Warren Harding [2] | 4-Mar-1921 | 2-Aug-1923 | Calvin Coolidge | 4-Mar-1921 | 3-Aug-1923 |
| | 30 | | R | Calvin Coolidge | 3-Aug-1923 | 4-Mar-1925 | vacant | 2-Aug-1923 | 4-Mar-1925 |
| 35 | | 1924 | R | Calvin Coolidge | 4-Mar-1925 | 4-Mar-1929 | Charles Dawes | 4-Mar-1925 | 4-Mar-1929 |
| 36 | 31 | 1928 | R | Herbert Hoover | 4-Mar-1929 | 4-Mar-1933 | Charles Curtis | 4-Mar-1929 | 4-Mar-1933 |
| 37 | 32 | 1932 | D | Franklin Roosevelt | 4-Mar-1933 | 20-Jan-1937 | John Garner | 4-Mar-1933 | 20-Jan-1937 |
| 38 | | 1936 | D | Franklin Roosevelt | 20-Jan-1937 | 20-Jan-1941 | John Garner | 20-Jan-1937 | 20-Jan-1941 |
| 39 | | 1940 | D | Franklin Roosevelt | 20-Jan-1941 | 20-Jan-1945 | Henry Wallace | 20-Jan-1941 | 20-Jan-1945 |
| 40 | | 1944 | D | Franklin Roosevelt [2] | 20-Jan-1945 | 12-Apr-1945 | Harry Truman | 20-Jan-1945 | 12-Apr-1945 |
| | 33 | | D | Harry Truman | 12-Apr-1945 | 20-Jan-1949 | vacant | 12-Apr-1945 | 20-Jan-1949 |
| 41 | | 1948 | D | Harry Truman | 20-Jan-1949 | 20-Jan-1953 | Alben Barkley | 20-Jan-1949 | 20-Jan-1953 |
| 42 | 34 | 1952 | R | Dwight Eisenhower | 20-Jan-1953 | 20-Jan-1957 | Richard Nixon | 20-Jan-1953 | 20-Jan-1957 |
| 43 | | 1956 | R | Dwight Eisenhower | 20-Jan-1957 | 20-Jan-1961 | Richard Nixon | 20-Jan-1957 | 20-Jan-1961 |
| 44 | 35 | 1960 | D | John Kennedy [3] | 20-Jan-1961 | 22-Nov-1963 | Lyndon Johnson | 20-Jan-1961 | 22-Nov-1963 |
| | 36 | | D | Lyndon Johnson | 22-Nov-1963 | 20-Jan-1965 | vacant | 22-Nov-1963 | 20-Jan-1965 |
| 45 | | 1964 | D | Lyndon Johnson | 20-Jan-1965 | 20-Jan-1969 | Hubert Humphrey | 20-Jan-1965 | 20-Jan-1969 |
| 46 | 37 | 1968 | R | Richard Nixon | 20-Jan-1969 | 20-Jan-1973 | Spiro Agnew | 20-Jan-1969 | 20-Jan-1973 |
| 47 | | 1972 | R | Richard Nixon [4] | 20-Jan-1973 | | Spiro Agnew [4] | 20-Jan-1973 | 10-Oct-1973 |
| | | | | | | | vacant | 10-Oct-1973 | 6-Dec-1973 |
| | | | | | | 9-Aug-1974 | Gerald Ford | 6-Dec-1973 | 9-Aug-1974 |
| | 38 | | R | Gerald Ford | 9-Aug-1974 | | vacant | 9-Aug-1974 | 19-Dec-1974 |
| | | | | | | 20-Jan-1977 | Nelson Rockefeller | 19-Dec-1974 | 20-Jan-1977 |
| 48 | 39 | 1976 | D | James Carter | 20-Jan-1977 | 20-Jan-1981 | Walter Mondale | 20-Jan-1977 | 20-Jan-1981 |
| 49 | 40 | 1980 | R | Ronald Reagan | 20-Jan-1981 | 20-Jan-1985 | George H. W. Bush | 20-Jan-1981 | 20-Jan-1985 |
| 50 | | 1984 | R | Ronald Reagan | 20-Jan-1985 | 20-Jan-1989 | George H. W. Bush | 20-Jan-1985 | 20-Jan-1989 |
| 51 | 41 | 1988 | R | George H.W. Bush | 20-Jan-1989 | 20-Jan-1993 | Danforth Quayle | 20-Jan-1989 | 20-Jan-1993 |
| 52 | 42 | 1992 | D | William Clinton | 20-Jan-1993 | 20-Jan-1997 | Albert Gore | 20-Jan-1993 | 20-Jan-1997 |
| 53 | | 1996 | D | William Clinton | 20-Jan-1997 | 20-Jan-2001 | Albert Gore | 20-Jan-1997 | 20-Jan-2001 |
| 54 | 43 | 2000 | R | George W. Bush | 20-Jan-2001 | 20-Jan-2005 | Richard Cheney | 20-Jan-2001 | 20-Jan-2005 |
| 55 | | 2004 | R | George W. Bush | 20-Jan-2005 | 20-Jan-2009 | Richard Cheney | 20-Jan-2005 | 20-Jan-2009 |
| 56 | 44 | 2008 | D | Barack Obama | 20-Jan-2009 | 20-Jan-2013 | Joseph Biden | 20-Jan-2009 | 20-Jan-2013 |
| 57 | | 2012 | D | Barack Obama | 20-Jan-2013 | 20-Jan-2017 | Joseph Biden | 20-Jan-2013 | 20-Jan-2017 |
| 58 | 45 | 2016 | R | Donald Trump | 20-Jan-2017 | *Incumbent* | Michael Pence | 20-Jan-2017 | *Incumbent* |

(1) Elected under the original "first place; second place" voting scheme    (2) Died in office of natural causes.    (3) Assassinated.    (4) Resigned.

# Candidates for President and Vice President

| Election Year | Winning Candidates | | | Losing Candidates [1] | | |
|---|---|---|---|---|---|---|
| | Party | President | Vice President | Party | President | Vice President |
| 1789 | F | George Washington | John Adams | | | |
| 1792 | F | George Washington | John Adams | | | |
| 1796 | F | John Adams | Thomas Jefferson [2] | | | |
| 1800 | D-R | Thomas Jefferson | Aaron Burr | | | |
| 1804 | D-R | Thomas Jefferson | George Clinton | F | Charles C. Pinckney | Rufus King |
| 1808 | D-R | James Madison | George Clinton | F | Charles C. Pinckney | Rufus King |
| 1812 | D-R | James Madison | Elbridge Gerry | F | De Witt Clinton | Jared Ingersoll |
| 1816 | D-R | James Monroe | Daniel Tompkins | F | Rufus King | John E. Howard |
| 1820 | D-R | James Monroe | Daniel Tompkins | | no opposition | |
| 1824 | D-R | John Quincy Adams | John Calhoun | D-R | Andrew Jackson | Nathan Sanford |
| 1828 | D | Andrew Jackson | John Calhoun | N | John Quincy Adams | Richard Rush |
| 1832 | D | Andrew Jackson | Martin Van Buren | N | Henry Clay | John Sargeant |
| 1836 | D | Martin Van Buren | Richard Johnson | W | William Harrison | Francis Granger |
| 1840 | W | William Harrison | John Tyler | D | Martin Van Buren | Richard M. Johnson |
| 1844 | D | James Polk | George Dallas | W | Henry Clay | Theodore Frelinghuysen |
| 1848 | W | Zachary Taylor | Millard Fillmore | D | Lewis Cass | William O. Butler |
| 1852 | D | Franklin Pierce | William King | W | Winfield Scott | William Graham |
| 1856 | D | James Buchanan | John Breckinridge | R | John C. Fremont | William Dayton |
| 1860 | R | Abraham Lincoln | Hannibal Hamlin | D | John Breckinridge | Joseph Lane |
| 1864 | R | Abraham Lincoln | Andrew Johnson [3] | D | George B. McClellan | George Pendleton |
| 1868 | R | Ulysses Grant | Schuyler Colfax | D | Horatio Seymour | Francis Blair, Jr. |
| 1872 | R | Ulysses Grant | Henry Wilson | D | Horace Greeley | B. Gratz Brown |
| 1876 | R | Rutherford Hayes | William Wheeler | D | Samuel J. Tilden | Thomas Hendricks |
| 1880 | R | James Garfield | Chester Arthur | D | Winfield S. Hancock | William English |
| 1884 | D | Grover Cleveland | Thomas Hendricks | R | James G. Blaine | John Logan |
| 1888 | R | Benjamin Harrison | Levi Morton | D | Grover Cleveland | Allen Thurman |
| 1892 | D | Grover Cleveland | Adlai Stevenson | R | Benjamin Harrison | Whitelaw Reid |
| 1896 | R | William McKinley | Garret Hobart | D | William J. Bryan | Arthur Sewall |
| 1900 | R | William McKinley | Theodore Roosevelt | D | William J. Bryan | Adlai Stevenson |
| 1904 | R | Theodore Roosevelt | Charles Fairbanks | D | Alton B. Parker | Henry Davis |
| 1908 | R | William Taft | James Sherman | D | William J. Bryan | John Kern |
| 1912 | D | Woodrow Wilson | Thomas Marshall | P | Theodore Roosevelt | Hiram Johnson |
| 1916 | D | Woodrow Wilson | Thomas Marshall | R | Charles E. Hughes | Charles Fairbanks |
| 1920 | R | Warren Harding | Calvin Coolidge | D | James M. Cox | Franklin Roosevelt |
| 1924 | R | Calvin Coolidge | Charles Dawes | D | John W. Davis | Charles Bryan |
| 1928 | R | Herbert Hoover | Charles Curtis | D | Alfred E. Smith | Joseph Robinson |
| 1932 | D | Franklin Roosevelt | John Garner | R | Herbert Hoover | Charles Curtis |
| 1936 | D | Franklin Roosevelt | John Garner | R | Alfred M. Landon | Frank Knox |
| 1940 | D | Franklin Roosevelt | Henry Wallace | R | Wendell L. Wilkie | Charles McNary |
| 1944 | D | Franklin Roosevelt | Harry Truman | R | Thomas E. Dewey | John Bricker |
| 1948 | D | Harry Truman | Alben Barkley | R | Thomas E. Dewey | Earl Warren |
| 1952 | R | Dwight Eisenhower | Richard Nixon | D | Adlai E. Stevenson II | John Sparkman |
| 1956 | R | Dwight Eisenhower | Richard Nixon | D | Adlai E. Stevenson II | Estes Kefauver |
| 1960 | D | John Kennedy | Lyndon Johnson | R | Richard Nixon | Henry Lodge |
| 1964 | D | Lyndon Johnson | Hubert Humphrey | R | Barry M. Goldwater | William Miller |
| 1968 | R | Richard Nixon | Spiro Agnew | D | Hubert Humphrey | Edmund Muskie |
| 1972 | R | Richard Nixon | Spiro Agnew | D | George McGovern | R. Sargent Shriver |
| 1976 | D | James Carter | Walter Mondale | R | Gerald Ford | Robert Dole |
| 1980 | R | Ronald Reagan | George H.W. Bush | D | James Carter | Walter Mondale |
| 1984 | R | Ronald Reagan | George H.W. Bush | D | Walter F. Mondale | Geraldine Ferraro |
| 1988 | R | George H.W. Bush | Danforth Quayle | D | Michael S. Dukakis | Lloyd Bentsen |
| 1992 | D | William Clinton | Albert Gore | R | George H.W. Bush | Danforth Quayle |
| 1996 | D | William Clinton | Albert Gore | R | Robert Dole | Jack Kemp |
| 2000 | R | George W. Bush | Richard Cheney | D | Albert Gore | Joseph Lieberman |
| 2004 | R | George W. Bush | Richard Cheney | D | John F. Kerry | John Edwards |
| 2008 | D | Barack Obama | Joseph Biden | R | John S. McCain III | Sarah H. Palin |
| 2012 | D | Barack Obama | Joseph Biden | R | Willard Mitt Romney | Paul Davis Ryan |
| 2016 | R | Donald Trump | Michael Pence | D | Hillary Clinton | Timothy Kaine |

(1) Second-place loser only.   (2) Jefferson was a Democratic-Republican.   (3) Andrew Johnson was a Democrat.

# Results of Presidential Elections, 1789 to 1872

| Term | Year | Winner Candidate (party) | EV | PV | Amp./Min. | Victory Margin EV | PV | Loser Candidate (party) | EV | PV | Amp./Min. | Other EV (1) |
|---|---|---|---|---|---|---|---|---|---|---|---|---|
| 1 | 1789 | George Washington | 69 / 100.0% | | | n.a. / n.a. | | John Adams (F) | n.a. / n.a. | | | |
| 2 | 1792 | **George Washington** (F) | 132 / 100.0% | | | n.a. / n.a. | | John Adams (F) | n.a. / n.a. | | | |
| 3 | 1796 | John Adams (F) | 71 / 51.4% | | | n.a. / n.a. | | Thomas Jefferson (D-R) | n.a. / n.a. | | | 1 |
| 4 | 1800 | Thomas Jefferson (D-R) | 73 / 52.9% | | | n.a. / n.a. | | Aaron Burr (D-R) | n.a. / n.a. | | | |
| 5 | 1804 | **Thomas Jefferson** (D-R) | 162 / 92.0% | | | 148 / 84 | | Charles Pinckney (F) | 14 / 8.0% | | | |
| 6 | 1808 | James Madison (D-R) | 122 / 69.3% | | | 75 / 42.9 | | Charles Pinckney (F) | 47 / 26.7% | | | 7 |
| 7 | 1812 | **James Madison** (D-R) | 128 / 59.0% | | | 39 / 18.0 | | De Witt Clinton (F) | 89 / 41.0% | | | 1 |
| 8 | 1816 | James Monroe (D-R) | 183 / 84.3% | | | 149 / 68.7 | | Rufus King (F) | 34 / 15.7% | | | 4 |
| 9 | 1820 | **James Monroe** (D-R) | 231 / 98.3% | | | 230 / 99.1 | | | | | | 4 |
| 10 | 1824 | John Quincy Adams (2) (D-R) | 84 / 32.2% | 0.1 / 30.9% | 1.3% | (15) / -5.7 | (0.038) / (10.4) | Andrew Jackson (2) (D-R) | 99 / 37.9% | 0.2 / 41.4% | -3.4% | 78 |
| 11 | 1828 | Andrew Jackson (D) | 178 / 68.2% | 0.6 / 55.9% | 12.3% | 95 / 36.4 | 0.141 / 12.2 | **John Q. Adams** (N) | 83 / 31.8% | 0.5 / 43.7% | -11.9% | |
| 12 | 1832 | **Andrew Jackson** (D) | 219 / 76.0% | 0.7 / 54.7% | 21.3% | 170 / 59.0 | 0.229 / 17.8 | Henry Clay (N) | 49 / 17.0% | 0.5 / 36.9% | -19.9% | 20 |
| 13 | 1836 | Martin Van Buren (D) | 170 / 57.8% | 0.8 / 50.8% | 7.0% | 97 / 33.0 | 0.213 / 14.2 | William Harrison (W) | 73 / 24.8% | 0.5 / 36.6% | -11.8% | 51 |
| 14 | 1840 | William Harrison (W) | 234 / 79.6% | 1.3 / 52.9% | 26.7% | 174 / 59.2 | 0.146 / 6.0 | **Martin Van Buren** (D) | 60 / 20.4% | 1.1 / 46.8% | -26.4% | |
| 15 | 1844 | James Polk (D) | 170 / 61.8% | 1.3 / 49.5% | 12.3% | 65 / 23.6 | 0.039 / 1.5 | Henry Clay (W) | 105 / 38.2% | 1.3 / 48.1% | -9.9% | |
| 16 | 1848 | Zachary Taylor (W) | 163 / 56.2% | 1.4 / 47.3% | 8.9% | 36 / 12.4 | 0.138 / 4.8 | Lewis Cass (D) | 127 / 43.8% | 1.2 / 42.5% | 1.3% | |
| 17 | 1852 | Franklin Pierce (D) | 254 / 85.8% | 1.6 / 50.8% | 35.0% | 212 / 71.6 | 0.220 / 6.9 | Winfield Scott (W) | 42 / 14.2% | 1.4 / 43.9% | -29.7% | |
| 18 | 1856 | James Buchanan (D) | 174 / 58.8% | 1.8 / 45.3% | 13.5% | 60 / 20.3 | 0.494 / 12.2 | John Fremont (R) | 114 / 38.5% | 1.3 / 33.1% | 5.4% | 8 |
| 19 | 1860 | Abraham Lincoln (R) | 180 / 59.4% | 1.9 / 39.6% | 19.8% | 108 / 35.6 | 1.004 / 21.5 | John Breckenridge (D) | 72 / 23.8% | 0.9 / 18.2% | 5.6% | 51 |
| 20 | 1864 | **Abraham Lincoln** (R) | 212 / 91.0% | 2.2 / 55.0% | 36.0% | 191 / 82.0 | 0.405 / 10.1 | George McClellan (D) | 21 / 9.0% | 1.8 / 45.0% | -35.9% | |
| 21 | 1868 | Ulysses Grant (R) | 214 / 72.8% | 3.0 / 52.7% | 20.1% | 134 / 45.6 | 0.305 / 5.3 | Horatio Seymour (D) | 80 / 27.2% | 2.7 / 47.3% | -20.1% | |
| 22 | 1872 | **Ulysses Grant** (R) | 286 / 81.3% | 3.6 / 55.6% | 25.7% | 220 / 62.5 | 0.764 / 11.8 | Horace Greeley (D) | (3) / n.a. | 2.8 / 43.8% | -25.0% | 66 |

# Results of Presidential Elections, 1876 to 1960

| Term | Year | Winner Candidate (party) | EV | PV | Amp./Min. | Victory Margin EV | Victory Margin PV | Loser Candidate (party) | EV | PV | Amp./Min. | Other EV (1) |
|------|------|------|------|------|------|------|------|------|------|------|------|------|
| 23 | 1876 | Rutherford Hayes (R) | 185 50.1% | 4.0 47.9% | 2.2% | 1 0.3 | (0.253) (3.0) | Samuel Tilden (D) | 184 49.9% | 4.3 50.9% | -1.1% | |
| 24 | 1880 | James Garfield (R) | 214 58.0% | 4.5 48.3% | 9.7% | 59 16.0 | 0.009 0.1 | Winfield Hancock (D) | 155 42.0% | 4.4 48.2% | -6.2% | |
| 25 | 1884 | Grover Cleveland (D) | 219 54.6% | 4.9 48.9% | 5.8% | 37 9.2 | 0.058 0.6 | James Blaine (R) | 182 45.4% | 4.9 48.3% | -2.9% | |
| 26 | 1888 | Benjamin Harrison (R) | 233 58.1% | 5.4 47.8% | 10.3% | 65 16.2 | (0.095) (0.8) | **Grover Cleveland** (D) | 168 41.9% | 5.5 48.6% | -6.7% | |
| 27 | 1892 | Grover Cleveland (D) | 277 62.4% | 5.6 46.0% | 16.4% | 132 29.7 | 0.363 3.0 | **Benjamin Harrison** (R) | 145 32.7% | 5.2 43.0% | -10.4% | 22 |
| 28 | 1896 | William McKinley (R) | 271 60.6% | 7.1 51.0% | 9.6% | 95 21.3 | 0.601 4.3 | William Bryan (D-P) | 176 39.4% | 6.5 46.7% | -7.3% | |
| 29 | 1900 | **William McKinley** (R) | 292 65.3% | 7.2 51.6% | 13.7% | 137 30.6 | 0.858 6.1 | William Bryan (D-P) | 155 34.7% | 6.4 45.5% | -10.8% | |
| 30 | 1904 | **Theodore Roosevelt** (R) | 336 70.6% | 7.6 56.4% | 14.2% | 196 41.2 | 2.547 18.8 | Alton Parker (D) | 140 29.4% | 5.1 37.6% | -8.2% | |
| 31 | 1908 | William Taft (R) | 321 66.5% | 7.7 51.6% | 14.9% | 159 32.9 | 1.269 8.5 | William Bryan (D) | 162 33.5% | 6.4 43.0% | -9.5% | |
| 32 | 1912 | Woodrow Wilson (D) | 435 81.9% | 6.3 41.8% | 40.1% | 347 65.3 | 2.174 14.4 | Theodore Roosevelt (P) | 88 16.6% | 4.1 27.4% | -10.8% | 8 |
| 33 | 1916 | **Woodrow Wilson** (D) | 277 52.2% | 9.1 49.2% | 2.9% | 23 4.3 | 0.578 3.1 | Charles Hughes (R) | 254 47.8% | 8.5 46.1% | 1.7% | |
| 34 | 1920 | Warren Harding (R) | 404 76.1% | 16.1 61.7% | 14.4% | 277 52.2 | 7.006 26.8 | James Cox (D) | 127 23.9% | 9.1 34.9% | -11.0% | |
| 35 | 1924 | **Calvin Coolidge** (R) | 382 71.9% | 15.7 54.1% | 17.9% | 246 46.3 | 7.339 25.2 | John Davis (D) | 136 25.6% | 8.4 28.8% | -3.2% | 13 |
| 36 | 1928 | Herbert Hoover (R) | 444 83.6% | 21.4 58.2% | 25.4% | 357 67.2 | 6.376 17.3 | Alfred Smith (D) | 87 16.4% | 15.0 40.8% | -24.5% | |
| 37 | 1932 | Franklin Roosevelt (D) | 472 88.9% | 22.8 57.3% | 31.6% | 413 77.8 | 7.060 17.7 | **Herbert Hoover** (R) | 59 11.1% | 15.8 39.6% | -28.5% | |
| 38 | 1936 | Franklin Roosevelt (D) | 523 98.5% | 27.5 60.2% | 38.3% | 515 97.0 | 10.797 23.7 | Alfred Landon (R) | 8 1.5% | 16.7 36.5% | -35.0% | |
| 39 | 1940 | **Franklin Roosevelt** (D) | 449 84.6% | 27.2 54.7% | 29.9% | 367 69.1 | 4.939 9.9 | Wendell Wilkie (R) | 82 15.4% | 22.3 44.8% | -29.3% | |
| 40 | 1944 | **Franklin Roosevelt** (D) | 432 81.4% | 25.6 53.3% | 28.0% | 333 62.7 | 3.596 7.5 | Thomas Dewey (R) | 99 18.6% | 22.0 45.8% | -27.2% | |
| 41 | 1948 | **Harry Truman** (D) | 303 57.1% | 24.1 49.4% | 7.7% | 114 21.5 | 2.137 4.4 | Thomas Dewey (R) | 189 35.6% | 22.0 45.0% | -9.4% | 39 |
| 42 | 1952 | Dwight Eisenhower (R) | 442 83.2% | 33.8 54.9% | 28.4% | 353 66.5 | 6.464 10.5 | Adlai Stevenson (D) | 89 16.8% | 27.3 44.4% | -27.6% | |
| 43 | 1956 | **Dwight Eisenhower** (R) | 457 86.1% | 35.6 57.4% | 28.7% | 384 72.3 | 9.842 15.9 | Adlai Stevenson (D) | 73 13.7% | 25.7 41.5% | -27.7% | 1 |
| 44 | 1960 | John Kennedy (D) | 303 56.4% | 34.2 49.7% | 6.7% | 84 15.6 | 0.119 0.2 | Richard Nixon (R) | 219 40.8% | 34.1 49.5% | -8.8% | 15 |

# Results of Presidential Elections, 1964 to 2016

| Term | Year | Winner Candidate (party) | EV | PV | Amp./Min. | Victory Margin EV | Victory Margin PV | Loser Candidate (party) | EV | PV | Amp./Min. | Other EV (1) |
|---|---|---|---|---|---|---|---|---|---|---|---|---|
| 45 | 1964 | **Lyndon Johnson** (D) | 486 90.3% | 42.8 60.8% | 29.5% | 434 80.7 | 15.678 22.3 | Barry Goldwater (R) | 52 9.7% | 27.1 38.5% | -28.9% | |
| 46 | 1968 | Richard Nixon (R) | 301 55.9% | 31.7 43.4% | 12.5% | 110 20.4 | 0.812 1.1 | Hubert Humphrey (D) | 191 35.5% | 30.9 42.3% | -6.8% | 46 |
| 47 | 1972 | **Richard Nixon** (R) | 520 96.7% | 46.7 60.2% | 36.4% | 503 93.5 | 17.839 23.0 | George McGovern (D) | 17 3.2% | 28.9 37.2% | -34.1% | 1 |
| 48 | 1976 | James Carter (D) | 297 55.2% | 40.8 50.0% | 5.2% | 57 10.6 | 1.678 2.1 | **Gerald Ford** (R) | 240 44.6% | 39.1 48.0% | -3.4% | 1 |
| 49 | 1980 | Ronald Reagan (R) | 489 90.9% | 43.6 50.5% | 40.4% | 440 81.8 | 8.162 9.4 | **James Carter** (D) | 49 9.1% | 35.5 41.0% | -31.9% | |
| 50 | 1984 | **Ronald Reagan** (R) | 525 97.6% | 54.2 58.5% | 39.1% | 512 95.2 | 16.717 18.0 | Walter Mondale (D) | 13 2.4% | 37.4 40.4% | -38.0% | |
| 51 | 1988 | George H.W. Bush (R) | 426 79.2% | 48.6 53.1% | 26.1% | 315 58.6 | 6.926 7.6 | Michael Dukakis (D) | 111 20.6% | 41.7 45.5% | -24.9% | 1 |
| 52 | 1992 | William Clinton (D) | 370 68.8% | 44.9 42.9% | 25.9% | 202 37.5 | 6.059 5.8 | **George H.W. Bush** (R) | 168 31.2% | 38.8 37.1% | -5.9% | |
| 53 | 1996 | **William Clinton** (D) | 379 70.4% | 47.4 49.2% | 21.3% | 220 40.9 | 8.203 8.5 | Robert Dole (R) | 159 29.6% | 39.2 40.7% | -11.1% | |
| 54 | 2000 | George W. Bush (2) (R) | 271 50.4% | 50.5 47.8% | 2.7% | 5 0.9 | (0.531) (0.5) | Albert Gore (D) | 266 49.4% | 51.0 48.3% | 1.2% | 1 |
| 55 | 2004 | **George W. Bush** (R) | 286 53.2% | 61.9 50.6% | 2.6% | 35 6.5 | 2.978 2.4 | John Kerry (D) | 251 46.7% | 58.9 48.1% | -1.5% | 1 |
| 56 | 2008 | Barack Obama (D) | 365 67.8% | 69.3 52.9% | 15.0% | 192 35.7 | 9.700 7.4 | John McCain (R) | 173 32.2% | 59.6 45.5% | -13.3% | |
| 57 | 2012 | **Barack Obama** (D) | 332 61.7% | 65.4 50.9% | 10.8% | 126 23.4 | 4.857 3.8 | Mitt Romney (R) | 206 38.3% | 60.6 47.1% | -8.8% | |
| 58 | 2016 | Donald Trump (R) | 304 56.5% | 63.0 46.3% | 10.2% | 77 14.3 | (2.839) (2.1) | Hillary Clinton (D) | 227 42.2% | 65.8 48.4% | -6.2% | 7 |

**Notes:**

(1) Includes electoral votes received by other candidates, those cast by faithless electors, those not counted, and the votes of electors who abstained.

(2) Horace Greeley was supposed to receive 66 electoral votes. However, when he died before the Electoral College voted, his electoral votes were cast as follows: 42 for Democrat Thomas A. Hendricks, 18 for B. Gratz Brown, 2 for Charles J. Jenkins, 1 for David Davis, and by resolution of the House of Representatives, 3 were not counted.

Incumbents are shown in **boldface type.**

**Legend:** EV = electoral votes; PV = popular votes (in millions)

Amp./Min. = Electoral College amplification / minimization; i.e., candidate's EV percentage minus PV percentage.

## Best and Worst Electoral Performances by Winning Candidates

| | 538-Electoral-Vote Era | | | Post War Period | | | 1860 to 2016 | | |
|---|---|---|---|---|---|---|---|---|---|
| | Result | Candidate (party) | Year | Result | Candidate (party) | Year | Result | Candidate (party) | Year |
| **Electoral Votes** | | | | | | | | | |
| Highest percentage | 97.6% | Reagan R | 1984 | 98.5% | Roosevelt D | 1936 | 98.5% | Roosevelt D | 1936 |
| Lowest percentage | 50.5% | Bush R | 2000 | 50.5% | Bush R | 2000 | 50.5% | Bush R | 2000 |
| Largest % point margin | 95.2 | Reagan R | 1984 | 95.2 | Reagan R | 1984 | 97.0 | Roosevelt D | 1936 |
| Smallest % point margin | 0.9 | Bush R | 2000 | 0.9 | Bush R | 2000 | 0.9 | Bush R | 2000 |
| Most votes | 525 | Reagan R | 1984 | | | | | | |
| Fewest votes | 271 | Bush R | 2000 | | | | | | |
| Largest vote margin | 512 | Reagan R | 1984 | | | | | | |
| Smallest vote margin | 5 | Bush R | 2000 | | | | | | |
| **Popular Votes** | | | | | | | | | |
| Highest percentage | 60.8% | Johnson D | 1964 | 60.8% | Johnson D | 1964 | 61.7% | Harding R | 1920 |
| Lowest percentage | 42.9% | Clinton D | 1992 | 42.9% | Clinton D | 1992 | 39.6% | Lincoln R | 1860 |
| Largest % point margin | 23.0 | Nixon R | 1972 | 23.0 | Nixon R | 1972 | 26.8 | Harding R | 1920 |
| Smallest % point margin | -2.1 | Trump R | 2016 | -2.1 | Trump R | 2016 | -2.1 | Trump R | 2016 |
| **EV vs PV Percentage** | | | | | | | | | |
| Largest | 40.4 | Reagan R | 1980 | 40.4 | Reagan R | 1980 | 40.4 | Reagan R | 1980 |
| Smallest | 2.6 | Bush R | 2004 | 2.6 | Bush R | 2004 | 2.6 | Bush R | 2004 |
| **Number of States Won** | | | | | | | | | |
| Most (tie) | 49 | Nixon R | 1972 | 49 | Nixon R | 1972 | | | |
| (tie) | 49 | Reagan R | 1984 | 49 | Reagan R | 1984 | | | |
| Fewest | 24 | Carter D | 1976 | 23 | Kennedy D | 1960 | | | |

## Best and Worst Electoral Performances by Losing Candidates

| | 538-Electoral-Vote Era | | | Post War Period | | | 1860 to 2016 | | |
|---|---|---|---|---|---|---|---|---|---|
| | Result | Candidate (party) | Year | Result | Candidate (party) | Year | Result | Candidate (party) | Year |
| **Electoral Votes** | | | | | | | | | |
| Highest percentage | 49.5% | Gore D | 2000 | 49.5% | Gore D | 2000 | 49.5% | Gore D | 2000 |
| Lowest percentage | 2.4% | Mondale D | 1984 | 2.4% | Mondale D | 1984 | 1.5% | Landon R | 1936 |
| "Best" % point margin | -0.9 | Gore D | 2000 | -0.9 | Gore D | 2000 | -0.9 | Gore D | 2000 |
| Worst % point margin | -95.2 | Mondale D | 1984 | -95.2 | Mondale D | 1984 | -97.0 | Landon R | 1936 |
| Most votes | 266 | Gore D | 2000 | | | | | | |
| Fewest votes | 13 | Mondale D | 1984 | | | | | | |
| "Best" margin | -5 | Gore D | 2000 | | | | | | |
| Worst margin | -512 | Mondale D | 1984 | | | | | | |
| **Popular Votes** | | | | | | | | | |
| Highest percentage | 48.4% | H. Clinton D | 2016 | 49.5% | Nixon R | 1960 | 49.5% | Nixon R | 1960 |
| Lowest percentage | 37.1% | Bush R | 1992 | 37.1% | Bush R | 1992 | 18.2% | Breckinridge D | 1860 |
| "Best" % point margin | 2.1 | H. Clinton D | 2016 | 2.1 | H. Clinton D | 2016 | 2.1 | H. Clinton D | 2016 |
| Worst % point margin | -23.0 | McGovern D | 1972 | -23.0 | McGovern D | 1972 | -26.8 | Cox D | 1920 |
| **EV vs PV Percentage** | | | | | | | | | |
| Smallest | +1.2 | Gore D | 2000 | +1.2 | Gore D | 2000 | +5.6 | Breckinridge D | 1860 |
| Worst | -38.0 | Mondale D | 1984 | -34.1 | McGovern D | 1972 | -38.0 | Mondale D | 1984 |
| **Number of States Won** | | | | | | | | | |
| Most | 27 | Ford R | 1976 | | | | | | |
| Fewest (tie) | 1 | McGovern D | 1972 | | | | | | |
| (tie) | 1 | Mondale D | 1984 | | | | | | |

# Electoral Performance of Winning Candidates as a Group

| | 538-Electoral-Vote Era | | | Post War Period | | |
|---|---|---|---|---|---|---|
| | In All Elections | Elections With An Incumbent Candidate | Elections With No Incumbent Candidate | In All Elections | Elections With An Incumbent Candidate | Elections With No Incumbent Candidate |
| Number of Elections | 14 | 9 | 5 | 18 | 11 | 7 |
| **Electoral Vote Won** | | | | | | |
| Median | 68.3% | 70.4% | 56.5% | 68.3% | 70.4% | 56.5% |
| Average | 71.0% | 76.1% | 62.0% | 71.0% | 75.3% | 64.2% |
| High | 97.6% | 97.6% | 79.2% | 97.6% | 97.6% | 83.2% |
| Low | 50.5% | 53.2% | 50.5% | 50.5% | 53.2% | 50.5% |
| **Popular Vote Won** | | | | | | |
| Median | 50.5% | 50.6% | 47.8% | 50.5% | 50.6% | 49.7% |
| Average | 51.2% | 52.6% | 48.7% | 51.6% | 52.7% | 49.7% |
| High | 60.8% | 60.8% | 53.1% | 60.8% | 60.8% | 54.9% |
| Low | 42.9% | 42.9% | 43.4% | 42.9% | 42.9% | 43.4% |

| | 1860 to 2016 | | | 1804 to 2016 | | |
|---|---|---|---|---|---|---|
| | In All Elections | Elections With An Incumbent Candidate | Elections With No Incumbent Candidate | In All Elections | Elections With An Incumbent Candidate | Elections With No Incumbent Candidate |
| Number of Elections | 39 | 24 | 15 | 51 | 29 | 22 |
| **Electoral Vote Won** | | | | | | |
| Median | 70.4% | 76.6% | 60.6% | 69.7% | 76.6% | 61.2% |
| Average | 71.7% | 75.7% | 65.4% | 71.5% | 75.6% | 66.2% |
| High | 98.5% | 98.5% | 83.6% | 98.5% | 98.5% | 85.8% |
| Low | 50.5% | 52.2% | 50.5% | 50.5% | 52.2% | 50.5% |
| **Popular Vote Won** | | | | | | |
| Median | 51.6% | 52.5% | 51.0% | | | |
| Average | 51.9% | 52.6% | 50.7% | | | |
| High | 61.7% | 60.8% | 61.7% | | | |
| Low | 39.6% | 41.8% | 39.6% | | | |

# Electoral Performance of Losing Candidates as a Group

| | 538-Electoral-Vote Era | | | Post War Period | | |
|---|---|---|---|---|---|---|
| | In All Elections | Elections With An Incumbent Candidate | Elections With No Incumbent Candidate | In All Elections | Elections With An Incumbent Candidate | Elections With No Incumbent Candidate |
| Number of Elections | 14 | 9 | 5 | 18 | 11 | 7 |
| **Electoral Vote Won** | | | | | | |
| Median | 31.7% | 29.6% | 35.5% | 31.7% | 29.6% | 35.5% |
| Average | 28.2% | 23.9% | 36.0% | 27.9% | 24.0% | 33.9% |
| High | 49.5% | 46.7% | 49.5% | 49.5% | 46.7% | 49.5% |
| Low | 2.4% | 2.4% | 20.6% | 2.4% | 2.4% | 16.8% |
| **Popular Vote Won** | | | | | | |
| Median | 43.9% | 40.7% | 45.6% | 44.7% | 41.0% | 45.6% |
| Average | 43.5% | 42.0% | 46.0% | 43.8% | 42.2% | 46.3% |
| High | 48.4% | 48.1% | 48.4% | 49.5% | 48.1% | 49.5% |
| Low | 37.1% | 37.1% | 42.3% | 37.1% | 37.1% | 42.3% |

| | 1860 to 2016 | | | 1804 to 2016 | | |
|---|---|---|---|---|---|---|
| | In All Elections | Elections With An Incumbent Candidate | Elections With No Incumbent Candidate | In All Elections | Elections With An Incumbent Candidate | Elections With No Incumbent Candidate |
| Number of Elections | 39 | 24 | 15 | 51 | 29 | 22 |
| **Electoral Vote Won** | | | | | | |
| Median | 29.4% | 22.2% | 33.5% | 27.2% | 20.4% | 32.8% |
| Average | 27.1% | 23.6% | 32.6% | 27.0% | 23.6% | 31.4% |
| High | 49.5% | 47.8% | 49.5% | 49.5% | 47.8% | 49.5% |
| Low | 1.5% | 1.5% | 16.4% | 1.5% | 1.5% | 14.2% |
| **Popular Vote Won** | | | | | | |
| Median | 44.4% | 42.3% | 45.6% | | | |
| Average | 42.3% | 41.6% | 43.4% | | | |
| High | 49.5% | 48.6% | 49.5% | | | |
| Low | 18.2% | 27.4% | 18.2% | | | |

# Best and Worst Electoral Performances by Incumbent Winners

| | 538-Electoral-Vote Era | | | | Post War Period | | | | 1860 to 2016 | | | |
|---|---|---|---|---|---|---|---|---|---|---|---|---|
| | Result | Candidate (party) | | Year | Result | Candidate (party) | | Year | Result | Candidate (party) | | Year |
| **Electoral Votes** | | | | | | | | | | | | |
| Highest percentage | 96.7% | Nixon | R | 1972 | 96.7% | Nixon | R | 1972 | 98.5% | Roosevelt | D | 1936 |
| Lowest percentage | 53.2% | Bush | R | 2004 | 53.2% | Bush | R | 2004 | 52.2% | Wilson | D | 1916 |
| Largest % point margin | 95.2 | Reagan | R | 1984 | 95.2 | Reagan | R | 1984 | 97.0 | Roosevelt | D | 1936 |
| Smallest % point margin | 35.0 | Bush | R | 2004 | 35.0 | Bush | R | 2004 | 4.3 | Wilson | D | 1916 |
| Most votes | 525 | Reagan | R | 1984 | | | | | | | | |
| Fewest votes | 286 | Bush | R | 2004 | | | | | | | | |
| Largest vote margin | 512 | Reagan | R | 1984 | | | | | | | | |
| Smallest vote margin | 35 | Bush | R | 2004 | | | | | | | | |
| **Popular Votes** | | | | | | | | | | | | |
| Highest percentage | 60.8% | Johnson | D | 1964 | 60.8% | Johnson | D | 1964 | 60.8% | Johnson | D | 1964 |
| Lowest percentage | 49.2% | Clinton | D | 1996 | 49.2% | Clinton | D | 1996 | 49.2% | Clinton | D | 1996 |
| Largest % point margin | 23.0 | Nixon | R | 1972 | 23.0 | Nixon | R | 1972 | 25.2 | Coolidge | R | 1924 |
| Smallest % point margin | 2.4 | Bush | R | 2004 | 2.4 | Bush | R | 2004 | 2.4 | Bush | R | 2004 |
| **EV vs PV Percentage** | | | | | | | | | | | | |
| Largest difference | 39.1 | Reagan | R | 1984 | 39.1 | Reagan | R | 1984 | 39.1 | Reagan | R | 1984 |
| Smallest difference | 2.6 | Bush | R | 2004 | 2.6 | Bush | R | 2004 | 2.6 | Bush | R | 2004 |
| **Number of States Won** | | | | | | | | | | | | |
| Most (tie) | 49 | Nixon | R | 1972 | | | | | | | | |
| (tie) | 49 | Reagan | R | 1984 | | | | | | | | |
| Fewest | 27 | Obama | D | 2012 | | | | | | | | |

# Best and Worst Electoral Performances by Incumbent Losers

| | 538-Electoral-Vote Era | | | | Post War Period | | | | 1860 to 2016 | | | |
|---|---|---|---|---|---|---|---|---|---|---|---|---|
| | Result | Candidate (party) | | Year | Result | Candidate (party) | | Year | Result | Candidate (party) | | Year |
| **Electoral Votes** | | | | | | | | | | | | |
| Highest percentage | 44.6% | Ford | R | 1976 | 44.6% | Ford | R | 1976 | 44.6% | Ford | R | 1976 |
| Lowest percentage | 9.1% | Carter | D | 1980 | 9.1% | Carter | D | 1980 | 9.1% | Carter | D | 1980 |
| "Best" % point margin | -10.6 | Ford | R | 1976 | -10.6 | Ford | R | 1976 | -10.6 | Ford | R | 1976 |
| Worst % point margin | -81.8 | Carter | D | 1980 | -81.8 | Carter | D | 1980 | -81.8 | Carter | D | 1980 |
| Most votes | 240 | Ford | R | 1976 | | | | | | | | |
| Fewest votes | 49 | Carter | D | 1980 | | | | | | | | |
| "Best" margin | -57 | Ford | R | 1976 | | | | | | | | |
| Worst margin | -440 | Carter | D | 1980 | | | | | | | | |
| **Popular Votes** | | | | | | | | | | | | |
| Highest percentage | 48.0% | Ford | R | 1976 | 48.0% | Ford | R | 1976 | 48.6% | Cleveland | D | 1888 |
| Lowest percentage | 37.1% | Bush | R | 1992 | 37.1% | Bush | R | 1992 | 23.2% | Taft | R | 1912 |
| "Best" % point margin | -2.1 | Ford | R | 1976 | -2.1 | Ford | R | 1976 | + 0.8 | Cleveland | D | 1888 |
| Worst % point margin | -9.4 | Carter | D | 1980 | -9.4 | Carter | D | 1980 | -17.7 | Hoover | R | 1932 |
| **EV vs PV Percentage** | | | | | | | | | | | | |
| Smallest | -3.4 | Ford | R | 1976 | -3.4 | Ford | R | 1976 | -3.4 | Ford | R | 1976 |
| Worst | -31.9 | Carter | D | 1980 | -31.9 | Carter | D | 1980 | -31.9 | Carter | D | 1980 |
| **Number of States Won** | | | | | | | | | | | | |
| Most | 27 | Ford | R | 1976 | | | | | | | | |
| Fewest | 7 | Carter | D | 1980 | | | | | | | | |

# Electoral Performance of Incumbents as a Group

| | 538-Electoral-Vote Era | | | Post War Period | | |
|---|---|---|---|---|---|---|
| | All Incumb. | Winners Only | Losers Only | All Incumb. | Winners Only | Losers Only |
| **Electoral Vote Won** | | | | | | |
| Median | 61.7% | 80.4% | 31.2% | 61.7% | 78.3% | 31.2% |
| Average | 61.6% | 78.3% | 28.3% | 63.5% | 76.6% | 28.3% |
| High | 97.6% | 97.6% | 44.6% | 97.6% | 97.6% | 44.6% |
| Low | 9.1% | 53.2% | 9.1% | 9.1% | 53.2% | 9.1% |
| # of winners | 6 | 5 | 0 | 8 | 8 | 0 |
| # of losers | 3 | 0 | 3 | 3 | 0 | 3 |
| **Popular Vote Won** | | | | | | |
| Median | 50.6% | 54.7% | 41.0% | 50.6% | 54.1% | 41.0% |
| Average | 50.7% | 55.0% | 42.0% | 51.2% | 54.6% | 42.0% |
| High | 60.8% | 60.8% | 48.0% | 60.8% | 60.8% | 48.0% |
| Low | 37.1% | 49.2% | 37.1% | 37.1% | 49.2% | 37.1% |
| # of winners | 6 | 6 | 0 | 8 | 8 | 0 |
| # of losers | 3 | 0 | 3 | 3 | 0 | 3 |

| | 1860 to 2016 | | | 1804 to 2016 | | |
|---|---|---|---|---|---|---|
| | All Incumb. | Winners Only | Losers Only | All Incumb. | Winners Only | Losers Only |
| **Electoral Vote Won** | | | | | | |
| Median | 67.9% | 81.3% | 31.2% | 65.3% | 78.9% | 31.2% |
| Average | 61.7% | 77.0% | 24.6% | 60.7% | 76.9% | 24.9% |
| High | 98.5% | 98.5% | 44.6% | 98.5% | 98.5% | 44.6% |
| Low | 1.5% | 52.2% | 1.5% | 1.5% | 52.2% | 1.5% |
| # of winners | 17 | 17 | 0 | 20 | 20 | 0 |
| # of losers | 7 | 0 | 7 | 9 | 0 | 9 |
| **Popular Vote Won** | | | | | | |
| Median | 51.3% | 54.7% | 41.0% | | | |
| Average | 50.3% | 54.5% | 40.1% | | | |
| High | 60.8% | 60.8% | 48.6% | | | |
| Low | 23.2% | 49.2% | 23.2% | | | |
| # of winners | 17 | 17 | 0 | | | |
| # of losers | 7 | 0 | 7 | | | |

# Full Text of Certain Constitutional Provisions and Amendments Relating to the Presidency, Vice Presidency, and Presidential Elections

## ARTICLE II, SECTION 1 of the Constitution of the United States of America

*The executive Power shall be vested in a President of the United States of America. He shall hold his Office during the Term of four Years, and, together with the Vice President, chosen for the same Term, be elected, as follows:*

*Each State shall appoint, in such Manner as the Legislature thereof may direct, a Number of Electors, equal to the whole Number of Senators and Representatives to which the State may be entitled in the Congress: but no Senator or Representative, or Person holding an Office of Trust or Profit under the United States, shall be appointed an Elector.*

*The Electors shall meet in their respective States, and vote by Ballot for two Persons, of whom one at least shall not be an Inhabitant of the same State with themselves* [sic]. *And they shall make a List of all the Persons voted for, and of the Number of Votes for each; which List they shall sign and certify, and transmit sealed to the Seat of the Government of the United States, directed to the President of the Senate. The President of the Senate shall, in the Presence of the Senate and House of Representatives, open all the Certificates, and the Votes shall then be counted. The Person having the greatest Number of Votes shall be the President, if such Number be a Majority of the whole Number of Electors appointed; and if there be more than one who have such Majority, and have an equal Number of Votes, then the House of Representatives shall immediately chuse* [sic] *by Ballot one of them for President; and if no Person have a Majority, then from the five highest on the List the said House shall in like Manner chuse the President. But in chusing* [sic] *the President, the Votes shall be taken by States, the Representation from each State having one Vote; A quorum for this purpose shall consist of a Member or Members from two thirds of the States, and a Majority of all the States shall be necessary to a Choice. In every Case, after the Choice of the President, the Person having the greatest Number of Votes of the Electors shall be the Vice President. But if there should remain two or more who have equal Votes, the Senate shall chuse from them by Ballot the Vice President.*

*The Congress may determine the Time of chusing the Electors, and the Day on which they shall give their Votes; which Day shall be the same throughout the United States.*

*No Person except a natural born Citizen, or a Citizen of the United States, at the time of the Adoption of this Constitution, shall be eligible to the Office of President; neither shall any Person be eligible to that Office who shall not have attained to the Age of thirty five Years, and been fourteen Years a Resident within the United States.*

*In Case of the Removal of the President from Office, or of his Death, Resignation, or Inability to discharge the Powers and Duties of the said Office, the Same shall devolve on the Vice President, and the Congress may by Law provide for the Case of Removal, Death, Resignation or Inability, both of the President and Vice President, declaring what Officer shall then act as President, and such Officer shall act accordingly, until the Disability be removed, or a President shall be elected.*

[two additional irrelevant paragraphs of Section 1 omitted]

# THE TWELFTH AMENDMENT

Passed by Congress on 9 December 1803.
Ratified by the requisite number of states on 15 June 1804.

A portion of Article II, section 1 is superseded by this 12th Amendment.

*The Electors shall meet in their respective states and vote by ballot for President and Vice-President, one of whom, at least, shall not be an inhabitant of the same state with themselves; they shall name in their ballots the person voted for as President, and in distinct ballots the person voted for as Vice-President, and they shall make distinct lists of all persons voted for as President, and of all persons voted for as Vice-President, and of the number of votes for each, which lists they shall sign and certify, and transmit sealed to the seat of the government of the United States, directed to the President of the Senate; the President of the Senate shall, in the presence of the Senate and House of Representatives, open all the certificates and the votes shall then be counted. The person having the greatest number of votes for President, shall be the President, if such number be a majority of the whole number of Electors appointed; and if no person have such majority, then from the persons having the highest numbers not exceeding three on the list of those voted for as President, the House of Representatives shall choose immediately, by ballot, the President. But in choosing the President, the votes shall be taken by states, the representation from each state having one vote; a quorum for this purpose shall consist of a member or members from two-thirds of the states, and a majority of all the states shall be necessary to a choice. And if the House of Representatives shall not choose a President whenever the right of choice shall devolve upon them, before the fourth day of March next following, then the Vice-President shall act as President, as in case of the death or other constitutional disability of the President.\* The person having the greatest number of votes as Vice-President, shall be the Vice-President, if such number be a majority of the whole number of Electors appointed, and if no person have a majority, then from the two highest numbers on the list, the Senate shall choose the Vice-President; a quorum for the purpose shall consist of two-thirds of the whole number of Senators, and a majority of the whole number shall be necessary to a choice. But no person constitutionally ineligible to the office of President shall be eligible to that of Vice-President of the United States.*

\*superseded by Section 3 of the 20th Amendment

---

# THE FIFTEENTH AMENDMENT

Passed by Congress on 26 February 1869.
Ratified by the requisite number of states on 3 February 1870.

### Section 1.
*The right of citizens of the United States to vote shall not be denied or abridged by the United States or by any State on account of race, color, or previous condition of servitude.*

### Section 2.
*The Congress shall have power to enforce this article by appropriate legislation.*

---

# THE NINETEENTH AMENDMENT

Passed by Congress on 4 June 1919.
Ratified by the requisite number of states on 18 August 1920.

*The right of citizens of the United States to vote shall not be denied or abridged by the United States or by any State on account of sex.*

*Congress shall have power to enforce this article by appropriate legislation.*

---

# THE TWENTIETH AMENDMENT

Passed by on 2 March 1932.
Ratified by the requisite number of states on 23 January 1933.

Article I, Section 4, of the Constitution was modified by Section 2 of this amendment. In addition, a portion of the 12$^{th}$ Amendment was superseded by Section 3 of this amendment.

### Section 1.
*The terms of the President and the Vice President shall end at noon on the 20$^{th}$ day of January, and the terms of Senators and Representatives at noon on the 3$^{rd}$ day of January, of the years in which such terms would have ended if this article had not been ratified; and the terms of their successors shall then begin.*

### Section 2.
*The Congress shall assemble at least once in every year, and such meeting shall begin at noon on the 3$^{rd}$ day of January, unless they shall by law appoint a different day.*

### Section 3.
*If, at the time fixed for the beginning of the term of the President, the President elect shall have died, the Vice President elect shall become President. If a President shall not have been chosen before the time fixed for the beginning of his term, or if the President elect shall have failed to qualify, then the Vice President elect shall act as President until a President shall have qualified; and the Congress may by law provide for the case wherein neither a President elect nor a Vice President shall have qualified, declaring who shall then act as President, or the manner in which one who is to act shall be selected, and such person shall act accordingly until a President or Vice President shall have qualified.*

### Section 4.
*The Congress may by law provide for the case of the death of any of the persons from whom the House of Representatives may choose a President whenever the right of choice shall have devolved upon them, and for the case of the death of any of the persons from whom the Senate may choose a Vice President whenever the right of choice shall have devolved upon them.*

### Section 5.
*Sections 1 and 2 shall take effect on the 15th day of October following the ratification of this article.*

### Section 6.
*This article shall be inoperative unless it shall have been ratified as an amendment to the Constitution by the legislatures of three-fourths of the several States within seven years from the date of its submission.*

# THE TWENTY-SECOND AMENDMENT

Passed by Congress on 21 March 1947.
Ratified by the requisite number of states on 27 February 1951.

## Section 1.

*No person shall be elected to the office of the President more than twice, and no person who has held the office of President, or acted as President, for more than two years of a term to which some other person was elected President shall be elected to the office of President more than once. But this Article shall not apply to any person holding the office of President when this Article was proposed by Congress, and shall not prevent any person who may be holding the office of President, or acting as President, during the term within which this Article becomes operative from holding the office of President or acting as President during the remainder of such term.*

## Section 2.

*This article shall be inoperative unless it shall have been ratified as an amendment to the Constitution by the legislatures of three-fourths of the several States within seven years from the date of its submission to the States by the Congress.*

# THE TWENTY-THIRD AMENDMENT

Passed by Congress on 16 June1960.
Ratified by the requisite number of states on 29 March 1961.

## Section 1.

*The District constituting the seat of Government of the United States shall appoint in such manner as Congress may direct:*

*A number of electors of President and Vice President equal to the whole number of Senators and Representatives in Congress to which the District would be entitled if it were a State, but in no event more than the least populous State; they shall be in addition to those appointed by the States, but they shall be considered, for the purposes of the election of President and Vice President, to be electors appointed by a State; and they shall meet in the District and perform such duties as provided by the twelfth article of amendment.*

## Section 2.

*The Congress shall have power to enforce this article by appropriate legislation.*

# THE TWENTY-FOURTH AMENDMENT

Passed by Congress on 14 September 1962.
Ratified by the requisite number of states on 23 January 1964.

## Section 1.

*The right of citizens of the United States to vote in any primary or other election for President or Vice President, for electors for President or Vice President, or for Senator or Representative in Congress, shall not be denied or abridged by the United States or any State by reason of failure to pay any poll tax or other tax.*

## Section 2.

*The Congress shall have power to enforce this article by appropriate legislation.*

---

# THE TWENTY-FIFTH AMENDMENT

Passed by Congress on 6 July 1965.
Ratified by the requisite number of states on 10 February 1967.

Article II, Section 1, of the Constitution was affected by this amendment.

## Section 1.

*In case of the removal of the President from office or of his death or resignation, the Vice President shall become President.*

## Section 2.

*Whenever there is a vacancy in the office of the Vice President, the President shall nominate a Vice President who shall take office upon confirmation by a majority vote of both Houses of Congress.*

## Section 3.

*Whenever the President transmits to the President pro tempore of the Senate and the Speaker of the House of Representatives his written declaration that he is unable to discharge the powers and duties of his office, and until he transmits to them a written declaration to the contrary, such powers and duties shall be discharged by the Vice President as Acting President.*

## Section 4.

*Whenever the Vice President and a majority of either the principal officers of the executive departments or of such other body as Congress may by law provide, transmit to the President pro tempore of the Senate and the Speaker of the House of Representatives their written declaration that the President is unable to discharge the powers and duties of his office, the Vice President shall immediately assume the powers and duties of the office as Acting President.*

*Thereafter, when the President transmits to the President pro tempore of the Senate and the Speaker of the House of Representatives his written declaration that no inability exists, he shall resume the powers and duties of his office unless the Vice President and a majority of either the principal officers of the executive department or of such other body as Congress may by law provide, transmit within four days to the President pro tempore of the Senate and the Speaker of the House of Representatives their written declaration that the President is unable to discharge the powers and duties of his office. Thereupon Congress shall decide the issue, assembling within forty-eight hours for that purpose if not in session. If the Congress, within twenty-one days after receipt of the latter written declaration, or, if Congress is not in session, within twenty-one days after Congress is required to assemble, determines by two-thirds vote of both Houses that the President is unable to discharge the powers and duties of his office, the Vice President shall continue to discharge the same as Acting President; otherwise, the President shall resume the powers and duties of his office.*

---

## THE TWENTY-SIXTH AMENDMENT

Passed by Congress on 23 March 1971.
Ratified by the requisite number of states on 1 July 1971.

*The right of citizens of the United States, who are eighteen years of age or older, to vote shall not be denied or abridged by the United States or by any State on account of age. Congress shall have the power to enforce this law through appropriate legislation.*

# About the Author
## B.C. Jackson

Mr. Jackson is an avocational author with a strong interest in politics, economics, and international affairs. He is a self-professed news junkie who loves detail, data, the visual presentation of data, and analysis of all sorts.

In his day job the author advises private companies on strategic corporate-development and financial issues, including the sale of a company, effecting acquisitions, raising capital, and structuring joint ventures.

Mr. Jackson holds degrees in politics, international economics, and corporate finance from Princeton University, Johns Hopkins University's School of Advanced International Studies, and New York University's Graduate School of Business Administration.

He lives in the suburbs of New York City.

The author may be contacted by sending an email to u.s.presidency.book@gmail.com

www.ingramcontent.com/pod-product-compliance
Lightning Source LLC
Chambersburg PA
CBHW060808270326
41928CB00002B/23